MARTYRDOM

MARTYRDOM

The Psychology, Theology, and Politics of Self-Sacrifice

Rona M. Fields

*with Contributions from Cóilín Owens, Valérie Rosoux,
Michael Berenbaum, and Reuven Firestone*

Contemporary Psychology
Chris E. Stout, Series Editor

Westport, Connecticut
London

Library of Congress Cataloging-in-Publication Data

Martyrdom : the psychology, theology, and politics of self-sacrifice / Rona M. Fields . . . [et al.].
   p. cm. — (Contemporary psychology)
  Includes bibliographical references and index.
  ISBN 0-275-97993-8
  1. Martyrdom. I. Fields, Rona M. II. Contemporary psychology (Praeger Publishers)
BL626.5.M37 2004
303.6—dc22   2003025654

British Library Cataloguing in Publication Data is available.

Library of Congress Catalog Card Number: 2003025654
ISBN: 0–275–97993–8
ISSN: 1546-668x

First published in 2004

Praeger Publishers, 88 Post Road West, Westport, CT 06881
An imprint of Greenwood Publishing Group, Inc.
www.praeger.com

Printed in the United States of America

∞™

The paper used in this book complies with the Permanent Paper Standard issued by the National Information Standards Organization (Z39.48–1984).

10 9 8 7 6 5 4 3 2 1

Copyright Acknowledgments

Contents

Illustrations

PREFACE

Eric Berne said, "It takes three generations to make one neurotic," and I believe that is also so to make a book. I owe much to my parents and grandparents and to the extended family they provided as my heritage. I have an equal debt to the people who in different ways in various parts of the world stimulated my research and directed me to the paper trails and the people paths that ultimately provided answers to my questions. Then there is a huge debt to the many social scientists, philosophers, and scholars who preceded me and wrote marvelously and extensively. My late teacher and mentor, Magda B. Arnold, whose life and work inspired my own, is paramount among these. And of course, I have been most fortunate in the collaborators for this volume. Each of them might easily have occupied their talents on a far more prestigious and lucrative project but agreed instead to work with me because we are concerned about martyrdom as an idea dominating this moment in human history.

I thought my next book would be *Terror's Children*. That manuscript has been growing in fits and starts over the past fifteen years and presented in papers and articles and chapters in other books. But maybe that will be the next one. My editor at Greenwood Press, Debora Carvalko, gave me so much initial reinforcement to pursue this book, that I yielded to temptation and became immersed and, for the past eight months, as monomaniacal as I could be while continuing my clinical practice and professional commitments. I came to know her when I was working on a chapter for the four-volume set, *The Psychology of Terrorism,* which was also one of her special projects for Greenwood/Praeger. The chapter on the Palestinian suicide bomber was written with Salman Elbedour, who also studies children growing up in violence and especially the Palestinian children in Gaza and the Palestinian Territories. We argued endlessly about the use of the term martyrdom ascribed to such deeds. He also opposed the idea of identifying them as terrorists. I could sympathize with that because I am all too aware of how such terminology is politically determined. That collaboration was a difficult one for both of us even though we share the same political perspective and respect each other as scholars. It was the idea of martyrdom, which, like the infamous hanging chads of the Florida presidential ballots, could neither determine nor successfully be ignored.

This debate compelled me to re-examine my research and experience, but not limited as before by the data-based clinical or social psychology research methodologies I taught and used for most of my professional life. Rather, I wanted to look at the meaning and connections I had learned after so many years and so much data. I wondered about the individuals I'd encountered who didn't fit the normative and predictable expectancies. I thought more about the many who were raised amid violence, hatred, and torture, but rejected that model for their own lives. I thought about all the anthropological and archeological studies that fascinated me and had coalesced somewhat when I taught social anthropology. And all the knowledge I'd acquired in my years of human rights work with torture survivors, refugees, and migrants. And then, of course, there is my own and my family's history.

How this book came about is the subject of yet another book, my autobiography, which is yet to be written. For now, I want to acknowledge and thank first of all, my wonderful collaborators. Cóilín Owens and I have worked together on many projects dating back to 1977. Most of these concerned Irish culture, the language, the history, and the politics of that magical and turbulent island nation. I knew his lecture on *Murder in the Cathedral* and I realized how that work introduced my own thinking on the psychology of Thomas à Becket—the prototypical martyr.

But I also knew how overcommitted he is and appreciate his taking the time to share this project by setting aside many other priorities. Michael Berenbaum and I met fortuitously while he was organizing and directing the then nascent Holocaust Museum. Dr. Judith Issroff, a psychiatrist who shared our profound interest in that signal history, introduced us. I met with Michael several times again after I had for several years become immersed in the Czech Jewish Holocaust experience of my own family. I wanted to know a theologian's thinking on martyrdom. Especially, I wanted to know the connections with the politics of memory, which is, of course, exemplified in Holocaust museums and the Shoah Foundation that he went on to found and organize in such an extraordinary and effective achievement. I also realized that to do justice to this project, I had to find an expert on the politics of memory and that search required months of contacting by phone and Internet many scholars I knew and others to whom I was referred. When I was talking with Professor Dan Druckman of the George Mason Institute for Conflict Analysis and Resolution about my search, he immediately recommended Valérie Rosoux, who had been a guest lecturer at his institute and at Johns Hopkins some months earlier. Everyone who heard her or had read any of her articles and monographs in French or English was enthusiastic in recommending her. I contacted her on-line and hoped she would find this appealing. We wrote letters, e-mails, had a brief telephone chat and, Voila!, she agreed. Even though her first language is French, she writes so well in English that her essay required very little editing to be perfect.

The hardest part of this project became the Conversation chapter. I conceived this book as a conversation in process and the section designed as conversation among the collaborators, in that respect, is the most important part of the book. My intention is that this conversation will spark conversations among many, many people all over the world. I hope that our essays have been provocative, stimulating, and knowledgeable, but in no way definitive or pretentious. We know we have skimmed the surface and want the readers to join us in digging more deeply and expanding more widely.

Since we are spread over half the globe, Valérie in Belgium, Michael in California, Cóilín in Virginia, and me in Washington, D.C., the only way we could converse is two-by-two in on-line chat room form. That required getting used to, and took much more time than I originally thought it would. But this is certainly more rapid than the old rabbinical commentaries circulating through various kinds of pre-postal services. We have something amounting to instant communication. But all of that could never have been collated coherently single-handedly. My editorial assistant, Randy Blocker, Sergeant Major, U.S. Army (Retired), put his technological genius to work in our behalf and, our two heads and four hands and two computers at his direction, managed the job.

Each of us has acknowledgments and the advantage of my position is that I can write mine first. For reviewing and critically commenting on these essays, I owe an enormous debt of gratitude to Paidraig O'Snadaigh, historian, poet, and publisher of books in Gaelic; Curator of the Irish National Museum, retired. Eva Selucka, in Brno, Czech Republic, an economist, linguist, and, I like to believe, my spiritual sister, reviewed and contributed her valuable insights for my essay. Bedrich and Yerka Kopold, scholars and veterans of the Czech Battalion, were my hosts and guides through archival materials, introductions and geography of Czechoslovakia, and all parts east. Fabiola Letelier del Solar, Pedro Matta, Mireya Garcia, and Denis Trabmann (*mis primo*) helped me understand the surreal world of Chile under Pinochet, that is, as much as a rational mind can comprehend the bizarre. In the process, my involvement in the Parque Por La Paz became my introduction to the psychology attending the politics of memory. Bobby Sands and Patsy O'Hare, friends of my son Sean, were on a trajectory unfathomable and, Thank God, improbable for my American adolescent who shared with them the no-go areas of Derry and Belfast in 1972 and the pain of Operation Motorman. Sean McKenna, senior and junior, were amongst the many Irish men and women devastated by torture and imprisonment and consumed by their political passion who were important in my studies. Many years later, in Galang, an island in the vast archipelago that constitutes Indonesia, I enhanced my understanding of the realities of refugee flight and asylum. I encountered the memories and memorialization and confronted the horror of mothers who immolated themselves to provide a chance for their children to be resettled rather than repatriated. I realized that sometimes the soldiers of a host regime were more humanitarian than the officials of the humanitarian agencies that are charged with protecting the lives and ensuring the appropriate legal designation of the helpless survivors of catastrophe.

Nasser Shansab, Nabi and Arian Misdaq, and Azzim Nassirzia provided me with an expanded context for considering Islamic thought and practices concerning death, memorializing, and martyrdom in Jihad (*Shaheed*). Theirs is an Afghan perspective and, even at that, far from homogenous. Aicha Laidi (*lemsine*), Algerian feminist, writer and soul sister of the past 20 years, offered yet a different insight into Islamic thinking and a woman's experience in Islam.

My Palestinian graduate students at American University of Beirut in 1982 and 1983 taught me much more than I could teach them. We shared in so much horror, pain, suffering, and fear. Sawson and Samir Huelelah came to my aid when my own government agents acted to leave me, unprotected, vulnerable, and adrift in Beirut. Members of the Democratic Front for the Liberation of Palestine sheltered me in 1983. They helped me get safely back to Israel. With the help of Professors Ibrahim and Janet AbuLughod, friends and colleagues from our graduate student days at the University of Illinois, I was able to meet and learn so much in company with Palestinians. At the same time, I have valued and cherished my Israeli colleagues and friends—Ma'Ariv journalist, artist and humorist, Eldad Zakowitz; Kibbutz Megiddo and Lili; Kibbutz Amir where I too briefly lived my adolescent dream and picked apples from 4 to 8 A.M. and worked with the *matpelot* (children's caretakers) in the afternoons. Cols. Jacob Evan and Eli Dolev provided very important knowledge about the psychology and psychological services for members of the Israeli Defense Forces from the inception of the State of Israel through the mid-eighties. Eliane Montouchet, one of our little group at the University of Illinois in the mid-fifties, became my French connection. We share a fascination with Rouen, its history, and the evolution of justice and law in that place and internationally.

There is no way I can list and mention the wonderful, brilliant, generous people whose experience and perspective enlarged my own. Suffice then, if anyone reading this book remembers—the point at which our lives touched and inspired what is written herein, accept my appreciation and apologies for missing mention of my gratitude.

Acknowledgments by the Contributors

Cóilín Owens—I would like to thank Rona Fields for her energetic engagement in many difficult causes, Lucretia Bailey for her stimulating conversations about Eliot's dramatic ideas, and Pádraig O Snódaigh for his perusal of this essay.

Valérie Rosoux—First of all, I would like to thank Rona M. Fields for her confidence and her enthusiasm as well as her uncommon determination. As leader of the adventure, her role was decisive. The experience of co-writing a book is always a real challenge. It is even more on such a sensitive issue. This book would have never been published without her perseverance and a remarkable ability to motivate the members of the team, Cóilín Owens, Michael Berenbaum, and myself. I also would like to express my gratitude towards two of my colleagues at the University of Louvain, Amine Ait-Chaalal and Tanguy de Wilde d'Estmael, co-directors of the Center for the International Crisis and Conflicts Studies. Their constant support and their immense knowledge have helped me for years now to understand more fully the dynamics of international relations. Finally, I want to place in bold relief the unceasing support of my husband, Paul. His encouraging attitude and his insightful suggestions are milestones on my way.

Michael Berenbaum—I want to thank my co-authors for their forbearance as the illness of my mother last fall and her death this past winter cost me three months of work and so much more. I was tardy in meeting deadlines and not quite reliable in my promised submission. Through all this, Rona was both persistent and understanding. She was also accommodating when she needed to be and insistent that the job get done. Apologies are in order; so too, gratitude. Permit me also to thank my friend Reuven Firestone, a distinguished Jewish scholar of Islam, for dealing with martyrdom in Islam and thus enhancing my understanding and ours. If there is to be healing in this difficult relationship, it will come from the scholarship of men and women like Reuven Firestone; persons of faith, whose religious world view embrace the other and who, rooted in their own religious tradition, can fully see the majesty of another faith even through difficult times.

INTRODUCTION

The idea of martyrdom has, of late, been connected with terrorism through suicide bombing—killing others while killing oneself. This phenomenon has a political and, some would claim, religious linkage. Martyrdom is attributed to those who sacrifice themselves or have been victims for a cause. Self-sacrifice, mortification, and even self-immolation are generally acknowledged means to martyrdom; they are also the means to suicide and the cause for the self-inflicted death may be any of a variety of subjective presumptions. The ancient Celtic practice of sacrificing oneself to shame the enemy by starving (not necessarily to death) on his doorstep has been, in the past century, converted into hunger strikes by the Irish to protest continued British military depredations on Irish soil. Similarly, the hunger strike is used by young Kurds to protest the denial of their right to their identity by the Turkish authorities.

Voluntary death, suicide, incorporates two significant symbols: power and purity. A cosmic war carries the symbolism of sacrifice and martyrdom. The origins of suicide/homicide are found in the practices of the twelfth- to thirteenth-century Islamic sect, Ismaeli, whose highest initiates into the secrets of the order became the instruments of assassination and in the process sought martyrdom. "It is thought they were given hashish (the word assassin means, literally, user of hashish) and exposed to luxuriant sexual pleasures as a foretaste of the pleasures of paradise they were promised should they achieve their martyrdom" (Lifton 1979, p. 158). However, two centuries earlier, Pope Urban II, in recruiting crusaders to take back Jerusalem, promised forgiveness of venial sins and immediate assumption to Paradise for anyone who met death at the hands of infidels. One might say that Muhammad accepted the laws of war as practiced by the Christian nations of his time. The practices of the Ismaeli sect may be compared with those of the Zealots of the period preceding and following the Maccabees, generally referred to in Judaism as the Rabbinic period. And, as we shall see when we examine the theology of martyrdom, homicide/suicide might have been exemplified in the story of Samson. Important as the Ismaeli practice may be in illuminating the altered state of consciousness implicit in suicide/homicide or terrorism, the practice, whether drug induced or passion inspired, has deep roots in human social behaviors.

Today, Shi'ite clerics quote their icon, "Death with dignity is preferable to life in humiliation," attributed to Inam Hussein, who was assassinated as he declared his legitimacy as the rightful heir to his grandfather, Mohamed. He is their penultimate martyr and the prototype for acts of martyrdom, notably, suicide/homicide.

Unlike the self-abnegation of the Celts, suicide bombings are intended to kill bystanders, in other words, suicide/homicide is in contrast the act attributed to martyrdom. Death is, of course, the ultimate transformative experience and imbued with psychological and cultural symbolism.

But heroism is distinguished from martyrdom because it implies fighting against odds and either winning and staying alive, or death in the process of bringing down the enemy.

Whether any individual or group is ascribed martyrdom has been the function of the politics of memory. Contemporaneous ascription of martyrdom implies deliberation and determination of the act. Historically, in literature and theology, martyrdom has not been deliberate choice. In fact, in the opera, *Dialogues of the Carmelites*, when the nuns offer to take the place of the priests who are to be slaughtered by the French revolutionaries for their continuation of banned religious practices, the Mother Superior admonishes them that they cannot choose death in order to be martyrs. It is explicitly stated by the Mother Superior that their religious duty is to live and practice their faith. But, as the libretto unfolds, the nuns, having chosen not to be killed are, in fact killed one by one, all except the one who *wanted* to be a martyr!

But this is quite different from contemporary suicide bombers or kamikaze pilots of the Pacific in the Second World War. The connection between terrorism and martyrdom has, of late, been asserted in the designation of suicide bombers, a political connection asserted and debated. The presumption of connection between terrorism and the idea of martyrdom through suicide bombing is neither new nor unique to Islamic ideology.

Concurrently, there has been a growing literature on the politics of memory. International institutions are enacted out of the politics of memory as war crimes and crimes against humanity require the institution of international tribunals, international courts, and transitional justice systems. With instant communication of events on the battlefield has come the recognition that the standard of habeas corpus, literally meaning the presence of the body, is no longer requisite to prove mass murders, torture, and culpability.

Suits for recompense for slavery, the Holocaust, torture, and disappearances in the dirty wars of Central and South America have utilized new technology for establishing victimization and heroism and, finally, might alter the assignment of martyrdom.

The politics of memory incorporates victimology but produces heroes and saints.

These are powerful psychological and political images. Yet martyrdom has historically been connected with religion and religious violence; ideology and commitment with profession of faith and violent opposition to religious; religious beliefs and practices.

The psychology of the martyr was suggested by Freud and Jung in their exploration of human imagination and identity. Psychoanalytic studies of *thanatos*, or the death driving force, also connects suicide and homicide as contradiction to *libido*, or the life force. But Jung, in writing about archetypes, refers to the summit of life when the hidden immortal emerges from the consciousness of the mortal and to the enlargement of personality by the great idea. The idea of the martyr as such is embedded in several Jungian archetypes and not made explicit as an archetype in itself. But it has established an archetype in the psyche of Irish Catholics in the form of the hunger strike—self-sacrifice to shame the alleged oppressor. In *Totem and Taboo*, Freud explores the phenomenon of self-inflicted death and self-sacrifice, the sacrificial offering, and the distinctions between sublimation and suppression.

In studies of altruism and altruistic behavior the concept of risking or giving up one's life for another is close to the idea of heroism, but in a circumstance of violence and war the soldier who dies in combat is not essentially defined as a martyr. Depending on the circumstances of his death rather than the fact of it, he may eventually be attributed martyrdom. Soldiers on a mission commit their lives to their comrades and the mission. They may be heroes, but those in "The Charge of the Light Brigade" were not acting in the mindset of martyrdom. Heroes they may be to those whose cause they espoused, but not martyrs. The psychoanalytic construct of martyrdom presumes the individual to have made a *quid pro quo*. The altruist thinks first and foremost about the well-being of others and acts without regard to self—selflessly, and the martyr acts selflessly. Or, does the martyr act with self-consciousness? Is martyrdom solely a product of religious violence? Can secular torture victims be considered martyrs if they withstand the torturer's torments to extract information that would be deleterious to the victim's companions or cause? But on a multiaxial scoring system predicated on monotheistic taboos, can this motivation be codified? If martyrdom is the objective, what happens when it is engineered through homicide or suicide?

Is a person a martyr only if remembered as such? Memory and meaning are psychological phenomena emanating from the connative (the kind of knowing that is not derived from rational cues, or intuitive sensing) processes. It is formulated in language through mediating processes in the brain. The essay on the psychology and sociology of martyrdom will examine the psychodynamic and social processes linked with martyrdom. And because emotion and motivation happen in the brain, the central nervous system and its circuitry transport the idea to the part of the brain that is continually engaged in choices that govern behavior, that is, martyrdom.

The essays and the book itself are intended to be provocative and stimulate wider discussion rather than to be a scholarly definitive work on the subject. It is expected that by exploring from each discipline the scope of thinking on martyrdom, this volume will provide a foundation for widespread popular discussion.

Chapter 1: A Literary Preamble

Martyr and martyrdom are considered in terms of history and literature based in Christianity and derived from the ancient Greeks who invented the word. This section introduces the tensions between the sacred and the mundane, self-denial, and the assertion of belief that characterized the life and death of the martyr in Christian thought. While some of the individuals celebrated in literature are ascribed martyrdom in the Catholic Church or generally in Christendom, others are literary fictions whose behaviors symbolize these tensions and ideological conflicts.

The purpose of cult is the glory of God through prayer and the edification and instruction of the believer. The purpose of literature, on the other hand, is to instruction and entertainment of those who are willing to suspend, temporarily, imaginative disbelief. Literature achieves its ends with various degrees of logical discrimination and subtlety of expression. So while religious ceremonies—including the recollection of the saints and martyrs—are the official, communal, and impersonal commemorations of witness, literary and dramatic versions are unofficial, private, and personal reflections on the same subjects. Literary expressions that take into consideration contrary positions and respect the intelligence and cultivate self-criticism in the readers are morally and aesthetically superior to those that advocate a doctrinal, or sectarian case, or merely pander to a sense of tribal victimization.

Since virtue is less interesting than vice, the lives of the saints are less dramatic than the deaths of martyrs. Successful literary representation of the deaths of true martyrs requires a double struggle—with the enemies outside the martyr and also with the daemons within. Martyrdom is dramatically redemptive suffering. It thus contrasts with suffering considered as arbitrary or accidental, and not acceptance in the spirit of love and obedience to the will of God. It also contrasts with suffering that is non-dramatic, but endured in a spirit of hope or even transfiguring joy, as we see attested in the lives of the saints.

Eliot's *Murder in the Cathedral* is a dramatic example, which through his analysis exemplifies the psychological political and theological issues around martyrdom that are elaborated in the other sections of this book. The words of Thomas à Becket are echoed in the sermons of Martin Luther King. The chorus in the drama previews the dilemmas of popular respondents to contemporary martyrs, Gandhi and King. The distinction of these figures in literature is their having been defined and attributed martyrdom through the institution that incorporates and celebrates their deeds. Martyrdom outside that institution is not so definitively recognized. This essay touches on several classic examples of heroes turned martyr through the literature and the politics of its authors.

Chapter 2: The Psychology and Sociology of Martyrdom

Theoretical concepts of Freud and Jung on death and transformation, on Archetype and Race Memory provides the substrata for this discussion. But equally fundamental is the newer science of neuropsychology, the brain and behavior. It is, after all, through brain processing that motivation and emotion are translated from conception to action.

Altruism and aggression must be examined in terms of the motivational dynamics and also the social context in which they are manifested. Motivation and personality as defined by Magda Arnold are based in the neuropsychology of emotion. Weaving together the theoretical formulations of Lorenz, Pincus, Fromm, Maslow, Arnold, and Adler provides a dynamic framework for examining motivation and personality of martyrs and of martyrdom. Other giants in social psychological theory provide a context for examining extreme circumstances and the evolution of human capacity for shaping their psychological and social behavior. Lifton's *Death in Life* and *The Broken Connection* provide insight and perspectives, while Erikson's *Life History and the Historical Moment*, as well as his biographies of Gandhi and Luther, conveys psychological insights into the lives and development of revolutionaries and martyrs. Viktor Frankl and Jean Piaget have theoretical frameworks for examining moral development and meaning, learned or social memory, and intuitive or faith experience.

We examine diverse lives through these constructs, some of which are universally recognized as martyrs and many of which have a narrower base of recognition.

Finally, through social anthropology and psychohistory, we consider the societal function in the attribution of martyrdom and indeed in the process of memorialization out of memory.

Chapter 3: The Politics of Martyrdom

This section is aimed at observing the links between martyrdom and politics. To do so, it focuses on the representation of those who commemorate martyrdom. There is much at stake. Indeed, the analysis shows that the figure of martyr is revealed as particularly useful to maintain national identity, especially in a crisis situation.

The perspective adopted is based on one specific case: the political uses of national martyrs in France. Do the French authorities refer to any martyrs? In which circumstances? For what reasons? In doing so, do they have any impact on the population or do they encounter a form of resistance within the civil society?

In order to address these questions, we have divided this section into three main parts. The first one describes the *selective* character of national memory. The analysis of attitudes adopted by French authorities toward fallen soldiers and more broadly toward victims of war reveals the selective aspect of official memory. It indicates the importance of two main kinds of national martyrs: the sacrificial figure of the *Poilu*, the ordinary French soldier, in the First World War and the mythical figure of the *Résistant*, in the Second World War. By contrast, the reality of the Algerian war explains the quasi-impossibility of French leaders commemorating any martyrs of the nation in relation with this war.

The second part stresses the *fluctuating* character of national memory. The rhetoric of official memory works by building symbolic bridges between today and yesterday; the primary movement being not from the past to the present but the other way around. The examination of the French case shows that official representations of the past fluctuate according to two main variables. The first one is the context—that is to say the national and international circumstances and the political aims that are pursued by the leaders. The second variable results from the generation effect. Thus, we will see that the time factor is often a determining element in explaining the conversion of a victim—or even a traitor—into a martyr and vice versa.

The third and final part of the section underlines that the political use of martyrdom is inevitably a *limited* process. Admittedly, official discourses about the past can be powerful tools for inspiring mass devotion and self-sacrifice. However, they cannot be imposed by decree. Indeed, the citizens who are exposed to the official interpretation of the past do not always internalize it. The potential gap between the official and the individual representations of the same event allow questioning the factors determining the degree of population adherence. Research thus far shows that the impact of official memory on the population depends on three main variables: individual experience, popular expectations, and the personal legitimacy of the official representative.

Chapter 4: The Theology of Martyrdom

Michael Berenbaum turned to Reuven Firestone, a rabbi and an expert in Islamic thought at Hebrew Union College in Los Angeles, to sketch the issue of martyrdom in Islamic thought. Berenbaum strongly felt that it required an expertise far beyond his own. Firestone traces the origin of Islamic thought back to its pre-Islamic roots and into the climate of the region and the nature of social arrangements. He draws parallels with Christian and Jewish thought.

Like Judaism, Scripture (the Qur'an) and Tradition (the Hadith) have authority for the believers. The early followers of Mohamed, Firestone argues, were subject to the kind of treatment one encounters in Christianity and Jewish martyrology. Islam has elements of the Garden, Gehenna, and the Fire that have parallels in Christian and Jewish thought. Scripture maintains that one should not consider those killed in the path of God as dead.

Later tradition shapes the notion of battlefield martyrs, martyrs in this world and the next. Martyrdom, Firestone maintains, became a means of extolling certain behavior and a way of ensuring that those who behaved accordingly entered the Garden. Death in combat became established as the noblest way to depart this life. These traditions reached their apogee in Shi'ite religion, where it became an important part of ritual and shape the creation of heroes, paradigms of self-sacrifice. The Shi'ite faith emphasized redemptive suffering. Far more prevalent in Shi'ite ritual than other forms of Islamic faith, these religious views have been absorbed into Sunni Muslim faith as well and shape the context for contemporary political movements.

Chapter 5: A Conversation among the Collaborators

The four collaborating authors question each other's essays and answer questions of their own while linking the four perspectives on martyrdom with each other. They examine the impact of a martyrology theologically, psychologically, and in building national cohesion and international politics. They discuss the interaction between religious and secular martyrdom and the psychology of memory and the politics of memorialization. This conversation is provocative and stimulating as the collaborators bounce ideas off each other.

Reference

Lifton, R. J. (1979). *The broken connection: On death and the continuity of life.* New York: Simon and Schuster.

PART I

CHAPTER 1

A LITERARY PREAMBLE

Cóilín Owens

Martyrdom

Christian History

The word "martyr" derives from the Greek for a first-hand witness (*martus*, μάρτυς): one whose knowledge derives from personal observation. Its first appearances in Christian literature—Matthew 18:16 and Mark 14:63—carry this original meaning: that the Apostles were "witnesses" of Christ's activities and sayings. However, since this witness got them into trouble with the law, where they were regarded as unreliable citizens in refusing to pay respects to the state deities, the word began to carry the added significance of conveying the risk of physical punishment, or even death, for their persistence. The beginnings of this use may be observed in such passages as Acts 22:20 and Apocalypse 2:13 and 13:6. Thus tradition has it that beginning with St. Stephen and all of the original Apostles, martyrdom was the price that the early witnesses to the Christian faith were likely to pay. Within the lifetime of the first generation of the Christian era, therefore, the term took on the meaning that it has retained to the present day: one who out of devotion to any aspect of Christian faith or practice, suffers torture and death at the hands of a hostile regime or populace.

In the course of early Church history, with the demise of the original witnesses to Christ's ministry, the term took on the significance of bearing the testimony of religious faith to which one was not a personal witness—a reversal of its original meaning. Another effect of the experience of the disabilities and threat under which Christians in the late Roman Empire lived was the emergence of the distinction between martyrs (those who suffered death for their beliefs) and confessors (those who suffered lesser inconveniences for the same cause, informally known as "white martyrs" in contrast with "red martyrs"). Although there are inconsistencies in the usage, it is clear that early Christians did not use the term for any but the orthodox believers; thus, heretics, schismatics, and apostates who might happen to suffer execution for their religious beliefs were not afforded the honor of the name. The term did not, of course, apply to persons suffering execution or death for causes other than those of religious belief, such as political or ethnic allegiances, vendettas, or criminal executions. By the time of the Reformation, however, it took on the broader meaning of one who suffers death (or even torture) for the sake of any religious or political cause. Thus in today's popular culture, voracious, self-promoting, and ecumenical to a fault, the lives of figures such as James Dean, Marilyn Monroe, and John Lennon may be found catalogued under the subject heading "Martyred Pop Icons." Where market opportunity is the only rule and victimization a commodity, the word "martyr" is bandied about without any regard for its high and hard-won historical integrity. Thus although one is likely to encounter it in current usages that are often consciously ironical or hyperbolic ("he's a martyr to the bottle"), much current usage is self-serving and betrays a trendy pseudo-masochism.

During two hundred and fifty of the years preceding the edict of the Emperor Constantine (A.D. 313), Christians within the Roman Empire were under some degree of disapproval, impediment, or active persecution. These persecutions originated in the perceived disrespect to the state gods (in Christians' unwillingness to participate in state occasions honoring these gods), in the damage to local economies that traded on official shrines, and in personal vendettas. Since refusal to worship the official state gods was regarded as treason, and Christians had not yet been granted the exemptions granted to the monotheistic Jews, Christians in the late Roman Empire were constantly in danger of persecution. These persecutions were intermittent—being especially vindictive during the reigns of Nero, Domitian, and Diocletian—but Christians in the late Empire generally enjoyed a tolerance such as that afforded Jews in the same period.

Under these persecutions, Christians suffered ascending degrees of civil disability: assemblies forbidden, books and sacred objects destroyed, and churches leveled. To judge by contemporary accounts, Christian martyrs were tortured and executed with a sadistic vindictiveness reserved for those deemed to be the direst threats to the political order. They were subjected to imprisonment, whipping, the rack, dismemberment, fire, and rape. They endured enslavement and various forms of execution: beheading, drowning, strangulation, crucifixion, and exposure to the elements or to wild animals. Considering that their eternal salvation—a higher stake than physical survival—depended on their unwillingness to abjure their faith in Jesus as redeemer, they were willing to endure these barbaric sufferings. There are many accounts of apostasies among those so challenged. But as the numbers of those martyred grew, and the numbers of local martyrologies (lists of martyrs) multiplied throughout the empire—in Pontus, Egypt, Greece, and Rome itself—the commemorations of these martyrs became celebrated public events. These martyrologies were the most popular literature in the early Church. Relics and shrines became objects and venues of prestige and pious pilgrimage. The title of martyr so grew in prestige that new questions needed answering: could one consciously seek out death for Christ's sake—by vandalizing the shrines of the Roman gods, or insulting the magistrates, as some fanatics were moved to do, for example—and thus assure both historical fame and eternal salvation in the one stroke? Could one become a martyr by accident? Would martyrdom alone atone for one's sins? Was a life of heroic Christian witness—in prison or exile, for example—that did not actually end in violent death, that of a martyr?

The orthodox positions on these questions gradually emerged: that it was rash to seek out death, but reprehensible to avoid it; that one was obligated to proclaim one's faith only if challenged, and then one was not permitted to deny it; and that the title of martyr was denied to those who deliberately vandalized official shrines and suffered the consequences. In these formulations, the early Church sought to preserve the peace with the indifferent—but hostile if provoked—officials of the Empire, while also preserving the moral integrity of the individual Christian and acknowledging the Providential order that governed all.

The subsequent worldwide spread of Christianity followed the commercial routes, the slave trade, imperial expansion, and colonial outreach. As it challenged local belief systems and the attendant social, political, and economic orders, it often encountered official retaliation, through various forms of interdiction, ranging from restriction of speech, constraints on proselytizing, expulsion, and death. As Christian belief—despite its contrary principles—became identified with imperialism and colonial exploitation, its adherents who suffered death at the hands of anti-colonial activists might lay claim to the title of martyr. Similarly, the religious wars that followed the Reformation produced victims of conscience on several sides. These developments introduced new complications bearing upon the circumstances and motivations of the executioners and executed alike. Whatever the problems surrounding any historical circumstance, local martyrologies have developed in almost every region of the globe where Christianity has flourished. And these martyrologies continue to grow. Thus there are martyrologies in countries as dispersed as Uganda, Japan, Egypt, El Salvador, and Canada, and with dates ranging from the first to the twentieth centuries in the Christian era.

The Roman Catholic Church has an authorized Martyrology ("Martyrology"), a catalog or list of martyrs, arranged in the order of their anniversaries, together with brief biographies. The names of some early Christian martyrs are mentioned in every Mass (in the Eucharistic Prayer, immediately after the Apostles: "Linus, Cletus, Clement, Sixtus, Cornelius, Cyprian, Lawrence, Chrysogonus . . . Cosmas and Damian"), and the yearly liturgical calendar contains the names of scores of individual martyrs (e.g., St. Emigdius, Bishop & Martyr, August 9; St. Vibiana, Virgin and Martyr, September 1; Saints Isaac Jogues, John de Bebeuf and Companions, Martyrs, September 26; St. Ursula and Companions, Virgins and Martyrs, October 21) whose anniversaries are universally commemorated. Thus the consciousness of the bonds of blood between contemporary Christians and those who suffered the loss of their earthly lives for the sake of the Kingdom is officially maintained, even in liberal, tolerant, or indifferent political and cultural climates. These figures remind contemporary Christians that their beliefs, however politely tolerated, are in significant ways at odds with popularly held views: with regard to the uses of political power, social responsibility, personal integrity, and metaphysical or spiritual assumptions.

Some Modern Literary Examples

Popular cultural representations of Christian martyrdom—such as the Hollywood film *Quo Vadis* (1951)—maintain the tradition of the Martyrology while also providing a comfortable and historical distancing from contemporary life. A more recent, and relevant, example is the film *Romero* (1989) that underlines the Christian witness of the Salvadorean archbishop murdered for his option for the poor. Thoughtful examples of the literature of martyrdom in twentieth-century fiction are George Bernard Shaw's *Saint Joan* (1923), Graham Greene's fine novel, *The Power and the Glory* (1940), Shusaku Endo's *Silence* (tr. 1969), and Brian Moore's *Black Robe* (1985). The orthodox masterpiece, however, is T. S. Eliot's verse play, *Murder in the Cathedral* (1935).

The secular analogue here is Yeats's celebration of the blood sacrifice of the leaders of the Easter Rising in Dublin. Centuries of adjustment to British imperial interests had dried up Ireland's flower garden. "The Rose Tree" concludes with the memorable lines:

O plain as plain can be
There's nothing but our own red blood
Can make a right Rose Tree. (Yeats 206)

Yet that is not Yeats's last word. In his more deeply considered reflection, "Easter 1916," he admits to qualms about possible English good faith, to reservations both personal and cultural about the executed leaders. He also admits that their example has caused him to revise his own position, and that in some mysterious way, the course of history has been changed because through these possessed men, something divine has finally intervened in the daily round of grubbing and gossip. The language of this poem conveys all of these complexities, converging on the ringing—and by now immemorial—paradox: "A terrible beauty is born" (Yeats 202–205).

Graham Greene's *The Power and the Glory* (1940) is a classic representation of the pursuit and death of an unlikely martyr. Greene visited Mexico in 1938 during the religious persecution undertaken under the guise of political revolution by Plutarco Elias Calles, and based his novel on his travels there. It pursues the final stages of the ministry of a disheveled and alcoholic priest who is an outlaw in his own provinces of Tabasco and Chiapas. His dedication to his priestly ministry is stronger than his sense of unworthiness, and so he persists until his final apprehension. The arresting lieutenant is a fanatical idealist, a "good man" who seeks to root out all traces of superstition among the peasantry. These two main characters contrast with another pair: Padre José, a conforming priest who, accepting marriage, has turned from his ministry of service to the people of God, and so no longer enjoys their respect; and the "gringo," a bank

robber and murderer on the run from the law. The lieutenant suc-
ceeds in capturing the priest who had paused, as he reached the border and safety, to give the last rites to the dying gringo. Although he
does not realize it, the priest's execution has its evangelical influence.
There are several indications that this persecution will not eliminate
the Church; beyond what he can know, his death affects the spiritual
welfare of his community. Nevertheless, despite its clear Christian
ideas, and no doubt because of the moral ambiguities surrounding the
priest, the Roman Holy Office voiced its unofficial displeasure.

This novel—at once a thriller and a morality tale—implies many
parallels between the priest's activities and the passion and death of
Jesus: riding a mule, his sympathy with and service to the poor, his be-
trayal, his spiritual crisis, and eventual execution. He is a figure of
spiritual hope, in dual contrast with the material optimism of the lieutenant and the spiritual despair of Padre José. His sacrifice has an effect beyond what he can himself observe; despite his sense of personal
failure, the action of grace can be seen on Tench, the embittered ex-
patriate dentist, and in the conversion of the little boy. Both are minor
characters with but tangential relationships with the central action,
yet their brief witness of the priest's witness is sufficient for the Holy
Spirit to enter their lives. By such means, the novel sets the scientific
and materialist view of the world—represented by the bones and the
lieutenant—against the Christian, where the action of grace takes its
own mysterious course. It weaves this dualistic theme—the struggle
between good and evil—through the vivid details of the pursuit.
Nevertheless, full of well-drawn figures and graphic landscapes, it
avoids moral simplicities: the lieutenant is, by his lights, a good man;
and the priest, by his, seems a bad one, and unworthy of the role for
which Providence has singled him out. Greene was appalled by the social conditions in Mexico, but saw in its squalor and corruption an un-
masking of true spiritual desolation. He considers that it is better to
keep hold of a small bastion of religious comfort against the inroads
made by hypothetical happiness based on materialism than to succumb
to despair. Thus he shows in this unsentimental novel that despite the
degradation and hardship undergone by the priest and his people, the
mystery of God's love shines through. The impoverished are closest to
grace; the furthest away from it are the morally complacent and pious.
In Francois Mauriac's words, *The Power and the Glory* expresses "the
utilization of sin by Grace." No doubt it was for this reason that the
Holy Office was not pleased, regarding the novel as presenting an ec-
centric rather than an emotionally transparent subject.

If pressed for a clarification, the Holy Office might have observed that as his execution approaches, the terrified priest does not burst into visionary prayer as do many of the heroes of the Martyrology, but can only face it fortified by whisky. He has not desired martyrdom, but only to do what he knows he has undertaken: his duty. He has a natural father's love for his daughter, and a true priest's love for his people. He has taken the burden of sin upon himself. The various images of renewal—including the unexpected arrival of another priest at the end—signify the mysterious ways of Providence. Thus, in the tradition of Christian martyrdom, we see in the shedding of the blood of this otherwise unremarkable man the fertilization of the seeds of faith.

Murder in the Cathedral

When he declared himself a royalist in politics, a classicist in literature, and an Anglo-Catholic in religion in 1934, the American poet Thomas Stearns Eliot was turning his back on the earlier work—notably *Prufrock and Other Observations* (1917) and *The Waste Land* (1922)—those theme songs of the Lost Generation and the most widely influential expressions of literary modernism. With his verse play, *Murder in the Cathedral*, he turned from the modishness he had himself in large part established, and from poetry to the theater. In his "Dialogue on Dramatic Poetry," Eliot maintained that the greatest drama would always be poetic. He wrote the play for the 1935 Canterbury Festival, and revised it for subsequent productions in 1937 and 1938. His four poetic dramas have for a common theme the lives of the saints. Of them, *Murder in the Cathedral* is the only one with a non-contemporary setting, his most obviously religious, and his most poetic.

Eliot's subject, Thomas à Becket, was born of Norman parentage in London in 1118. He was educated at the University of Paris, where he studied theology and canon law. These disciplines prepared him to enter Church politics, and on his return to England, he became secretary to Theobald, the Archbishop of Canterbury, Kent. During his secretariat he became a close friend of the young man who later became King Henry II. Henry appointed him chancellor in 1155. Charged with governing ecclesiastical benefices, he taxed the Church to help with the French war in which he served as commander, envoy, and knight. In recognition of these services, and despite opposition, Henry awarded him the See of Canterbury in 1162. But once charged with ecclesiastical responsibilities, he resisted Henry's attempts to manipulate him. This led to open conflict between them over taxes and court jurisdiction. Rejecting Henry's *Constitutions of Clarendon*, which defined Church-State relations, Thomas, with the Pope's backing, quit England in 1164 and excommunicated some of Henry's counselors. On the basis of a shallow truce, Thomas returned from France in 1170, but within a month of this return he was murdered on December 29th (the complicated relationship between Henry and Thomas is gracefully summarized by Lacey Baldwin Smith). Thomas was canonized in 1172, and his shrine at Canterbury became a place of pilgrimage made famous in literary history by Chaucer.

In dramatizing the martyrdom of St. Thomas à Becket, Eliot follows Tennyson (*Becket*, 1884). He has successors, Christopher Fry (*Curtmantle*, 1961) and Jean Anouilh (*Becket; or, The Honor of God*, 1960). In contrast with these writers, Eliot set aside the general historical context in order to dilate the central issue, Becket's martyrdom. The action of the play takes place during the month of December, between Thomas's return from France and his death at Canterbury. In the course of the action, the Chorus, representing the ordinary Christians, is moved from a spiritless adjustment to the reduced, but natural, circumstances of daily life to the recognition that they were resistant to both the larger historical moment and the even larger moment in salvation history. Similarly, the priests are caught up—against their timorous temperaments—in facing the implications of their Christian ministry. But most significantly of all, Thomas, by his sequence of confrontations with the four tempters, has his own motives—which are over-determined by public and private circumstances—purified in the crucible of progressively insidious invitations to compromise. The design of the drama, which has these four tempters return as his four assassins, epitomizes the congruence of private and public, of spiritual and political threats to Thomas's life. The rich range of rhetorical and structural borrowings—from the verse, dramatic, and liturgical traditions—give the play a powerful emotional force, so that we can agree that it is justly celebrated as perhaps the most successful verse play in the modern repertoire. It is, by the same token, a uniquely penetrating moral and spiritual examination of the convention of Christian martyrdom, in which the attendant historical and moral dimensions are scrupulously and eloquently examined.

Murder in the Cathedral is similar to the *Agamemnon* of Aeschylus in its celebration of a sacred place and its arrangement as a series of episodes linked by choral odes. The chorus is used expressively to provide exposition, a stereo-optic view of the action, and thus intensify its dramatic force. This tragic structuring implicitly raises the question of whether or not this is a tragic play, as well as the relationship between Christian martyrdom and Greek tragedy and the disparate visions that underlie each. At the same time, it is like the medieval morality play, *Everyman*, in its versification and as a drama with biblical echoes of temptation overcome. In this case, the dramatic sequence of tempters ironically extends the accounts (Matthew 4:1–11and Luke 4:1–13) of Jesus in the desert, where this classic trio are followed by the especially insidious fourth, presenting the attractions of martyrdom itself. Thomas's temptations are similar to those of Christ in the desert: to sensual appetite, to political power, and to divinity. In an ironic twist, Eliot has the Fourth Tempter address Thomas in the very words Thomas used to the Women of Canterbury; it is at that moment that Thomas achieves his victory over temptation: "The last temptation is the greatest treason: / To do the right deed for the wrong reason."

Eliot wrote this play in the form of a poetic drama to challenge the naturalistic bias of post-eighteenth-century drama, and, in his own words, to "present at once two aspects of dramatic and musical order" ("Poetry and Drama" 146). Indeed, the immediately distinctive qualities of the play are to be found in its rhetorical range. The verse draws on a variety of forms: the doggerel of the quarrels between Becket and Knights; the easy, near-blank verse for dialog with the Priests and Women's Chorus; the three-stress lines of the women's domestic talk; and the long complexes of pleading or of praise in subtle, rhythmic blank verse. These variations set off the lamentations of the Women, the insidious, sometimes crabbed, four-stress rhyming verse for the Tempters, and the throes of anguish of Becket's inner struggle. This dramatic verse is backed by the interspersed hymnody, the formal rhetoric of the sermon, and the Knights' prose apologiae. Behind all of this are the hymnal background and the prose of interlude and finale. These colorations bear out Eliot's purposes in exploiting the acoustic peculiarities of churches for which this liturgical play was written.

Similarly, Eliot's borrowings from church ritual, from pre-Shakespearean drama, while running the risk of archaism, take us back to the roots of western drama and language. By observing the unities of place, time, and action, the drama coalesces into a classic intensity. The rhythms of the verse are hypnotic and sensuous, providing an apprehension of experience that is not possible in prose, implying a religious view of life with its values beyond human measure. So while much of the language is modern, its versification medieval, it expresses the timeless theme of the redemption of the Christian community. The subtle range of the poetry, the evocative power of the images, purifies both our appreciation of the moral issues and our sense of language as a conveyor of emotional and spiritual distinctions. *Murder in the Cathedral* is neither a play of mere historical situation or of character; both are subordinate to the universal theme of the relationship between the phenomena of human action and the spiritual dimension of our lives. In other words, the subtle music of the language is the objective correlative of the order of grace underlying the otherwise simply realistic components of the physical action. One of the major thematic implications of these effects is the statement about the limitations of action if detached from the larger order of divine Providence.

In a similar vein, this poetic language is permeated with recurrent images of the redemption of the barren lands. As David Jones observed, the language of *Murder in the Cathedral* is permeated with

> ... recurrent images of ... *The Waste Land*, the seasons, beasts and birds, the everyday tasks, the blood of redemption ... gathered together and resolved in a significant pattern. They all fit together in the scheme of God's Providence: the blood of redemption restores fertility to the Waste Land ... so that the natural rhythm of the seasons can remain undisturbed, ... [so that] men can perform their seasonal tasks and give articulate praise not just for themselves, but for the beasts as well, and all creatures are secured in their ordained places, fulfilling their role in the "eternal design." (pp. 78–99)

A major symbol in the play is the wheel: the wheel of fortune becomes that of the still center of redemptive grace which redeems life on the shifting circumference where time is measured in hours and seasons. These contrasting aspects represent the stoic acceptance of the flux of events as they present themselves or the awareness that these apparently random or determined events are redeemed by the stillness at the wheel's center. This contrast appears early in the play when the Chorus, and then the Priests, express their apprehensions about their reduced circumstances and hopes. The members of the Chorus are forced to accept their fragmented lives, "living and partly living," they cling to their piety and the flux of events. The Priests, on the other hand, are practical, worldly, and sanguine: they hope that nothing will happen; they hope to manage by fulfilling the daily prescriptions of the law. In the course of the play they all come to realize their dependence upon a larger system of values, embodied at this historical moment, by Thomas.

Between them, the trio of priests combine in expressing a hierarchy of understanding of Thomas's return: the first fears for the Church, the second is primarily concerned with Thomas's comfort, but the third comes closest to Thomas's understanding of events to come. Nevertheless, these opening speeches are full of ironies—as indeed is Thomas's own. This can be seen, for example, in the ways in which they use the thematic word, "Peace." In their casual and apparently thoughtless juxtaposition of its sacred and profane meanings, they introduce what will become the major epiphany of the work. With unconscious irony, Thomas addresses the Chorus in his opening greeting:

Peace. And let them be, in their exaltation.
They speak better than they know, and beyond your understanding.
They know and do not know, what it is to act or suffer.
They know and do not know, that action is suffering
And suffering action.

As the subsequent action shows, this address is too full of moral complacency: a pastiche of false epigrams, the stuff of ecclesiastical public relations speech or formal sermonizing. Thomas is in need of redemption as are his spiritual charges.

The theme of the play is the conflict between the Christian and modern or materialist view of human nature. These can be summarized by contrasting the Christian view of human nature as wounded by sin, living by divine grace, and seeking perfection by the exercise of love, with the modern materialist view that man is a psychological animal living by social law, and seeking security by adjustment to the environment. In his role as representative of the Church, Thomas comes into public conflict with the claims of the realm on Church property, appointments, and income. And in his role as leader of the Christian community, he must both preach and set an example of a life lived by Christian principles, reminding them that they do not live by the natural or social laws alone, but by reference to the divine law of the gospel of charity. But more profoundly, he must confront these counterclaims in his own conscience, bound as he is to the principle of integrity: he must practice what he preaches.

In the opening chorus, the ordinary citizens express their impotence, their sense of foreboding, and their apprehension about actions forced on them from without. They have resigned themselves to the rhythms of the natural seasons, seeking respite from the prospect of their redemption through violent martyrdom. They are apprehensive that they may find themselves living in "interesting times"—at the intersection of time defined temporally or historically, *chronos*, and time understood sacramentally, *kairos*. Like Saint Peter, when identified as an associate of the arrested Christ, they seek immediate respite from the approaching axial moment. These women are already preoccupied with the management of their own domestic lives. Yet despite this, their central action is on the spiritual plane: waiting for God's Providence to reveal itself—the moment of *kairos*. Thus beneath their complaints and apprehension, we are enabled to see salvation at work in the consciousness of the Chorus.

The dramatic development of the play follows the sequence of tempters who approach Thomas, offering him Peace on escalating terms. With their entrance, the focus of the drama switches from the public to the private realm, from the import of the political situation to the impact of the impending conflict on Thomas's conscience. The Four Tempters may be read as representing aspects of Thomas's own personality; and between them, they comprise a dramatic projection of the wrestling within Thomas's soul. They parallel—and dramatically play one-upmanship on Jesus's three temptations in Luke 4:1–13 and Matthew 4:1–11. The First is ingratiating; in jigging doggerel, he presents the case for the World and the Flesh overlaid with a patina from the Past (and thus a nostalgic separation from the real experience of the present with its premonition of Future). But for Thomas, there is no going back; he easily rejects the lure offered by sensuous self-indulgence. The Second Tempter approaches offering temporal power: to build a better world by using his political power to build a just world. Thomas's response comes in eloquent rhetoric, structured acoustically in natural breath lengths, full of antithesis and alliteration, with firm cumulative effects. His answer is that his calling is not to build political power, but to remind those who do that it cannot be established without reference to God's Providence:

Temporal power, to build a good world
To keep order, as the world knows order.
Those who put their faith in worldly order
Not controlled by the order of God,
In confident ignorance, but arrest disorder,
Make it fast, breed fatal disease,
Degrade what they exalt.

The Third Tempter is an English Country Gentleman. He appeals to Thomas's patriotism, but as a conspirator, a member of "a happy coalition / Of intelligent interests," tempting Thomas to sedition and treachery against the legitimate ruler, Henry II. He would thus appear to be superimposing a perverted Future on the Present—by rendering to God without rendering to Caesar. Thomas replies, quoting *Judges* and *Samson Agonistes*, that he has considered this before, but that he must act alone. The contradiction in Thomas's thinking—the rejection of temptation to willing action (seeking power) leads to willing his own destruction—shows a will incompliant with God's will. This is immediately mocked by the Fourth Tempter, who offers a subtler and more sinister lure than those proposed by his predecessors. This is the temptation to martyrdom itself, the wrong use of the Future. It appeals to Thomas's spiritual pride, offering what Thomas agrees with, spiritual eminence, the vision of eternal grandeur:

Seek the way of martyrdom, make yourself the lowest
On earth, to be high in heaven.
And see far off below you, where the gulf is fixed,
Your persecutors, in timeless torment,
Parched passion, beyond expiation.

He quotes Thomas's own words,

You know and do not know, what it is to suffer.
You know and do not know, that action is suffering,
And suffering action . . . that the wheel may turn and still
Be forever still.

Thomas's response, in the most famous lines of the play, "The last temptation is the greatest treason—To do the right deed for the wrong reason." He sees his own error and pride in seeking to do good action without love, without acknowledging his dependence on grace, in aspiring to enjoy heaven without God. This, the finest temptation, appeals only to the saints.

In refuting these tempters, Thomas summons all of his spiritual and intellectual resources. His refutation might be read in terms of his grasp of a Christian sense of history, the alignment and assessment of his personal account with that of history and eternity. The first tempts him back to his past, but Thomas necessarily rejects a past vision—whether pious or profligate—dissociated from the demands of the present reality and his responsibility to the future. The second tempts him with present temporal power, attempting to stake

all on a present dissociated from past history and from the Day of
Judgment (holiness hereafter), an alternative Thomas also must reject. The third and fourth are temptations to the misuse of the future
or apocalyptic dimension, the first by using the power of the church
for earthly, temporal profit; and the second by claiming the promise
of heaven for the wrong reasons: for the personal glory of a creature,
rather than for the love of God.

Summoning all his emotional, intellectual, and spiritual resources,
he assesses the temptations. He reviews his personal history and puts
it in the perspective of the public consciousness. He must reject the
desire to turn the wheel himself rather than accept the Will of the
Prime Mover. In this summative meditation on his own biography, his
place in secular history, and the Providential order, he makes his inspired decision. In this respect his position is different from that of
the Chorus, who ache to dissociate their personal lives from the demands of history in order to live and half live. Thomas is the man in
whom the conflict is resolved and private and public integrated.
History is now and England, and on December 29th, Thomas dies; but
this death is simultaneously historic and personal, recapitulating St.
Stephen's death and the death of Christ—and emblematic of the passion of every Christian. But it is still Thomas à Becket who is murdered in the Cathedral.

Bewildered by this inspired summation, the lesser figures join in a
cacophonic chorus. The confusion is signified by the choral unison of
Priests and Tempters; their lives are in danger of losing their meaning. Similarly, the Chorus, Thomas's spiritual dependents, express
their horror, confusion, and hopelessness in images of panic: is their
Christian faith an illusion? All of this confirms Thomas's realization
that his decision is not autonomous: that his salvation is not his own
business alone, but involves the whole Church.

In a fine theatrical stroke, Eliot turns the theatre audience into a
church congregation attending to Thomas's sermon. The placement of
this Interlude in the aftermath of the Four Tempters ensures that the
religious atmosphere does not neutralize the theatricality of this passage. The sermon fulfills the traditional function: of being an expatia-
tion on the Gospel word to both the Chorus and the audience. It is also
an exposition of the progress of Becket's self-knowledge, as he comes
to recognize his place in the historical and eschatological scheme. The
center of the dogmatic drama of Becket's self-knowledge, the sermon is
an instruction in the Spirit, in the Nature of Peace. A meditation that
progresses from the feast of St. Stephen the first martyr through those

of the Holy Innocents and on to the 29th, it shows how the Word of the sermon anticipates the flesh of the drama (as in the Mass). It expresses the belief in the organic nature of all action: that a martyr's death is ours too. Taking a Providential perspective, it holds that a Christian martyrdom is never an accident. Still less is a Christian martyrdom the effect of a man's will to become a saint, as a man by willing and contriving may become a ruler of men. A true martyr is he who has become the instrument of God, who no longer desires anything for himself, not even the glory of being a martyr. The sermon is, then, Thomas's answer to the Fourth Tempter. It is the dramatic center of the play—more Protestant than Catholic in that sense—in that it centers on the Word rather than the Eucharist. As the center of the play, then, the sermon radiates both ways, linking Parts I and II. But in the second part, the sermon becomes dramatized: first in the liturgy of the holy days, but then more pointedly in Thomas's martyrdom.

Part II opens with the response of the Chorus to the sermon; their sensuous and intricate imaginings express their increased anxiety and insecurity. They vacillate between Christian and Pagan conceptions of time, the prospect of endless cycles contrasted with the Christian sense of final, apocalyptic deliverance. These desperate musings are cut short by the entrance of the Priests who, true to their official function, underline the significance of the liturgical calendar, marking the feasts of St. Stephen (December 26th), St. John the Apostle (December 27th), and the Holy Innocents (December 28th). This introduces the question of what will sanctify this day, the 29th; as we move through its sordid particulars, how will the Providential design reveal itself?

As the smell of roast pork circulates, the Knights enter, in an aura of appropriately contrastive bestiality. In an atmosphere rancorous with accusations of treason, they accuse Thomas of being in revolt against the king, to whom he actually owes the position even if he thinks it a debt he owes to God. Thomas replies that he has been loyal both to the king and his priestly order; but that the Church, the representative of Christ's law, is independent of the State. Seeing no compromise between these positions, the Chorus grows impassioned and hysterical. They acknowledge the corruption in nature, the interdependence of public and private, body politic and individual. They thus come to accept their part in the guilt for Thomas's martyrdom. Their acceptance of their role, however, brings disquiet, and not resignation. Eliot is here raising the question of whether this expression of guilt is morbid or true: is modern consciousness immune from this kind of guilt?

With his entry, Thomas promises that God's purposes will be made manifest in the day's actions: he has "a wink of heaven," a premonition that the true peace is in the resurrection. It is ironically appropriate that with this the Priests, ever preoccupied with ritual, call him to the Vespers, which mark the liturgical end of the day. Similarly, as he is martyred, the *Dies Irae* can be heard, and the Chorus sings of the emptiness beyond death and judgment. Without Calvary's intercession with the void, the emptiness, mankind is separated from God. Thus Thomas is a witness to salvation, a type of Christ, as are all Christians. What is out of time gives meaning to the temporal order: what is beyond history makes history itself sacramental. With this, the Knights enter with a jazzy mocking taunt (after Vachel Lindsay's "Daniel Jazz"). Now Thomas is becoming the incarnation of his own sermon, recognizing his own role in the redemptive plan: "I am here." Forming a symbolic circle around him on whom their own salvation depends, they murder him.

In this scene we see how the Church is washed in the blood of martyrs, beginning with the Lamb. Blood—for the women—is a symbol of their guilt and also of the redemptive blood of Christ. After this crime, there is no return to the quiet round of seasons; the axial event has intruded itself upon the natural round of seasons. Thus in the vacillations of the Chorus we see the reflection of the movements from private to public and to eternal—out-of-time—aspects of the event. The only way in which Thomas's death is not a waste is to see it from the point of view of salvation: that all nature is in need of redemption.

At this point, with the re-entry of the Tempters in the form of the murderous Knights, we encounter one of the most ironic scenes—dramatically and rhetorically—in the entire play. Each delivers a prosaic speech, in the manner of a modern press conference (and, indeed, reminiscent of the final scene in Shaw's *Saint Joan*). They plead for fair play, counting on our presumed sympathies with the underdog and our willingness to hear both sides of the case. In the contemporary prose of political debate, and claiming personal disinterest, they make the familiar appeals to patriotism. But they are ignorant of the perspectives to which we have been exposed; they are unaware of the incompatibilities over which they so blithely skate. These speeches—in their content and form—emphasize the divergence of the values of the world and from those of God. Arguments based on shallow and secular modern assumptions, they are patently dishonest, and, in this context, blasphemous. The effect of these bland defenses is the opposite of what they intend, showing that even the worst crimes can appear reasonable. This can be seen especially in the speech of the fourth Knight who, like his counterpart in his Tempter role, offers the subtlest argument—that Becket had determined upon a death by martyrdom: his death was not murder, but suicide. This may appear honest, but it is only as honest as its proponent is capable; it does not arise from a deep consciousness of the Providential order. Thus Eliot's Becket triumphs morally over the Knights as well as the Tempters (who are usually played by the same actors).

In the Coda to all of this tempestuous action, the Priests, ever concerned with the institution, miss the significance of the events they have just witnessed. The Chorus, on the other hand, seems to understand. In a summative hymn of nature, they see their historical situation *sub specie aeternatis:* that all of life's actions are sanctified by the sacrifice of Christ and of the martyrdom they have just witnessed. They give thanks for this sacrifice made on their behalf. They acknowledge that bearing witness means being involved, and not simply observing the sacrificial act. Like Greek tragic heroes, Christian martyrs recognize their place in an eternal order, and by refusing to strike back, turn what appears to be a defeat into a victory. The suffering is lost in the moral triumph.

Murder in the Cathedral is then a stylized dramatization of an historical event featuring the power struggle between Church and State. It is also a psychological study of a saint made understandable and relevant to modern world. On a deeper level, as the Christ-martyr parallels emerge, Calvary and Canterbury, the temptations and triumphs of Christ and Becket are clarified. It is thus a ritual drama on the death and resurrection of Christ: a meditation on the meaning of martyrdom and a celebration of the martyrdom, and a commemoration and celebration of that act, a sign of God's grace. The play ends with thanksgiving for sacrifice made on their behalf; bearing witness means being involved, not simply observing. Ending with the *Kyrie eleison*, it foreshadows the Mass as rendering of martyrdom into our time and days (and links with the passages that open and close *Little Gidding*). In its meditation on waiting—holy waiting—it rebukes, by anticipation, Samuel Beckett's *En attendant Godot* (1952).

Murder in the Cathedral is Eliot's effort to make liturgical drama a part of the living theatrical tradition—to write drama for serious people. It observes the traditional relations between priests, congregation, and choir. It employs dialog based on the responses of the Mass, and cites Christian hymns (*Te Deum* and Negro spirituals). It provides religious instruction, in providing a dramatized mediation on the significance of sainthood and martyrdom. In its combination of lyric and dramatic elements, it projects characters not as individuals with psychological conflicts. By eliminating all personal relationships, it dramatizes action in relation to the total pattern of events (e.g., the three Priests, the four Tempters and the four Knights are each distinguishable from one another): the real conflict is in the realm of the spiritual. It is a passion play rather than a tragedy of character.

Murder in the Cathedral represents Becket as the only character in the play who faces up to the realities and demands of history. The common people are still living in the pagan cycles of birth and death, seedtime and harvest, and they refuse to acknowledge their own part in the larger historical scheme, even as they benefit from it. The monarchy is blind to all but the present, temporal order, while the priests are haunted by an un-faith which fears that thing which is beyond death, even though that future should be by right their exclusive territory. They have sold out to the temporal order in their sure way by depending too much on the Archbishop and not enough on the Archbishop's God.

Murder in the Cathedral, then, projects the contemporary relevance of Becket's Christian martyrdom. An instructive contrast is Robert Bolt's play, *A Man for All Seasons* (1960) and Fred Zinnemann's later and successful film (1966). This popular dramatization of a man of conscience is grounded on stoic and existential ideas of personal integrity and not on that central to Christian martyrdom: bearing witness to Christ's redemptive love. Bolt's play thus makes a compromise with modern presumptions resisted by Eliot's greater vision.

References

Anouilh, Jean. *Becket; or, The Honor of God.* Trans. Lucienne Hill. New York: Coward-McCann, 1960.

Eliot, Thomas Stearns. *Murder in the Cathedral.* New York: Harcourt Brace Jovanovich, 1988.

————. "Poetry and Drama." *Selected Prose of T. S. Eliot.* Ed. Frank Kermode. New York: Harcourt, Brace, Jovanovich, 1975. 132–47.

Endo, Shusaku. *Silence.* Trans. William Johnston. Tokyo: Sophia University Press, 1969.

Fry, Christopher. *Curtmantle, a Play.* New York: Oxford University Press, 1961.

Greene, Graham. *The Power and the Glory.* New York: Viking Press, 1960.

Jones, David E. *The Plays of T. S. Eliot.* Toronto: University of Toronto Press, 1962.

"Martyrology." *The Catholic Encyclopedia.* 12 Dec. 2002 <http://www.newadvent.org/cathen>.

Moore, Brian. *Black Robe.* London: Jonathan Cape, 1985.

Shaw, George Bernard. *Saint Joan: A Chronicle Play in Six Scenes and an Epilogue.* New York: Brentano's, 1924.

Smith, Lacey Baldwin. *Fools, Martyrs, Traitors: The Story of Martyrdom in the Western World.* New York: Knopf, 1997.

Tennyson, Alfred Baron. *Becket.* London: Macmillan, 1884.

Yeats, William Butler. *The Collected Poems of W. B. Yeats.* London: Macmillan, 1963.

CHAPTER 2

The Psychology and Sociology of Martyrdom

Rona M. Fields

The Psychology of Martyrdom

George Bernard Shaw, writing on the execution of the leaders of the 1916 Irish rebellion, contended that it turned Padraic Pearse from a minor poet to a martyr. Of course Shaw was being glib. Since he didn't know the Irish language and Pearse wrote mostly in Irish—he could hardly judge his ranking as a poet. However, all World War I poetry is replete with themes and images of the blood sacrifice. Yeats, in one of his best-known poems, "The Blood Sacrifice," postulated that nationalism is grown out of the blood of martyrs. Other literary references to the executed leaders as martyrs in the poetry, ballad, and prose about the Irish Rebellion or Rising, raise the issue of the media role[1] in attribution of martyrdom. But Ireland was hardly the only place in which the rise of nationalism in Europe moved secular symbols from the religious icons that dominated nearly two millennia of western thought and were embedded in the archetypes of the psyche.

Adam Zamoyski, a political historian, best known for his work on Poland, identifies the ascendance of the nation between 1776 and 1871 as the transcendent power and central turning point of contemporary history. Zamoyski identifies the turning point as the date when the King of France, who ruled by Divine Right, was guillotined and replaced as the sovereign by the nation. In this idealized projection of "our Lord, Mankind" the nation, death is the service of which brought martyrdom and immortality. The notion of freedom through self-expression and the quest for happiness, self-fulfillment, and empowerment was conceived in highly religious terms without the oppressive dogma of the afterlife. "Fired by the urge to redeem mankind and—themselves, many young men struggled and died is a kind of crusade *immolating themselves rather than others*" (1999, p. 5).

Secularization remains tension laden at the very least. The social psychology of martyrdom may be viewed as the replacement of a religious ideal by the secular in the western world. The insurgence of humanism and scientism generate a political psychology consistent with the secular demands of democracy and rebellion. But the idea of martyrdom has important consistencies. The martyr gives him- or herself for the ideal, the soldier kills or may be killed for the cause. Even the secularization of martyrdom does not confuse these two forms of commitment.

This political and social shift is reflected in psychoanalytic and social theories in debates on predation and aggression as instinct or learned behavior. On the one hand, the dynamic etiology of motivation and emotion was attributed to the tension between the drive for life and the drive to death. All theorists and scientists reflecting on the human psyche have considered instinct in accounting for motives. In so doing they attributed to human nature, aggression and predation.

Breaking with analytic theories of instinct driven emotions, Erich Fromm (1973) embarked on a social psychological and anthropological study of human destructiveness as the driving force in human evolution and history. After comprehensive examination, Fromm concludes that the internal dynamics that drive human behavior evolve through survival and continuity functions rather than instincts for fight or flight or the demand for equilibrium (Cannon's Law). He incorporates the anthropological observations of Ruth Benedict, Quincy Wright, and E. A. Hoebel; that the propensity to war, which William James hypothesized as "The Moral Equivalents of War," that expressions of aggression more often provide exercise, sport, and amusement without destruction, and that the propensity to war is neither an instinct nor a psychological survival mechanism. The dichotomies presented by psychoanalysis as the source of the dynamic forces driving emotion, motivation, and behavior are contradicted by Fromm's argument. Significantly, through the cross-cultural relativistic approach, Fromm emerges with an absolutist and hierarchical theory of human behavior. In this he is in concert with Maslow and Frankl, perhaps the analytic link between the classic psychoanalytic theorists and the existential and cognitive perspectives. There are human behaviors and aspirations that are destructive of humankind and that is not a matter of cultural differences.

Fromm's thesis accesses the work of Piaget in cognition and Allport and Arnold on values and motivation. All recognize the contribution of environment and of the individual's position in the social and geographic matrix as they contribute to their mode of operation, values and aspirations. Each of these theorists of human behavior posits, as does Maslow (1968), a hierarchy of development. Taking this as the foundation for explaining personality and emotion makes it possible not only to measure but also to compare on the same axes, individuals, and groups from many milieus. Construction of a psychological theory of martyrdom can be incorporated into this amalgamated theoretical framework:

1. The motivation, emotion, and personality of the individual who becomes a martyr
2. Maturity and integrity
3. The social psychology of martyrdom or the context in which the phenomenon manifests
4. The psychology of memory. The neuropsychology of affective memory as a vehicle for martyr idealization. As well, the attribution inherent in and the critical juncture at which memorialization of a hero transforms into attribution of martyrdom. The sense of someone else having been sacrificed *for me* is the redemptive function of martyrdom.

Emotion, Motivation, and Personality

In Arnold's definition of motivation (1960), "perception of a good for action and move towards it," emotion is the physiological expression of the feeling state consequent to the sense judgment. Thus if martyrdom is perceived as a good for action it is motivated behavior. Taken from another direction, were Romeo and Juliet martyred for their love or for the contest between their families that would have separated them? In fact, they were victims of machinations to outwit their opponents that went tragically awry. We must deal with the psychodynamic engine that drives the ultimate sacrifice. Thus Romeo and Juliet were victims of their misguided, some would say, immature, efforts to thwart their families' constraints.

Recruiting for service in volunteer armies proceeds through proffered rewards as in many other jobs. The reward system for military recruits, however, historically has been predicated on fiscal and patriotic values. Even when military service is required, those more economically favored have bought their way out or traded their call up by sending a servant or a slave in their place. In the end, military recruits tend to be young, and drawn from the less educated and fiscally advantaged sectors. Recruiting tactics and recruit indoctrination is predicated, like religious conversion, on the transformative value of adherence to the ritual, dogma, and group identity. Thus, to be willing to "die for the cause" or to serve for the higher ideal becomes the pledge statement of commitment. But inherent in that pledge is confidence in the common belief—shared commitment. In military and paramilitary organizations the objective has always been to achieve the goal, the objective, win the battle, win the war, and the mission, as well as surviving the mission and ensuring the accomplishment and survival of the group. That is the commitment. Every military organization from the guerilla fighters of Judah Maccabee to the Mujahadin of Afghanistan, the commitment to fight for a cause is the same. In a recent interview, a respected Mujahid leader, Azzim Nasserzia, expressed anger at the widely propagandized idea that for Muslims, dying in Jihad is the objective and that suicide/homicide is a vehicle to paradise. In fact, in Islam, soldiers and civilians who die as a result of external aggression are regarded as *Shaheed* or martyrs. Usual rituals of washing the body and shrouding are done away with and *Shaheed* are buried in the clothes they were wearing at the time. This is an important distinction between Muslim and other soldiers slain in battle. The Pashtuns of Paktia wore the white shroud in most battles with Soviet forces to make sure they would be buried in it if they fell, rather than go to the next world in their worn out or dirty clothes. Nasserzia's own survival and the survival of the men under his command in more than ten years of guerilla warfare, first against the Soviets and then against the Taliban, is for him and his peers, proof of how well they fought and how intelligently he led. In discussing Massoud, the leader of the Northern Alliance who was assassinated by al Qaeda operatives on September 10, he said Massoud did not become a martyr for the way he died. He was already a great charismatic leader to whom greatness was attributed because of his abilities as a soldier and leader in combat. In Afghanistan today, two years after his death, his picture adorns every office and building, I was told. "Not because he died in Jihad, but because he successfully fought those forces, foreign and domestic that oppressed and destroyed his people and his homeland." Massoud remains a very controversial figure and is regarded as a hero by some, but by no means all of the many factions and historians of the Afghan struggle. His own personal history paralleled the history of his nation in a way that is typical of national heroes or redemptors. His grandfather was a General in the Afghan army that successfully defeated the British invasion. His father served as an officer in the army of the brief-lived Afghan Republic. Massoud himself, while a student at the University, participated in an Islamic opposition movement to the insurgent and increasingly violent Communists who eventually overthrew the Republic and sent his family into exile. According to his closest lieutenants who were with him at the time he was assassinated, he recognized the danger to his country and to the rest of the world represented by the Taliban and their allies, al Qaeda. He had traveled to Europe to speak to the European Union Parliament to awaken them to this danger. That is what made him a high priority target for assassination by these opponents. For him, as with soldiers historically, commitment to armed struggle may include death in the course of the armed struggle, but it is neither courted nor sought. That is why recruits are expected to be old enough to make that choice and trained sufficiently to succeed in overcoming the enemy rather than being their victim.

Of course, where children are forced to serve in armies or commandeered into fighting units, forced as slave labor, usually there is no commitment but survival. In such instances, in Liberia and Sierra Leone, the children are forced to kill or to be killed by their captors. In Mozambique, they were often forced to kill or torture a close family member or to be killed. The fact that they remained in the army is quite apart from loyalty or commitment. It is personal survival. And the will to life is so strong that in these and other kinds of morbid, forced-choice situations, the individual, even a child with little comprehension of past and future, chooses to live at all costs. This then is the psychological nub of martyrdom. A martyr is defined in all monotheistic religions (and in animist religious beliefs, as in the death of Crazy Horse) as one who knows that to profess their faith may result in death, but chooses to profess faith through their life. That is the common element of the secular and the religious martyr. But it is predicated on a *choice to live* to profess the faith. The act of living is itself a profession of faith, and the struggle to overcome obstacles to life is fueled by belief mixed with hope.

As for the act of choice, as we shall see, the neuropsychology of emotion incorporates a continual series of choices, or selections, from the myriad sensations transmitted to the brain. These choices are apparent when behavior is recognized as a sequence of deliberate actions (choices).

In November 1982, I was, with my Social Research graduate students from the American University of Beirut, interviewing survivors of the Sabra/Shatila Massacre. I wanted to do studies of the children aged 6 through 16, and needed to secure permission of parents or guardians. I visited with the mother of two of my subjects who had lost 11 members of her family in the massacre. She herself had not been in the house at the moment of the attack. She returned to find a grisly scene. As she described each of her slain loved ones and their condition her voice was flat and toneless. She held each of her two surviving children on either side of her. When she had finished her recitation, my students and I silently tasted our own tears, and she asked if we had any questions, anything else we wanted to know.

> I said, "Yes, how do you manage to wake up every morning?" She put her hands in front of her, palms up, and said, "Allah."

This was, of course, a profound declaration of faith by a thoughtful mature woman.

During the same time period, I examined Palestinian children who had been severely traumatized. They were not only traumatized during the massacre but also by violence before and after that event. Their projective stories and responses to the questions of legal socialization for most of the pre-adolescent boys revealed their suppressed guilt feelings. They had been angry and resentful about their mandatory paramilitary training. Boys who were aged 12 through 15 had been rebellious at an age where rebellion against parental and other authority is typical. Now their guilt and anger integrated with a new objective, revenge.

As one boy put it, "I *will have to kill* them now for the honor of my name!"

Four years later, several of the boys in that sample were among the group who shot and killed helpless people, including children, at the Rome and Vienna Airports.

They were killed and had probably accepted that their mission would be fatal. The single surviving captive expressed that expectation. Given that probability, speculation on suicidal acceptance, if not intention, is appropriate. The iconography in their homes depicted uncles, cousins, or brothers who had died or been killed in attacks against schools and villages in Israel, the attack against the Olympic athletes in the Israeli Team Village in Munich, and in hijacked airplanes.

Recruits to terrorist organizations are different from conventional military recruits in several ways that make them more accessible to the extremist ideology of suicide/homicide martyrdom and thus available to the politicization of their commitment. At the same time, recruits to paramilitary or terrorist organizations may join when they are motivated by vendetta but may mature to experience alternatives. That development depends on living long enough in a context that offers possibilities for political action and identity other than violence. In Piaget's terms, this means a social environment in which the growing child is able to experience a variety of roles and accessible goals. It would also mean an environment in which the guiding imagery is multidimensional and dynamic rather than the polarities of killing, as in good death vs. bad death.

During the past thirty years, I have used standardized psychological tests to examine members of paramilitary, or terrorist, groups, children growing up in conditions of violence and social change, and torture survivors. In many instances the three categories merge. In some instances, individuals have evolved from these three categories to become quite different. Several of these persons are included in this narrative. For the moment, however, it is important to consider the findings for the majority of those sampled in Northern Ireland, Israel, Palestine, Lebanon, South Africa, and Southeast Asia.

The data-based profile of a member of a terrorist or paramilitary organization is high state and trait Anger and low Guilt about angry behavior (although they are able to feel guilty about other behaviors and experiences). They manifest high state and trait Curiosity. This profile derives from the data of Spielberger's State Trait Personality Inventory with adult members of paramilitary organizations, including the IRA, UDA, PLO, and Comrades in South Africa (Fields, 1986, 1987, 1990, 1994, 2002). In addition such recruits are, for the most part, truncated in development of moral judgment and legal socialization at the level of retributive justice or vendetta. This combination profile is Righteous Indignation plus Risk Taker/thrill, Novelty Seeker. In the context of Moral Development Stage 2, this anger is vendetta and the course it takes involves high risk and novel experience. Already these points differentiate the prospective terrorist, even the suicide terrorist, from the individual whose death is imposed by others because of his or her expressed beliefs.

This description fits the definition laid out by Eric Hoffer in his 1951 thesis, *The True Believer*; as he called them, the "fanatic" in mass movements. Yet, as we shall see, there are, amongst insurgent or revolutionary groups, leaders and codes of discipline that indicate a search for a higher level of moral justice and these elements generally move to political action in preference to guerilla tactics. The profile is different from that of a sociopath or psychopath, who is totally lacking in guilt feelings. My database, which includes at least five hundred members of paramilitary organizations from diverse ethnic and cultural origins, socio-economic status, and religions, suggests a normal curve of distribution on such factors as intelligence, achievement motivation, and psychopathologies. What distinguishes them from regular military or other population samples is this particular profile. What they view as a "good for action," what they "move toward," motivation, and how they express their feelings about their choices are these parameters. It is reasonable to expect that a psychological profile may similarly distinguish those whose commitment to their beliefs choose to live to profess them. That is, the possibility of becoming a hero, a martyr, or a victim. This then, is an exploration of the psyche that is generally conceived to be opposite that of the terrorist.

Commitment is predicated on conscious choice emanating from motivation—the perception that is valued as a good for action and moved towards—or, in process, becomes the emotional engine driving towards the goal. Viewed in these terms, every behavior is motivated and every goal or objective is valued as a good for action. However, in evaluating a motivational system, it is possible and even necessary to have an absolute rather than a relativist measure. There are levels of effectiveness and coherence or integrity that are consistent cross culturally. And as we shall explore in this essay, the personality of the person who becomes a martyr is testament.

The major theorists of personality and emotion and of cognition present a dynamic matrix that is at once consistent and evolutionary. Adler provides several such matrices to explain courage and social interest. In his open system of dynamics, the individual is engaged in a ceaseless upward striving. In this, Adler's and Jung's theses of evolutionary development to maturity ultimately aimed at achieving integrity and unique identity of the individual comports with the Piagetian conception of the evolution of moral development from primitive, self-centered to the idea of universal equity (Ansbacher & Ansbacher, 1956).

Measurement of these stages is not only possible on a cross-cultural or transcultural basis, but also necessary if we view the evolu-

Figure 2.1
The Frontal Lobes

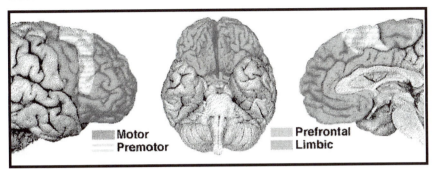

| Motor | Prefrontal |
| Premotor | Limbic |

The frontal lobes represent a large area of the brain. The brain centers within the frontal lobe have numerous interconnections with other parts of the brain. These include connections with emotion and mood centers, as well as cognitive centers. There are three general anatomical divisions of the frontal cortex: the limbic, the precentral, and the prefrontal cortices. *Source:* From *Structure of the Human Brain: A Photographic Atlas 3/E* by S.J. DeArmond, M. M. Fusco and M. M. Dewey, © 1974, 1976, 1989 by Oxford University Press, Inc. Used by permission of Oxford University Press, Inc.

tion of human civilization itself. Like the very young child, a primitive society comprehends goals in terms of immediate gratification rather than long-term good because they are so helpless and vulnerable in the face of natural events and unable to alter the conditions of their immediate environment. Parallel with these developmental and dynamic theses is contemporary knowledge in any major way of brain processes and development—behavioral neuropsychology. Mature development of the frontal and parietal lobes is critical to executive functioning and with it, the capacity to make moral judgments. Furthermore, these are the parts of the brain and the processing circuits that are the last to develop in the growth of the brain. All evidence indicates that full development is only established when the human individual is twenty to twenty-five years old.

However, the plan or intention for achieving the goal distinguishes and differentiates among the individuals aspiring to the same objectives. Thus many different individuals from diverse cultures may aspire to become icons in their milieu but their ultimate classification is dependent on two different dimensions. First, their own (usually learned) plan for achieving the goal and realistic efficacy. And second, recognition by others, either implicit or explicit, that the individual is indeed a heroic symbol.

The meaning of the act to the actor and to the wider audience may be at odds. To die for a cause in itself cannot be a measure of anything. Rather it is an accident or incident en route to a goal. It is measured by the recognition of the efficacy and universal value of the means and the goal. As Arnold defines it, life and death are not polarities but rather incorporated into the appraisal of a given situation:

> With each different aspect noticed, there is bound to be a change in emotion and emotional expression. In addition, a man may either abandon himself to the emotion or restrain it. (Arnold, 1960, p. 202)

Commitment to a cause, like love and hate, becomes a sentiment. While some emotions are action tendencies, a single emotional reaction that endures develops into a sentiment and various emotions grow out of it as distinct from attitudes and beliefs.

Mandated genocide, the annihilation of a group of people or their extermination because of their presumed genetic connection, places the victims outside the framework of "commitment to a cause" victimization. Yet even in the death camps, there was, as Frankl points out, the choice of how to meet death, and also the choice of the meaning to attribute to the deprivation of all other choice. Yet there were those amongst them who managed to fight, those who risked their lives to save others, and those who lost their lives in attempts to save others. Under these circumstances, personal survival itself was a heroic choice not always successful in action. Theologians and historians define the question of who and what was a martyr under these circumstances. Some would argue with considerable data that the people bestow it: survivors, colleagues, comrades, relatives, national groups, and communities, not by analysts (O'Snódaigh, personal communication, January 2003).

At this level we can differentiate between those who choose death as a homicidal act for martyrdom and those who have sacrificed themselves alone. Suicide is a deliberate and determined act that has had a central position in all psychiatry. As Schneidman says, "It is considered irrational in most societies . . . the taboos surrounding suicide, related to religion, sin, hereafter and the usurpation of divine right. . . ." Of the three kinds of taboos on which Schneidman remarks, those that imply action, discussion, and thought, suicide and murder cut across all three. The cultural and psychological relationships between suicide and death are complicated. "Suicide with its dark motivations for immortality punishment and reunion is spun from the same loom (taboos)" (Schneidman, Farberow, & Litman,

Figure 2.2
The Memory Circuit

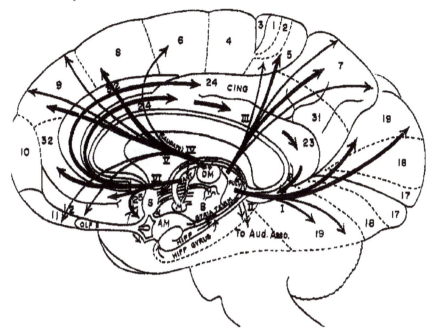

Circuits mediate imagination and affective memory. We identify things by recalling similar objects (relays from association cortex to limbic areas, and from there, via hippocampus-fornix circuit, to the brain stem and back to thalamic sensory nuclei and sensory association cortex) and remember their effect on us (affective memory circuit from association cortex to limbic areas, and from there, via hippocampus and postcommissural fornix, to anterior thalamic nuclei and cortical limbic areas). This results in imagining possible effects of this thing on us and possible ways of coping with it (imagination circuit from cortical limbic areas, via amygdala, to thalamic association nuclei and cortical association areas).

Notes: I–IV = imagination circuits: I = visual, II = auditory, III = somesthetic, IV = motor, V = olfactory imagination, VI = affective memory circuit. AM = amygdala, AT = anterior thalamic nucleus, B = brain stem, CING = cingulate gyrus, DM = dorsomedial thalamic nucleus, H=habenula, HIPP = hippocampus, M = mamillary body, OF = olfactory bulb, PULL = pulvinar, S = septal area, STRIA TERM = stria terminalis. *Source:* From *Emotion and Personality, v. II*, by Magda B. Arnold. © 1960 Columbia University. Reprinted by permission of the publisher.

Figure 2.3
Circuits Mediating Imagination and Affective Memory

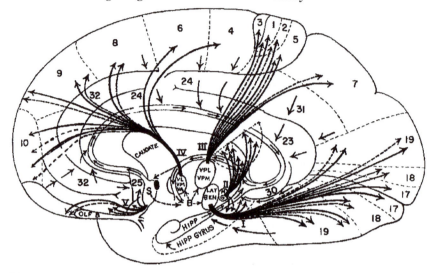

Motor memory is different from every other modality-specific memory. When we try to remember dancing or skating, or moving a pencil in a blind maze, we find ourselves imagining these actions or even visualizing them instead of remembering. Yet we know that we can dance or skate, and when we actually start dancing or skating, the movements are easy and familiar. The memory circuit—reception and registration, recall. Sensory impulses travel via thalamic sensory nuclei to cortical sensory and association areas, mediating sensory experience. Associated impulses are relayed to limbic areas, mediating appraisal. This appraisal of sense experience initiates spontaneous recall of similar things and situations, mediated via hippocampus, thalamic sensory nuclei, and the various association and limbic areas. Motor impulses travel via ventral thalamic nuclei to frontal areas.

Reception and registration. *Recall.* Arrows indicate the direction of conduction. Short arrows indicate the connections for appraisal and recall.

Notes: I = visual system, II = auditory system, III = somesthetic system (including taste), IV = motor system, V = olfactory system. Arabic numerals represent Bordmann areas. A = cortical auditory area. B = brain stem, HIPP = hippocampus, LAT GEN = lateral geniculate nucleus, MG = medial geniculate nucleus, OLF B = olfactory bulb, S = septal area, VA = anterior ventral nucleus, VM = ventromedial nucleus, VL = ventrolateral nucleus, VPL = ventroposterolateral nucleus, VPM = ventroposteromedial nuclei. *Source:* From *Emotion and Personality, v. II*, by Magda B. Arnold. © 1960 Columbia University. Reprinted by permission of the publisher.

1976, pp. 541–542). In this motivation for immortality, the suicide/homicide conceives martyrdom.

The political connection between terrorism and martyrdom engages yet another psychodynamic because the act of killing others while killing oneself becomes the political objective that incorporates the intention of vendetta. But in the process, and in contrast with the psychology of self-sacrifice, the vendetta motivation is at a lower level of moral development in the hierarchy of moral justice. In the neuropsychology of the brain, vendetta operates at a primitive level while a sense of universal moral judgment requires processing and mediation of experienced stimuli through the fully developed orbito-frontal cortex where decision and choice are formulated. Whereas impulsive, unconsidered reaction is through the hippocampus and is what Arnold references as unmediated because it proceeds in relays to the cortico-limbic system connecting with the hypothalamus through the cerebellum, this does not mean that it is outside the circuit of emotional memory. In fact, aggressive behavior (manifest as rage) results from stimulation of two places in the brain that are very much in the circuit—the amygdala and the lateral thalamus. How to explain aggressive violence as a repetitive response? Arnold's thesis can account for this in the undamaged human brain by reference to the frontal lobe mediation in emotional memory. This response may be viewed either as "hardwired as an emotional habit or appraised" through remembered imaginal processing as appropriate. Pincus and Tucker report that studies of violent juveniles found complex parietal seizure activity in the majority of the boys who committed the most violent acts. Behaviorally, they were likely to be "loose, mumbling and illogical in their thought processes" (1985, pp. 811–89). As we shall see when we examine the circuitry of emotional memory, these unmediated violent response sets are in effect short circuits that, when manifested in the human, are undeveloped or otherwise impaired (Arnold, 1984). It is relevant to understanding the etiology of the suicide/homicide and vendetta aggression as well as the notion of good death/bad death promulgated by totalitarian dictators, that aggression, fury, and rage are neither instinctive nor psychodynamic essentials. Viewed developmentally as well as in evolutionary development, the very young human being attempts and manifests a variety of responses to what seem to him or her to be amorphous stimuli. The response that communicates with the caretaker develops into an emotional habit. As the orbito-frontal lobes develop with a variety of transmissions and channels for action impulses, these emotional habits can alter, especially if

there is no organic damage. Furthermore, studies of the brain in sub-
human species indicate that the brain evolves with more frontal lobe
function in higher orders and in the human. The circuits also become
more complex (see Figure 2.4).

Separately, Viktor Frankl, Rollo May, Abraham Maslow, and
Robert Lifton recognize the existential psychology of choice and
moral judgment in the analysis of reality and moral action in their
writings on the psychology of meaning in a period of crisis. The neuropsychology of brain and behavior indicates that these choices and
their cognitive processing transpire in the most highly developed and
thus last to develop circuitry in the brain utilizing the frontal lobes.
Lifton, in writing about the psychology of survivors of brainwashing
and psychological torture (1979), remarks on the sustained focus of
the individuals' memories on issues transcending their immediate circumstances. They appear to be like the torture survivors I examined
in my earlier studies (Fields, 1973) to have a very high tolerance for
pain. This tolerance is enhanced by self-hypnosis.

Earlier scholars on religious experience have noted that the mental
powers acquired through the practice of self-denial and meditation
sustained victims of torture for their faith (Durkheim, 1965). At this
juncture, we might connect the behavioral neuropsychology of martyrdom. For such individuals, *the centrality of the emotional commitment,
or "sentiment," obscures perception and sensation of noxious experience.*
Lifton describes the survivors of brainwashing and other psycholog-
ical-deprivation techniques applied by the Chinese against captive
missionaries and attributes their mental survival to practicing meditation, recalling and reciting poetry, scripture and other literature to
themselves, and essentially living in their imaginal process to expand
their very limited, restricted physical environment. This capacity of
the human being to transcend an intolerable reality contradicts the
animalistic, instinct theories of behavior and the stimulus response
sets postulated by Skinner and others. It also puts to rest theories
that the violence of a terrorist group is a product solely or even primarily of others' domination and as a response to overwhelming danger to the life of their own people. Lifton provides this observation as
well:

> There is important structuring of the habit of violence. The use of a vi-
> olent style is by no means a matter of gradual accommodation, al-
> though there are elements of that, too . . . violence among terrorist
> groups can take on a form of transcendence even of ecstasy of its own.
> (Lifton, 1979, p. 158)

Figure 2.4
The Appraisal System

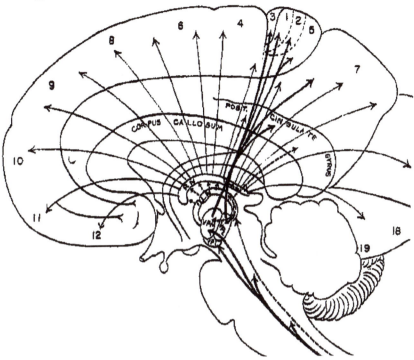

Peripheral fibers project in spinothalamic and spinoretier tracts to posterior cingulate gyrus. The associated somesthetic projection is also shown. (Appra . . . fibers from other sensory systems are not sketched.) The diffuse projection from the intralami . . . thalamic nuclei reaches every area of the cortex via the thalamic reticular nuclei.

Notes: Sensory . . . jection.—Projection of appraisal system.—Diffuse projection. Arabic numerals refer to Brodmann areas. CM = centrum medianum, ILN = intrelaminar nucleus, RN = reticular nucleus, ventropostero-inferior nucleus, VFL = Ventroposteroclateral nucleus, VPM = ventroposteromedical . . . cleus. *Source:* From *Emotion and Personality, v. II,* by Magda B. Arnold. © 1960 Columbia University. Reprinted by permission of the publisher.

In another dimension, Erik Erikson describes the psycho-social conflict with which the visionary great man at a particular junction of history. He described Luther as a young man, deeply and "pathologically upset, but possessed . . . by the vision of a new (or renewed) world order and by the need (and the gift) to transform masses of men . . . makes his individual "patienthood" representative of a universal one, and promises to 'solve for all what he could not solve for himself alone.'" Erikson continues:

> Finally, after all the new insights that totalitarianism, nuclear warfare and mass communication have forced us to face, it can no longer escape us that in all his past, man has based his ideologies on mutually exclusive group identities in the form of "pseudo-species": tribe, nation, caste, region, class and so on. The origin of man's identity problem thus is to be found in evolution itself. (Erikson, 1975, p. 47)

In my studies of survivors of terror trauma—particularly of torture and hostage survivors—one of the defining distinctions amongst them is in regard to the quality of the psychological aftermath between those who focused on helping others and empathy with others (altruism) and those who became self absorbed, centered on what was happening or would happen to them. The former suffered fewer measurable negative consequences. The latter were often disabled by their experience. This leads to another hypothesis: martyrdom, or the epitome of selflessness to help others through risks to self, may be the ultimate abandonment of selfishness that enables merging with the universal. But Frankl has another interpretation in *Logotherapy* (1962, 1967). Hyper-reflection, as he calls it in logotherapy, may be pathogenic. Excessive attention to one's own experience and feelings of fear, this anticipatory anxiety, confirms the fear and neurotic incapacity. In describing the effort to make sense of the apparently senseless suffering that is a dichotomous choice, Frankl quotes Nietsche: "He who has a why to live can bear with almost any how." When in the concentration camp, all familiar goals are snatched away; what remains is "the last of human freedoms, the ability to choose one's attitude in a given set of circumstances."

Frankl and Lifton each observed that some survivors of mass death and dehumanization choose to be "worthy of their suffering" and thus prove the human capacity to rise above outward fate (Allport, 1967, pp. xi–xii). At the same time, Frankl and Maslow both point out that an abnormal reaction to an abnormal situation is normal. In a time and situation where the will to die or even the death of the will to live was tantamount to suicide, the idea of one's own suffering as a sacrifice for a loved one's life became their sustenance. Frankl says:

> It was in the nature of this sacrifice that it should appear to be pointless in the normal world, the world of material success. But in reality our sacrifice did have a meaning. Those of us who had any religious

faith, I said frankly, could understand without difficulty. I told them of
a comrade who on his arrival in a camp had tied to make a pact with
Heaven that his suffering and death should save the human being he
loved from a painful death. For this man, suffering and death were
meaningful; his was a sacrifice of the deepest significance. He did not
want to die for nothing. None of us wanted that. (1962, p. 85)

Erik Erikson, in his essay, "The Revolt of Humanist Youth" (1975),
also refers to moral learning in company with ideological experi-
mentation as part of adolescence and of ethical consolidation as an
adult task. The step-by-step development results in a persistent lia-
bility that can always lead to individual regressions and joint retro-
gressions. In adulthood this can be seen either in a partial arrest on
the ideological level or backsliding to infantile conflicts over moral
interdicts. He says:

> Aggravated and specifically agitated youth, although highly sensitive
> to ethical positions and ready to put themselves on the line when a
> gifted leader seems to master the historical moment in the absence of
> ideological synthesis sometimes retrogressed to the logic, albeit in-
> verted of the moral position: protests are, as it were, hypermoralisti-
> cally turned against the establishment's morality. (p. 207)

When he wrote this essay, Erikson was analyzing the youth movement of the sixties in the United States. He wrote of the "turning
around of moralistic fury against the established wielders of punitive
power as enemies of childlikeness" and of youthfulness, and, of
course, of "the people." But it is not unrelated to the moral and ideological commitments that eventuated in the death of Romeo and Juliet
and Jeanne D'Arc. It applies, as well, to the psyche of the suicide
bomber. But Erikson does not suggest that this is martyrdom.

*The psychodynamic of a person who becomes a martyr begins with belief
and commitment to a cause greater than his or her own well being, but not
in contradiction of life and the self.* This dynamic evolves with maturity
because it is impossible for the immature brain to conceive a universal morality and judge an action to be taken beyond the feeling state
of the self. In that sense it is a self-concept but not an action plan.
Dying for a cause would negate the importance of living to fulfill that
cause and its attendant obligations. The martyr takes actions that
transcend but do not negate the self. Maturity is evidenced in taking
responsibility for the sequence of choices leading to confrontation
with mortality. While a religious martyr might say or believe "it's in

God's hands," that belief does not alter his or her recognition of their ultimate responsibility. The essence of martyrdom is the choice to live and the courage to take responsibility for life or death. Many people suffering chronic and terminal illnesses recognize that quitting would be easy but somehow wrong. Others choose to terminate their suffering and claim the right to die.

Perhaps less dramatically than Frankl's fellow concentration camp inmates, they make a choice between trying one and another treatment that is unpleasant or even painful but offers a possibility for life. When questioned about why they make such difficult choices, thoughtful patients have confided, "I must live to see my grandson's Bar Mitzvah, to be there for the family," or, "My spouse will go into a suicidal depression and I must maintain for both of us." These are not history-changing choices for life, but they reveal the essential nature of the ability and responsibility of ordinary people, not only heroic leaders nor icons of dissent against injustice, to choose. One woman with stomach cancer who had chosen hospice care continued to listen to Dr. Bernie Siegel's tapes for coping with stress and disease. Of course, her condition worsened, as might be expected in the course of such an illness. However, she blamed herself for lacking the ability to practice the exercises taught by the tapes to the degree necessary for healing. Not only do individuals choose their beliefs, many are convinced that the belief presages reality and that the strength of belief is testament to the psychological strength of the believer.

However, when we consider death as a psychic state in history and society, the issue of immortality becomes a psychological as well as theological issue. The individual's need to deny death, one's own and that of significant others, is more than a defense mechanism, but rather, as Lifton says:

> It represents a compelling universal urge to maintain a continuous symbolic relationship over time and space . . . symbolization of his ties with both his biological fellows and his history, past and future. (1974, p. 275)

Nowhere is this more commonly manifested than in the way an adult deals with or rather denies the death of a parent. In Judaism, the repetition of the Kaddish and the intensive communal recitation of the prayer during the period of Shiva, or the first week following the burial, is a psychological transition period in which the mourner bonds with the larger community in repeating praises and gratitude for the gift of life and the reinforcement of conviction. The Kaddish itself, in Aramaic, is an ancient formulaic prayer glorifying the Deity and the gift of life. Acceptance of the loss of the presence of the loved one is sought by expressing gratitude for the gift of life. A parallel practice of mourning is followed in Islam. Called *Martham*, this is the three days following burial during which people gather in the home of the next of kin with close relatives and recitation of the book of mourning. Like the Kaddish, these prayers are also statements celebrating the gift of life and the Creator. They are also a community effort to help the mourners return to the gift of life in commemoration of their loss. While there are differences in customs in many diverse cultures within Islam, they are essentially, like the Jewish Kaddish and Shiva, a means of remembering but remembering life as a fleeting time given by the Deity. In Christianity there is some variance, but generally the lighting of memorial candles, the dedication of a Mass, the acknowledgement of a gift in the name of the deceased, and in many Catholic celebrations, All Souls' Day, All Hallows' Day, and All Saints' Day provide annual ceremonies to facilitate the acceptance and recognition of death. At the same time, embedded and not inconsequential in all of these rituals and prayers is the formulaic phrase, "into life everlasting."

Another expression of the need for immortality, as Lifton says, is the theological idea of life after death common to all great religions and the ability to overcome death is exemplified in all of the great religious leaders around whom religions have been founded: Buddha, Moses, Christ, Mohamed. In this expression of immortality, it is the release from profane life to existence on a higher plane. This is the power of spiritual life to overcome death. Lifton identifies five different but related ideas of immortality in his essay, "The Sense of Immortality" (1979). Considered in these terms, we can identify in any particular instance of martyrdom one or more of these as critical or key to the distinction of this individual or this event. These are a sense of biological attachment, the power of the spiritual state to overcome death, the "works" or achievement, immersion in eternal nature, and the experience of transcendence of achieving a spiritual state so intense that time and death cease to exist. Indeed, these ideas of immortality, all of them together, are incorporated into the idea of martyrdom and into the individual who is martyred and the survivors who attribute martyrdom to that individual.

In their determination to expunge all opposition or challenge to their rule, Pinochet and his myrmidons publicly revoked the citizenship of the exiled former Defense Minister and Vice-President of

Chile, Orlando Letelier. Immediately following their pronouncement, the latter stood before an assemblage of Chilean exiles in New York and declared, "I was born a Chilean, I am a Chilean and I will always be a Chilean." These words are now engraved on his tombstone. In that statement and in the remarks that followed, he articulated his commitment to his cause and challenged his enemies. He expressed his belief as an *immortal progression that transcends the moment* and perhaps, as it turned out, his own lifetime. He refused to disappear. Torture and exile did not deter him from his intention and commitment. If anything, he became numbed to the risk of death. Letelier was constantly aware after his release from prison into exile, first in Venezuela and then in the United States, that he was being tracked by his Chilean enemies and by the less than sympathetic forces of the U.S. intelligence. He continued to plan and to organize the exile community and even to initiate a strategy for counter-revolution that he believed would happen within six years. He knew other colleagues in exile had been assassinated. He confided that he:

> *felt like I already died.* In prison each time they executed another prisoner, they deliberately announced his name, their taking him from his cell and the execution place was in earshot of my cell. . . . Many times they told me that I was next. I began to believe and stopped feeling anxious about my death. Now, *I no longer fear. . . . They will kill me*, but I will live while I am alive. Many people depend on me. I have an obligation to them and to the cause. (personal communication, 1976)

Pinochet and his DINA intelligence chiefs in concert with the United States CIA tried in every possible way to make him disappear. His assassination in the middle of Washington, D.C., assured the contrary, that he would not disappear.

A less-well-known member of the Allende government who became a *disaperacio*, Ernesto Traubmann y Riegelhaupt, contrived an illicit broadcasting apparatus to tell the world about the Pinochet coup and the horrors unleashed in Chile. He worked at it at first with a comrade and then, because it was becoming too dangerous, his comrade left and for another twenty-four hours Ernesto struggled alone to connect with the rest of the world. Tracing the radio signal, the army located and apprehended him. He was tortured to death and made to disappear. According to a witness, he refused to divulge the names and locations of his comrades under the most heinous tortures. He maintained his silence. Both men were killed at a time and age when they were socially and psychologically mature adults. Neither of these men professed a religious belief or creed as such. They professed their patriotism to their nation and their political ideals. That they are heroes, there is no question—insofar as their countrymen count them. Are they martyrs? Ironically, Letelier's death was at first attributed by authorities and even by a leading newspaper in the United States to left-wing elements creating a martyr for an anti-Pinochet campaign. The left-wing sympathizers in fact acted to shield from purview any of the less attractive aspects of his personal life and emphasized instead his courage and commitment. Taken together, in retrospect, the policy of assassination instigated martyrdom while the more prevalent practice of disappearances thwarted the ascension and attribution of martyrdom to most of the Chilean and Argentine victims of the dirty wars in those countries. There is an aspect of martyrdom as an ascription of heroism that revivifies and revitalizes believers in the cause. Absent the spectacle of what has been described in literature as "the Blood Sacrifice," that is to say, the publicly slain hero, there would seem to be lessened identification. As for assassinations and mass murders of political opponents and ethnic cleansing and genocide, the perpetrators have long assumed that without the evidence of bodies, *habeas corpus*, their culpability would remain unassigned. Pinochet, in fact, was so aware of that strategy that he, at one point shortly after the coup, was quoted as saying that perhaps Allende's body should have disappeared to save the trouble of having to account for the nature of his death. Additionally, there is the issue of the outcome of the quest. Theoretically, there can be a martyr for a lost cause, but, since winners write history and martyrdom cannot be such if it is not associated with some valued achievement, it is relatively rare that it happens. As treated elsewhere among these essays, two notable cases are Oliver Plunkett and Jeanne D'Arc (now saints). At the time of their murders they were not acknowledged, but later became icons for the political struggles of causes that were, at the time of their deaths, lost causes.

There is, perhaps, some primitive ideation of dualism intrinsic to this imagery through the notion of good death vs. bad death. This paradigm is utilized by dictators to maintain and enhance their position by repeatedly reminding their adherents that they are in danger of extinction (death of the good) which is a bad death if all means are not used to eliminate threat by "the other" (killing the other then becomes the good death). It is predicated on the belief that aggression is instinctive and the control and direction of aggression is a political rather than a psychological task. Because if we concede that, as Freud suggested, there is a mind-body dualism and that death and evil are instinctive motivating drives, we are compelled into a normative explanation for evil and destruction and we lose the capacity of the human being to transcend and become altruistic. We also lose the enormity of evil as a category. But on the public stage, as we shall see, the tyrant who orders the death of his opponents is utilizing this argument. The opponent would have killed or destroyed that which is deemed valuable and so must first be eliminated. Significant to the study of martyrdom is, of course, memory. And it is through the psychoneurology of memory and the brain that we have learned that there is not an instinctive life-death dualism driving human behavior.

At the same time, there is a social context for behavior and prosocial behavior that ranges from the essential survival modalities to the capacity for altruism, which, it must be said, has also been manifest in apes. In the latter, as Jane Goodall has remarked, altruistic behavior, though rare, appears associated with maternal social status or rank in the group. Offspring of high status mothers are more likely and able to risk and jeopardize themselves to save others. It is conceivable that this culture of caring among apes proceeds from the same apprehension as philanthropy among humans (personal communication, Dar es Salaam, 1984). That is, the individual whose upbringing has provided confidence and assurance is more likely able to take risks. Certainly contemporaneously, we find that the leaders and heroes who become martyrs are more likely to originate in middle-class economic circumstances. This is due neither to social determinism nor genetic advantages. It is, like the advantaged chimpanzees, because such individuals in childhood and adolescence have a measure of security and are able to image and experience themselves in a variety of roles and positions without jeopardizing themselves in hostile or novel circumstances. Studies of heroes and martyrs document the capability for altruism and the fearlessness of their convictions. Such studies also indicate that they are often individuals whose infancy and childhood have been relatively privileged and secure even when their identity group is itself disadvantaged or marginalized. This suggests that high achievement or resilience are more likely to be a consequence of position in the nuclear and extended family, the relationship of that primary group to the essential institutions of their cultural affinity. This social milieu is the critical field within which the individual integrates the developing self.

The fact that primates and humans in particular are engaged in continual choices, and the choices made as well as the capacity for future choices, directs the unique individual and provides the means to deal with the concepts of responsibility, courage, will, and possibility. Thus, as Abraham Maslow suggests:

> Man has his future within him, dynamically active at this present moment. . . . The future is in principle unknown and unknowable, which means that all habits, defenses and coping mechanisms are doubtful and ambiguous because they are based in past experience. Only the flexibly creative person can really imagine future, only the one who can face novelty with confidence and without fear. (May, 1967, p. 59)

This, while not intended to be the description of the martyr, it certainly is a definition of the kind of psychologically mature individual who might become a martyr. It also corresponds with Arnold's thesis on the capacity of the human brain to make choices on imagined, not experienced, future prospects and possibilities. What we learn about Gandhi's mode of operation and problem-solving paradigms, even in his early childhood, suggests his behavior as an adult, as a leader, and finally, as a hero/martyr. His life and work is a wonderful model of this thesis.

Gandhi's childhood and family circumstances fit well with these descriptions. His biographer, Pyaralel, describes the child he was, Moniya, (his childhood name) thus: "Unlike other children he was not given to crying he had a hearty ringing laughter and everybody liked to fondle him. He was the youngest and last son of a young mother and a much older, high status father raised in what was called a "joint family." His father had considerable status as the "prime minister of a small princely state" and head of a large extended family living together in one house. But he was adventurous, playful and apparently without fear. He sorely tested all who were close to him with his teasing and dissent. Also remarked was his "quality of tenacious and clever attachment which . . . made his parents feel that their relationship with him was a special one and made him in turn feel that his was the fate of a select being" (Erikson, 1975, p. 131).

Erikson, in *Childhood and Society* (1950), remarks on the confluence of the individual and the historical moment, as did psychoanalytic predecessors. But in elaborating on ego and identity in development, Erikson makes the observation that:

> A child has quite a number of opportunities to identify himself, more or less experimentally, with habits, traits, occupations and ideas of real or fictitious people of either sex. Certain crises force him to make radical

selections. However, the historical era in which he lives offers only a limited number of socially meaningful models for workable combinations of identification fragments. Their usefulness depends on the way in which they simultaneously meet the requirements of the organism's maturational stage and the ego's habits of synthesis. (p. 139)

Erikson has written extensively on Gandhi's militant non-violence. Yet, in his earlier career in activism, in South Africa, Gandhi countenanced and engaged in violence. Gandhi's life, contribution, and philosophy are neither uncomplicated nor unidimensional. The more we learn about him, the more we realize the complexity of the man. Significantly, Gandhi was murdered for the success of his beliefs and his symbolic importance in the nascent democracy of India. That he had achieved his political and moral objective before he was killed marked him as a hero and an icon. His successors in leadership were also assassinated but despite their heroic leadership and the manner of their deaths, they have never been accorded martyr appellation. For Gandhi, as for others we recognize as martyrs, the people, not the leaders, confer the status.

Significantly, another leader who became an icon for his movement and finally, a martyr, Martin Luther King, Jr., met Gandhi and was impressed by the man and his achievements. Of him, King said, "They followed him because of his absolute sincerity and his absolute dedication. Here was a man who achieved in his lifetime the bridging of the gulf between the ego and the id. Gandhi had an amazing capacity for self criticism (as cited in Carson, 1998, p. 128)." Gandhi's life, his childhood, and his identity provide insight into his philosophy and achievement. One of his biographers, B.R. Nanda, writing about Gandhi's pastimes as a child, and the way he programmed choice and decisions, said, "What was extraordinary was the way his adventures ended. In every case he posed for himself a moral problem for which he sought a solution by framing a proposition in moral algebra" (as cited in Erikson, 1975, p. 129).

Gandhi and his transmutation of the non-violent struggle for nationhood into a struggle for equality for the untouchables inspired King. And even as he took inspiration from the deeds and person of this man, he was, as Erikson defined it, a visionary who took inspiration from the beauty of nature as a manifestation of Divinity. He embarks on his autobiography with remarks on the setting of the sun and rising of the moon. At the time in his life when he became inspired by Gandhi and the power of non-violent mass movement for change, he remarks on his experience while standing on Cape Comorin at the juncture of the Arabian Sea, the Bay of Bengal and the Indian Ocean. He was entranced by the symbolism of this point where "you can see the setting of the sun and the rising of the moon simultaneously." From this he commented, "we have experiences when the light of day vanishes, leaving us in some dark and desolate midnight—moments when our highest hopes are turned into shambles of despair or when we are victims of some tragic injustice and some terrible exploitation. During such moments our spirits are overcome by gloom and despair and we feel there is no light anywhere. But . . . we look toward the east and discover that there is another light which shines even in he darkness and the 'spear of frustration' is transformed into 'a shaft of light'" (p. 128).

For Martin Luther King, Jr., as for Mahatma Gandhi, the epitome of moral justice is action that atones for social injustices. On March 22, 1959, Martin Luther King, Jr., sermonized the assassination of Gandhi and might have presaged his own violent death 11 years later:

> The world doesn't like people like Gandhi. That's strange, isn't it? They don't like people like Christ; they don't like people like Lincoln. They killed him—this man who had done all of that for India, who gave his life and who stabilized and galvanized 400 million people for independence . . . Here was a man of nonviolence, falling at the hands of a man with hate . . . and this is the story of history, but Thank God it never stopped here . . . The man who shot Gandhi only shot him into the hearts of humanity. (Sermon in Montgomery, as cited in Carson, 1998, p. 102)

King, perhaps more than any other contemporary icon, combined the religious and secular imagery and symbolism. He, after all, was a cleric and spoke fluently about God, quoted scripture, and appealed to Judeo-Christian moral values. Yet his was a secular, political objective. The nature of his life, his leadership, and his death meet the secular or nationalist martyr definition to which he himself contributed in his sermon about Gandhi's death; and then he seemed to invoke a different set of definitions and a more traditionally religious ideal of the martyr as the sacrificial innocent. In his own words he defined martyrdom four years later after the Birmingham bombing that killed four little girls in a church:

> In every battle for freedom there are martyrs whose lives are forfeited and whose sacrifice endorses the promise of liberty. The girls died as a result of the Holy Crusade of black men to be free. They were not Civil

Rights leaders as was Medgar Evers . . . they were youngsters—a tiny bit removed from baby food—and babies we're told, are the latest news from heaven. But they became the most glorious that they could have become. They became symbols of our crusade. They gave their lives to insure our liberty. They did not do this deliberately. They did this because something strange, something incomprehensible to men is reenacted in God's will, and they are home today with God. (Carson, 1998, p. 230)

King goes on to say that this innocent blood that was shed may serve as a redemptive force that brings new light. His description, in the same sermon, of death as the irreducible common denominator of all and a punctuation mark rather than a terminal point to life expresses his religious philosophy. It also echoes the blood sacrifice thesis. Later in his life and, in fact, shortly before his death, King's pronouncements always appeal to morality, the essential ethic of right and wrong, and also focus on the issue of power and justice. By the time of his assassination, King had become committed to the issues of universal justice—beyond the civil rights of blacks in America. He was leading a march for the right of janitorial workers, garbage collectors, to organize a union and set up collective bargaining when he was killed. In this progression, he moved, not in a direct path, from the historically religious ideology of martyrdom to embracing and embodying in his death the secular ideal.

The psychoanalytic theory that comes closest to identifying a personality or complex that might encompass the variety of individuals, who are identified as martyrs, is Alfred Adler's "redeemer complex." According to Adler, it:

Characterizes people who conspicuously but unknowingly take the attitude that they must save or redeem someone . . . it is always clearly the attitude of a person who finds his superiority in solving the complications of others. The redeemer complex may very well enter into medical endeavor or into . . . the ministry. In the most extreme cases we find the person. . . . acting as if he were sent by God, as if he could cure all the evils of mankind. (Ansbacher & Ansbacher, 1956, p. 186)

Even the original theorists of drive states as the motivators for human behavior, like Alfred Adler came later to the conclusion that the social element in personality is "determined by the individual's opinion of the facts and difficulties of life (Ansbacher & Ansbacher, 1956, p. 4). Thus the act of aggression itself is neither instinctual nor an expression of a motivating force. It is instead a response to an obstacle in the path of achieving an objective and at that, is appraised and it is selected as a "good for action."

Mother Teresa was attributed holiness and sainthood during her latter years, although, of course, it was only after her death that her beatification could be proposed. She and Mahatma Gandhi have in common their dedication to humanity and their selfless commitment to service. There is little doubt that each of them practiced self-denial ritualistically. Less than five years since her death, Mother Teresa was beatified and is well on her way to sainthood. Some might view her as a martyr although she did not die in the pursuit of her religious beliefs, but rather because she lived an ascetic life and selflessly devoted to the care of the helpless human discards of society. Beatification raises her above martyr within the organizational church because a miracle is attributed to her intervention. Viewed through the perspective of these several contrasting but iconic lives, we can recognize the idea of martyrdom contemporaneously imbued through the religious meaning, the sacrifice of pleasure in this life for the afterlife, or in the contemporary secular ideal as achieved by Gandhi and King. But there is an essential difference in their commitment as well as in the cause of death. Gandhi practiced self-denial (fasting and nonviolent civil disobedience) to obtain social and political change. That his tactics and person succeeded, there is no question. But Gandhi was a secular man whose public asceticism was one aspect of a multidimensional, very human person whose choices and behaviors in the private arena evidenced feeling, states, and emotional variations that were neither saintly nor transcendent. And he was quick to make that point. He considered self-criticism, public admission of mistakes, and admission of his humanity as the essential reminder that he did not want a religion built around him. The fact that he was Hindu distinguished his conception of martyrdom and his heroism as secular rather than religious might indeed provide an explanation.

Martin Luther King, Jr., although a preacher and the descendent of four generations of preachers, applied his knowledge of theology and religious practice to the secular and political goal of equality for, as he put it, "the Negro in America," with his commitment to nonviolence as the tactic in pursuit of that objective. Mother Teresa's mission was to provide comfort for the destitute dying. She did not seek their cure nor did she even change in the social and political circumstances that produced their condition. She, too, practiced self-denial. She lived well into old age and did not die of contagion from her patients nor assassination for her beliefs. Quite the contrary. She was committed to a missionary or evangelical creed. She did not allow any other ideological intrusion, or even persons espousing other beliefs, access into her client population.

Perhaps the place to start in a psychodynamic analysis is to conceptualize according to a Maslovian hierarchy. There are Basic Needs, which must be met for physical survival and socialization. Then there are the Being Needs, which are essential for spiritual gratification and self-realization. This is the hierarchy we attempt to define when we consider the question, survival for itself or survival for what. Frankl, Jung, Fromm, and Rollo May all respond to this question in terms of the essence of humanness. Jung writes of the greater consciousness in the development of the "persona" and the collective unconscious. The "persona" is the mask that contains and hides the unique human essence. At the foundation is the archetype formulated in the cauldron of the group unconscious, the mythology that is the cultural glue that binds the individual to the group of origin. Thus the individual, according to Jungian theory, has incorporated from early age the ideal of the hero and what makes a heroic act. The example of the Irish martyrs and saints, both religious and secular, provides dramatic elaboration for this thesis.

The ancient Celtic practice of the hunger strike has particular relevance when contrasted with the Palestinian suicide bomber. In pre-Christian times under Brehon Law, when an individual was offended or otherwise unjustly treated, they would take up station before the doorway of their antagonists' house. In that place, and exposed to all who passed by or had business with the inhabitant, the offended would go hungry and physically deteriorate. This was intended to shame the offender. When the latter wanted to resolve the complaint, he would have to make apology and ask forgiveness. The offended one then could demand recompense and grant forgiveness. If the faster died, the other was held by law responsible for the death and liable to make recompense to his family. Others have used the hunger strike. Gandhi went on seventeen hunger strikes in the course of his struggle for independence from Britain. In Britain, the suffragettes, as the women in the suffrage movement were identified, went on hunger strike for the vote. This stands in diametric contrast with the policy of impunity that protects tyrants and their systemic injustice and even protects the perpetrators of torture well beyond the end of their reign. The hunger strike in Irish society has been at various times condemned by the Catholic Church as a form of suicide, but is so interwoven with Irish history that the mythology tells us that St. Patrick himself went on hunger strike against God for forty-five days before God capitulated because such self sacrifice was seen by early Christians (who propagated the deeds of St. Patrick) as a godly quality. It remains a little unclear whether it was Patrick's self sacrifice or God's capitulation in the face of it that is the higher moral value in this case. But the hunger strike persists as non-violent civil disobedience to this day. Distinguished by the discipline and the decision of the political organization, these actions are undertaken by adults. Heroes transform to martyrs in a deliberate political statement. Although some hunger strikers have been individuals who were pacifists, others, most notably the ten young men who died on hunger strike in the Maze Prison in Northern Ireland in 1981, have been members of the IRA and incarcerated on charges including armed robbery, murder, bombing, or merely membership in an illegal organization. The first hunger striker in 1980 to reach the critical point was Sean McKenna, a young man whose father had been amongst the "hooded" men whose case was brought to the European Commission by the Irish government on charges of torture. Both father and son had been amongst the men who were tested using, among other instruments, the Thematic Apperception Test (TAT) scored by Arnold's criteria. This is significant because both father and son had been volunteers for hunger strikes. Neither man was permitted by his organization to fast to death in each of their separate instances. However, the younger man, who was a leader of the IRA inside the prison, was forcibly removed from his comrades to be placed on life support against his will. Sean McKenna, Jr. had been, like many of the other imprisoned Republican leaders, bent on political action more than violence *per se.* He, as his father did before him, viewed himself committed to the cause of a united thirty-two-county Ireland. His incarceration was on charges of attempted murder and membership in the IRA, but like all of the others convicted without charge or trial, these charges were at most unsubstantiated. He was deemed a security threat because, like the others again, he had a genealogy of Republicanism. His TAT stories were concerned with issues of right and wrong and about moral obligation to one's family and group. Neither he, nor his father, had been particularly pious, observant Roman Catholics and, like many Irish Republicans, they were critical of the attitudes of priests and diocesan leadership, but both viewed their religious identity as justification for their politics. McKenna did not die but remains permanently damaged by his ordeal. He suffered brain damage, the inevitable consequence of starvation. His father, too, was unable to sustain family life or a regular job after his release. His central nervous system damage was documented with standard psychoneurological screening tests: the Bender Gestalt, the Memory for Designs, and the Raven Progressive

Matrices. His condition matched the other hooding torture victims whose case was brought to the European Commission and then the European Court by the Irish government. Their interrogation torture incorporated sensory deprivation, sensory overstimulation, extreme physical and mental stress, sleep deprivation, malnutrition, and beatings. In fact, it was not altogether dissimilar to the techniques Lifton described as brainwashing. The father, Sean McKenna, Sr., died before he reached sixty years. The younger McKenna, after release from an earlier experience of interrogation, torture, and incarceration, similarly went on the run, feeling a need to keep moving to avoid capture, whether or not realistic.

The strategy used by the British government for breaking the first hunger strike included separating the strikers from each other and from all communication with the outside world, so that they could not become public martyrs. When they were separated and semi-isolated from everyone but the prison doctor and guards, they were asked, told, or otherwise informed that they could choose to have something to eat. In effect, the individual so damaged by the consequences to his central nervous system has restricted capacity for choice and judgment of his sensations and environment.

The Irish hunger strikers after McKenna got assurance from their families and comrades that they would be supported in their commitment. They knew that prolonged starvation produced confusion in every faculty. There was considerable disagreement amongst the IRA command and Sinn Fein leadership about the manner and objectives for a hunger strike. Although the British government described them as "thugs" and "Mafiosi," in fact, and on much of the psychological test data, they were not the immature vendetta-driven typical terrorists some of them had been when they first joined the *Fianna*, the Junior IRA, in their teens. In August 1971, when internment and torture were initiated, the vast majority of the first thousand men interned were either political activists or old guard who had been imprisoned in the fifties, like the elder McKenna. Their treatment and the subsequent actions of the British Army in Catholic enclaves became the irritants for vendetta. By 1972, youngsters at the most vulnerable age for recruitment into terrorism or the politics of vendetta had personally witnessed and experienced violence, injustice, and prolonged trauma. It is not surprising then that of the ten men who died on hunger strike in 1981, most were age 13 to 16 during that period, and at least one of them, Patsy O'Hara, was wounded in the leg by a soldier during Operation Motorman in the Bogside in Derry. Ten years later, he transformed from angry Fianna Scout into a very politicized leftist ideologue who had been imprisoned several times and was serving time for possession of weapons at the time he went on hunger strike. Patsy was psychologically and politically different from his comrade of the same age, who died the same day, Raymond McCreesh. McCreesh was quite religious and during his hunger strike was often seen praying alone and with his brother, Brian, a priest. These two young men, so different in life and beliefs, were committed to the same political idea and to the same means for achieving that goal.

But the most significant outcome of the hunger strike was the turn from dying for the cause to the ballot box. This was the contribution of the first man on the second hunger strike—Bobby Sands, a talented poet, student, musician, and athlete. He joined the IRA in 1972 at the age of 17 after having been forced to move out of predominantly Protestant areas in north Belfast and suburbs. He had personally been a target of UDA (Ulster Defense Association) attacks. Sands served his first sentence as a Special Category prisoner in Long Kesh at age 19. He was in a cage noted for its engagement in political studies, including Irish language classes and lectures and courses on Celtic Communism and Marxism. He read voraciously and wrote prolifically on a variety of topics, in addition to his poetry. Sands also played several musical instruments and engaged in endless political and philosophical arguments. One of his pastimes, "telling books," involved considerable imagination, at which he excelled. He was Camp Commander, elected by his fellow Republican prisoners, when he chose to be the first on hunger strike. Among the lesser known contextual issues that made the hunger strike an imperative was the treatment of the prisoners by the guards. They were being beaten, kicked, placed on short rations, and otherwise humiliated and battered. Their demands for political prisoner status were not some kind of propaganda ploy. They documented the brutality in smuggled notes, letters, and photos taken on minuscule cameras. The barbarism was routine and worsening when the decision was made to start the hunger strike. But the outcome was far more significant than anything initially anticipated. During the time of Bobby Sands's ordeal, a Nationalist Member of Parliament, Frank Maguire, suffered a heart attack. Even while the House of Commons demanded that the Secretary of State stop declaring his government's intention not to make concessions, the member of the House of Commons from southeast Fermanagh died. Bobby Sands became a candidate, selected by the Sinn Fein executive with the agreement of the other republican contenders and parties to become their registered contestant. This placed the question of his political status squarely on the parliamentarians. He was elected in a contest against a well-known Unionist, Harry West. The campaign officially began on the thirty-second day of Sands's hunger strike. During the nine-day campaign, Bobby Sands was represented by Owen Carron and was, despite his loss of weight and general fragility, cognizant during visits, able to participate in planning strategy, and continued to read poetry and works in the Irish language, as well as to communicate his thoughts. He was elected with a margin of approximately 1400 votes and this immediately made the H-Block's demands and Bobby Sands's continued imprisonment political issues for the rest of the world outside the Thatcher government and the Ulster Unionist parties. Interventions and intercessions from all over failed as Bobby grew weaker but no less determined. He is reported to have been able to speak, respond, and relate with his visitors despite encroaching blindness, deafness, enormous pain, and the distortions of what seemed to have been a stroke until his death on the sixty-sixth day of his hunger strike. He made it clear that it was his will that there would be no violence, no mass uprisings, and no reprisals after his death. That, in fact, he should be mourned in with dignity and in tradition. His wake and funeral were attended by at least 100,000 mourners, including international dignitaries (and Bobby Sands's eight-year-old son who had never really known his father) whose silence on the funeral march and graveside contributed to the solemnity and enormity of this sacrifice. After the death of the tenth man, 217 days after it had begun, the Republican leadership and the prisoners officially called off the hunger strike. The Secretary for Northern Ireland, James Prior, had negotiated a resolution granting the five demands without formally capitulating for the British government. Thus Prime Minister Thatcher was able to represent her victory and Sinn Fein became a political force that would not only stand for election, but would eventually become the main nationalist grouping in developing a government. Perhaps most significantly, they achieved international recognition of Irish republicanism as a political entity—that, contrary to the speeches of Thatcher and other Conservative Party voices, there had not been 800 years of "Irish thuggery," but rather 800 years of struggle for legitimacy of Irish political identity.

The Social Anthropology

Because the personality, and indeed the human brain itself, has been essentially identical through the millennia of human beings (or *homo sapiens*), our species may conceivably harbor the racial memory on which Jungian archetypes are predicated.

The existence of heroes presumes villains and aggression. Evidence from history and even archeological explorations of pre-history confirm that violent confrontations were an essential and repetitive expression of the primitive fear arising out of the constant regard "for the ever-lurking possibility of psychic danger" (Fromm, 1973, p. 482). If these archetypes and racial memory imposed the boundaries of human potential then we would have to interpret history as a continuing conflict between affinity groups, be they tribes, families, or non-state (pre-state) nations. How then might the psyche transcend the idea that retribution is the only option? Who would be able to conceive a higher level of moral development, much less achieve a level of morality, consistent with universal justice? But as my research on children growing up in conflict and violence has demonstrated, in every group, from Northern Ireland to the Khmer Rouge, I found some child or children at age 14 or thereabouts, who had ascended towards the third level of moral development—the level at which there is a sense of universal justice or ability to transcend vendetta and conceive of moral judgment in terms of universals rather than the parochialism that mandates intergenerational, intercommunal violence. Corollary with their scores on the Tapp-Kohlberg questions derived from Piaget's stages of moral development, are scores on the Arnold system of Thematic Apperception Test (TAT)[2] analysis. These indicate the motives and their hierarchy so that it is possible to determine a person's chances of achieving excellence. By examining an individual's motives through his or her imaginal expressions we can learn what moves the person to act in distinctive ways and how the synthesis of intelligence, creativity, attitudes, and values contributes to the behavior and future prospects of that individual. Like the questions of moral and legal development, the Motivation Index score is an absolute. The theory and criteria for scoring can be applied to any stimulus for story-telling whether real, imagined, ambiguous (as are the TAT stimulus cards), or precise. It is cross-culturally valid and can be applied to evaluate autobiographical anecdotes or interview material. For example, in my studies of members of paramilitary organizations in Northern Ireland, Israel, Lebanon, and South Africa, TAT story themes (imports) describing intentional vendetta corresponding with a T-K[3] score at Level II was often selected by adolescent and pre-adolescent boys recruited into violent actions.

There was the fourteen-year-old boy in a Khmer Rouge camp who declared in whispers his intention to become a doctor because so many people needed to be repaired and salvaged from their war wounds. He had no intention of vengeance but only struggled with finding a way to survive the pressures that compelled him and his peers to kill and torture and destroy anyone educated. He was, in his projections and responses to the questions on legal socialization, well on his way to Level III of the Piaget model of consciousness, even though his life experiences were so restricted. In order to go beyond that which is experienced and remembered, imagination is required. This transpires through a brain circuit that allows retrieval of memory images at will. As Arnold (1984, p. 216) points out, "since we can imagine movements and plan action . . . this relay station would have to connect with the frontal lobe as well." Thus frontal lobe development is critical to ascension to a level of moral judgment beyond that which one has personally experienced.

In *The True Believer*, a study of mass movements and the psychology of fanatics who lead and people mass movements, Eric Hoffer writes on self-sacrifice. He says that it is the least reasonable thing to give one's life for something symbolic like a button, a flag, a word, an opinion, a myth:

> when one's life is the most real of all things real. . . . Self-sacrifice cannot be a manifestation of tangible self-interest . . . the impulse to fight springs less from self-interest than from intangibles such as tradition, honor . . . and . . . hope. When there is no hope, people either run or allow themselves to be killed. (Hoffer, 1951, p. 74)

Hoffer's thesis is that self-sacrifice is instigated by a fervent hope and belief in the future. He describes the behavior of Jews on their return to Israel, thus:

> Jews fought recklessly when transferred to Palestine. And though it was said that they fought . . . because they had no choice—they had to fight or have their throats cut by the Arabs—it is still true that their daring and reckless readiness for self-sacrifice sprang not from despair but from their fervent preoccupation with the revival of an ancient land and an ancient people. They . . . fought and died for the cities yet to be built and the gardens yet to be planted. (p. 76)

Hoffer continues on the definition of self-sacrifice as distinct from fanaticism. He quotes Bergson, the philosopher, that strength of faith manifests itself, "not in moving mountains but in not seeing mountains to move (p. 76)."

Political historians may argue that the Jews in the Warsaw Ghetto fought at least as fervently in a situation of overwhelming opposition.

There may also be some argument about the reasoning behind their fight. From the testimony of fighters who survived and the journals of those who witnessed and fought but didn't survive, this was the ultimate choice: to die as victims of the Nazi genocide or to fight and take down with them as many of the enemy as possible. They had ample evidence that the plan was to empty the ghetto by transporting, outright murder, or starvation and ultimately armed might. There was ongoing effort to connect their action with the Polish resistance fighters and the Soviet Army moving from the East. Thus the struggle was not egregiously suicidal. In planning and execution the Warsaw Ghetto uprising was a reasoned, military action. That there were martyrs is recognized. There is no basis for comparison with suicide/homicide martyrdom.

Some children growing up in violence included in my data collection are remarkable adolescents who seem capable of imagining a higher morality. The fourteen-year-old I met in a United Nations Border Relief Organization (UNIBRO) camp in Thailand is one of the extraordinary exceptions I've found in each of the many war zones. In the instance of this young man whose fourteen years were lived in an environment of killing fields and whose experience of other ways of being was restricted, he'd nonetheless been able to image himself as a "redeemer," as Adler described it (Ansbacher & Ansbacher, 1956). The fact that he could make these mature choices and judgments could only be a consequence of this frontal lobe development at an extremely early age. But we have in history examples of others similarly endowed, although they are a tiny minority in any society. In each instance, the child found a model, an idea, and an identity that fit and provided an experimental vehicle within which the adolescent can try new ideas. The Khmer Rouge boy was born while his parents were actively engaged in warfare in Kampuchea. When we met in a UNIBRO camp, his experiences had broadened somewhat. Through a UNIBRO compromise with the Khmer Rouge leadership, the officials granted a blind eye to the nightly incursions into Cambodia and the shelling and shooting across the border. In return UNIBRO was allowed to bring into the camp foreign doctors along with food supplies. The French medical contingent worked under enormous constraints but they were observed and the effects of their work contrasted sharply with the otherwise routine hacking off wounded limbs and throwing away the human remains of mistakes. Remarkably, the boy also recognized and differentiated truth from lies. This is particularly remarkable because the philosophy and practice of the Khmer Rouge was to "invent reality" and construct history in total disregard of objective reality. After testing him, I asked him to take me to meet his parents. He begged for confidentiality, which was readily granted. We went to one of the huts, a bamboo stage raised on poles accessible by ladders. The sides were made of bamboo roll-down shades. In daytime, the scene was as in a theater. His father was sitting in the center foreground, holding between his feet a large piece of wood. As we watched, he slashed away at it, carving intricate designs, his knife flashing so rapidly that it made a blur of motion. He did not stop his work even as I interviewed him through his son and an Australian UN official who spoke Khmer. He told me that he and his sons (who were engaged in various tasks in other sections of the "stage") were farmers, as had been his father and grandfather in eastern Kampuchea. They were, he assured me, never soldiers and were driven off their land by the Vietnamese. In their flight for refuge, they'd become part of this group. They lived in the UNIBRO camp and made carvings to sell for cash. I bought several of his carvings from him and realized that they were tipped with bullets. When asked about the guerilla forays into Cambodia where they fought and burned villages, mined for rubies and sapphires, and the Khmer Rouge traded for weapons, he denied being a part of that. He insisted that he, a farmer, had no experience in soldiering and killing. As he told me this, he did not alter the rhythm of his knife flailing away at the piece of wood, mesmerizing flashes glinting off the metal; his sarong fell away from his thighs and shoulders and what looked like an intricately patterned bodysuit came into view. His entire body was covered, as his son pointed out surreptitiously, with tattoos. This is what the Khmer soldiers do to protect themselves from bullets. The tattoos are not painlessly acquired. The proportion of the body covered is also a symbol of the status and warrior experience of the bearer. Khmer Rouge ideology is rooted in construction of their own new reality. It is also based in a historical view of reality. It was common practice to redefine immediate experience and for children to be continually uncertain of their status in relation to parents and other adults. A father could praise a child with words and lunge out aggressively at the same moment. Growing up in this kind of system is the classic etiology of schizophrenia. Yet, here my young guide was able to choose to believe the evidence of his own senses and to imagine a different way of living.

Pincus describes the psychoneurology of schizophrenia as having everything on common with sensory deprivation. Both create or are manifest in the disturbance of the integrative function of the brain. Any environment that offers only a limited range of sensory stimuli, distorts the sense of time and contradicts and confounds the brain's effort to organize stimuli can produce alterations in cortical sensory processing that make hallucinations (Pincus & Tucker, 1985). In places where sensory deprivation torture has been employed, particularly on adolescents, there is a strong possibility of schizophrenia in the survivors. In societies that confound the sensory impressions of children and deny the accuracy of their experience, as did the Khmer Rouge, schizoid thinking is the probable outcome.

Individuals with sufficient self-confidence and an integrated belief system utilize the absence of sensory stimulation to remember or reorganize and reiterate meaningful experience. This is what was done by the imprisoned missionaries during their brainwashing as reported by Lifton (1974). The techniques of meditation develop this capacity, and there are other ways to learn and acquire this ability.

Studies of concentration camp survivors, many of whom were children in the camps, show a remarkable variety of patterns of moral development and motivation. One has only to read Arnost Lustig's *Children of the Holocaust* (1985) to realize that the experience of Theriesenstadt was so pathological that to have maintained a semblance of mental health, a child needed to shield himself from reality, affection, and all questions of right and wrong. What is remarkable to a psychologist interviewing survivors of these experiences is how so many managed to regain their own humanity and sustain faith, hope, and belief in others, themselves and in divine inspiration.

Eva was in her mid-teens when she was wrenched from her home in Slovakia and taken with her mother and aunt to Auschwitz. Her memory of the platform and the selection that sent her mother and aunt to die in the gas chamber and herself to Mauthausen and slave-labor in Germany, remains, sixty years later, as vivid as the day it happened. In retelling her story the psychologist realizes that Eva's emotionally significant recollections are of her survival modes. She does not ignore nor recast the horrors and hazards, the ugliness and grief. But she does tend to dwell on what might be scored as high achievement outcomes and effective modes of operation. Eva survived many traumatic experiences after Auschwitz. She returned to Czechoslovakia and lived in Brno, Moravia, for all the years under successive totalitarian regimes and managed to get educated in languages; took a five-year course towards a degree in Economics; and worked and supported herself and her two children after their father deserted to find refuge in Canada. Eva's intellect and capacity to adapt and recognize the mountains and assess the way to surmount them, undoubtedly served her well. Also significant is the fact that her childhood experiences in a middle-class family afforded her a solid foundation for emotional and legal socialization and moral development. Eva recalls wanting to survive because, as she put it, "I could not let myself go as long as there was the hope that somebody of my people had survived. I was thinking of my brother. He was a brilliant mathematician, but totally unable to take care of himself so I thought that I could aid him . . . I think the Jews fighting in '48 were happy they could fight for a country where nobody would call them 'dirty Jews' and could kill them at will. . . . But that they had arms and could, finally, after decades of helplessness, feel" (able to act for their own survival).

Then she told me a story that she remembered after seventy years as an early instance of the kind of critical thinking through which her personal survival philosophy evolved:

> I used to go to a Protestant school which was very open and liberal and visited also by Catholic and Jewish children. In the second class, when I was seven years old, I already read a lot and so I borrowed a book from the class library and therein was short stories for children. One story was about a widow who was noble but poor who had two sons. Now they had to sell the last horse they had, and so, how could the widow visit the Holy Mass on Sunday? So the sons drew the carriage instead of a horse to the church and back and the widow was happy about the goodness of her sons and prayed to the Holy Virgin to reward them, as they surely deserved. The next morning she found them dead in their little beds, so she knew the Holy Virgin had rewarded them by making them angels in heaven. I remember I was quite shocked and thinking whether it was not better to live than to become an angel. I'm sure the story had impressed me because I remember it so well. . . . That was also a way to educate children. (E. Seluczka, personal communication, 1989–2003)

That story was not the memory image that sustained her. Rather it was her capacity to critically evaluate and select her own meaning and values which is exemplified through her interpretation of that story which is what remained with her for so many years. Through all of the traumatic events as a slave laborer and then the horror of confinement in a boxcar full of women slaves left locked up on a siding with hostile crowds outside and no food or water, Eva rationed her emotions and activity, sustained her human concern for those worse off than she, including several young, pregnant women, and emerged from that experience, too, to search for her family because that was her reason for survival. Now, nearly eighty, she cared for her ailing husband for years before his death and has managed to overcome bouts with cancer, fractured bones, and many kinds of emotional turmoil. She continues to work as a translator, although no longer as a tour guide. She also pointed out a kind of distinction that is not often represented—the distinction between a martyr and suicide as a protest action to bring attention to an evil. Jan Palach, a young Czech, after the Soviets crushed the Prague Spring of 1968, publicly immolated himself to remind his countrymen that the Russians occupied them. He was inspired by the images of the Vietnamese nuns who had set themselves on fire in protest of the anti-Buddhist purges by a South Vietnamese administration. At the time, most of the bystanders and passers-by just continued about their business, but years later Palach is remembered.

This is an example of community identification or attribution through memory. It is likely to be the kind of ascription of martyrdom that is recognized when the political objectives of leadership or a critical mass of the community share the vision of the individual.

Probably it is the kind of intelligence in children that marks those who value life and choose it for themselves and for others that is represented in the projective stories of the children who score higher motivation index and legal socialization scores derived from the TAT and the Tapp-Kohlberg questions. Such children as adolescents are not as susceptible to recruitment in terrorist organizations. And of course, this is the kind of thinking and choice pattern that operated for Mahatma Gandhi and Martin Luther King, Jr., who valued their lives and their chosen belief so much so as to persist beyond threat and imminent annihilation.

Memory, Memorializing, and Remembering

The brain utilizes sensory icons much as the computer does. With the exception of the autonomic nervous system, the icons are formed through association and emotional memory. If there were racial archetypes transmitted to the unconscious, they would nonetheless have to be communicated through culture. So far as is known, there is no DNA equivalent to social or specific memories. There is, however, the human capacity to organize experience into rituals and communicate through the brain's processing circuitry. One of the very effective clinical techniques for dealing with neuroses and trauma,

Transactional Analysis, analyzes the repetitive, ritualized transactions of the subject in order to understand and change deleterious and dysfunctional social behaviors. Some of these behaviors are passed on from generation to generation out of awareness of the individuals. Other rituals have, like many neurotic defense mechanisms, been functional for group survival at some point in their history and incorporated into the group identity myth.

Human sacrifice was the center of religious experience for human beings thousands of years ago. The practice persists in some parts of the world today. In many societies it combined with cannibalism and formed the essential mystique of the group memory. Freud postulated in *Totem and Taboo* (1961) that the origin of sacrifice and ritual in general derived from the primordial killing and devouring of a patriarchal or dominant male by young males, who then expiated their guilt—a symbolic re-killing of a father figure transmogrified into a god and partaking of his being symbolically in a ritual of sacrifice and communion. This theory has been contested as fact but allowed as psychological process that contributes to social rituals. In the ancient world, at the time of the mythic forebear of monotheism, Abraham of Ur in the Chaldees, human sacrifice had given way to animal sacrifice for a subgroup of people. The significance of Abraham's ritual circumcision and the God-ordered sacrifice of his son, Isaac (which sacrifice was substituted by a ram provided by God), reiterates this expectation. Monotheists distinguished themselves through their abhorrence of human sacrificial offerings, yet ritualized not only animal sacrifice, but also self-sacrifice as an obligation to the deity. Along with it, monotheists evolved a thesis of disciplined self-denial as a means of both social control and individual achievement. Codified in the Ten Commandments or the codes of Hamurabi, these became the totems and taboos that distinguished the human capacity for choice and the human's brain capacity for memory. Animal sacrifice became and remains the dominant worship in what are now referred to as Animist religions. The blood sacrifice became the purification ritual. In times and places where human beings have had little control over their environment and where the forces of nature determine survival, the totem and taboo became the psychological lifeline for otherwise vulnerable, helpless human creatures. As human spirituality proceeded to monotheism, sacrificial animals became the means for expiation and the assurance, by the manner of their slaughter, that the human community would be favored with survival and the benefits of favor in the eyes of God. The idea of martyrdom probably began thus. Significantly, it was engaged as community action and provided a shared memory in ritual. As with all ritual, besides providing a framework or pattern for identity with the group it provides role models, expectations and imagination. The symbolism of sacrifice is universal among human societies. With the destruction of the Second Temple, animal sacrifice became transmogrified for Jews. The ritual of the scapegoat is retold as part of the High Holy Day liturgy. Psychologically the idea of the scapegoat or the bearer of the transgression is incorporated into the psychology of blame and guilt. Or was the ritual derived from these human behaviors? The anthropologists Victor Turner (1969) and Edmund Leach (1969) suggest that through sensory stimulation in rituals the emotions and values evoked are transferred to the ideological meanings of the culture. This comports well with learning theory and the neuropsychology of brain and emotion.

Through rituals of cleansing and purification, prayer and fasting, which are, after all, the practice of self-denial, expiation is achieved. What use then for the human psyche is the human blood sacrifice if what is deemed guilt can be expunged, or power over the unchained forces of threatened destruction can be achieved through these acts. Anthropologists argue that ritual operates where there are fundamental disharmonies within the social system that are not amenable to resolution by any of the intellectual procedures. Social psychologists studying individuals and societies in stress find recourse to ritual accentuated and advisable for the stressed individual in a clinical setting. Consistent with this perspective, the need for the hero icon in the social psyche becomes paramount. When that icon is the martyr or the hero/martyr the ritual sacrifice is revivified.

Crazy Horse, a Chief of the Lakota Sioux, became the hero/martyr for his people. As Black Elk tells the story of how Crazy Horse was bayoneted to death when he resisted the soldiers:

> Our people believe they did what they did because he was a great man and they could not kill him in battle and he would not make himself over into a Wasichu, as Spotted Tail and the others did. That summer, my father told me, the Wasichus wanted him to go to Washington with Red Cloud and Spotted Tail and others to see the Great Father there: but he would not go. He told them that he did not need to go looking for the Great Father. He said "My Father is with me, and there is no Great Father between me and the Great Spirit". . . . They could not kill him in battle. They had to lie to him and kill him that way . . . it does not matter where his body is, for that is grass, but where his spirit is, it will be good to be. (Niebuhr, 1972, pp. 121–122)

Archeological research documents the history of humankind in wars that destroy entire civilizations and natural disasters that turned densely populated areas into wastelands. But the human gene pool with all its diversity nonetheless crosses borders of ethnic and racial entities. Men and women crossed lines of enmity or taboos to mingle their DNA in creating new generations. Too often it is assumed that intermingling was the consequence of rape, enslavement, and conquest. But human beings have the capacity to go beyond the boundaries to love where vendetta would dictate hate. The richest contemporary catalog of data documenting survival through the intervention and love of the Other are the stories of Holocaust survivors. The Righteous Gentiles who helped Jews escape, those who hid Jews in their homes, those who became lovers, and those who fought to save individuals or whole communities. The Rwandan genocide provides some parallel cameos, and so too we can view historically the survival of ethnic Chinese amidst hostile indigenous populations in Asia, the New Christians of New Spain, the indigenous people of the Americas, and, of course, the indigenous pre-Celtic population of Ireland as various European groups invaded, occupied, and integrated within the island. From these and many other examples in human history we may assume that similar social forces shaped prehistory. Fight or flight are but two of many possibilities with which the human intellect contends its choice of action under perceived danger. The survival and progression of civilization is predicated on courses for survival more imaginative.

The Palais de Justice in Rouen, France, has a history that mirrors two thousand years of human search for the meaning of humanity and of repeated acts of inhumanity imposed in the name of the hegemony of one religious thesis over another. Rouen is not a grand capital but it is geographically and geologically gifted to be an administrative center and center for law and ideology. As such, it has been a nexus for the interactions of cultures and ideas. To this day, the Law School in Rouen is one of the most highly regarded in France. It is not a seaport, but a fluvial port; because of the deepness of the Seine River at this point it remains an important port in France. The Palais de Justice has undergone razing, rebuilding, renovation, and reconstruction over the past thousand years. But in the most recent renovation, to make a parking garage, the excavation revealed an ancient synagogue and yeshiva that had occupied the site well before the Palais De Justice was even conceived. And these were themselves later incarnations of an even earlier Jewish House of

Study, a Beit Midrash, that may have been constructed at the time Rouen was a Roman administrative center. The neighborhood surrounding the site has been identified as Jews Street from time immemorial. Close to the river, it provided a site for a Mikveh, or ritual bathhouse, and the other requisites for Jewish life. There is evidence that the enclave was inhabited and developed by Israelites who, either taken by the Romans from their ancient homeland or traveling and seeking new trade routes and markets for their commerce, had congregated here. But the indigenous inhabitants at the time of the Roman occupation were Gallic Celts (according to Josephus and other Roman historians, as well as to the folk belief of the region). They were, by religion, Druid. The Romans were, of course, pantheists and the Jews, fierce monotheists. The Celts had their temples and priestesses probably not very far from the Jewish house of worship. In fact, it would have been likely that the spot on which now stands the great and famous Cathedral of Rouen had originally been a far humbler house of Jewish worship. That would have been in a triangular line of connection with the Yeshiva and the Mikveh. The Romans were evangelistic in imposing their worship of their leaders and demigods, their pantheon of gods and goddesses. It is possible that the great cathedral was imposed on the site of a Roman or Druid temple. At the center of the enclave was the marketplace. Hundreds of years later in 1431, three hundred years after the razing of the Rouen yeshiva by the Crusaders, it was the site at which Jeanne d'Arc was burned to death. She had refused to retract her belief in her sacred visions, according to some accounts. According to others, she had recanted and was burned to death as a heretic. The Crusaders who antedated the Inquisition and auto-da-fé murdered Jews on their mission to free the Holy Land from the infidels. The Rouen Talmud was testament to the vitality and renown of the institution. Many of the teachers and scholars burned to death in the conflagration.

We do not know if the imposition of Roman worship was a contributor to the exodus of the Celts to Ireland but a thousand years before the crusaders burned that site, Celts from Normandy probably set sail in their little skin boats from what now is the seaport of LeHavre close by Rouen. A thousand years later, Normans, descendant from Viking, Celtic, Roman, and Teutonic mixtures of peoples that had, by then, become indigenous, invaded Britain in 1066 and, not long after, came to Ireland as another colonial plantation that became indigenous in its turn. It is quite possible in July to sail from that port to what is now Cork on a placid sea.

The Romans made Celts warriors in their legions. They were present in Jerusalem. The Israelites, or Jews as they then became known, were brought with the Romans to keep their accounts and collect their taxes. In all the Roman Empire and in many European and Asian empires before and after, Jews with their requisite literacy (a mitzvah, or religious obligation) became administrators and record keepers. Others, of course, were merchants traveling from place to place, carrying Chinese porcelains to trade for Turkish oils, and established small enclaves with a house of worship every six-days travel distance for their seventh-day Shabbat. And so one wonders, were the Israelites, Jews, amongst the passengers in the little boats? Did they land in Ireland long before their presence as Jews was noted in the twelfth century? All of which is to remind us that, besides making war, annihilating groups who held different beliefs, and the enormous cruelty of forcing conversions—human beings through the human brain have the capacity for imagination and transformation.

Erwin Traubmann married Ruth Erna, a Sudetan German woman who converted to Judaism, not long before he became one of 2000 Jewish men and boys ordered to be transported from Ostrava, Moravia, to make Eichman's first concentration camp in Nisko, Poland. For five years, Erwin fled the concentration camp and, in the next year, was variously on foot, transported, or force-marched from concentration camp to refugee camp to slave labor camp. In each place, with his comrade Edwin Safar with whom he had organized the Eggcentrics (a popular group of musicians in Ostrava) before the Anschluss, they made music, often after bitter days of heavy labor with hands half frozen or tattered by their work. They did not refer to their time in the Soviet camps as slave labor, although that is what the rest of the world and history labeled it. They worked for their food and keep and believed this was a fair exchange. When the orders were issued to form a Czech battalion in the Soviet Army they, along with thousands of other exiles, concentration camp escapees, and refugees, volunteered and were hastily trained by the Soviet Army. They were issued guns, uniforms, and very basic supplies. Their children and old people made up the rear of their column. Oxen drew their artillery. As they went along many farmers joined them, bringing their livestock with them. There were two airplanes and 14 women parachutists. I interviewed two of the surviving women, now in their early eighties. They are, in the winter of their lives, no less remarkable personages than they were in the ferocious winters of their march from the Urals to Prague.

When asked why women were chosen for this precarious task, they laughed and said, "women make smaller targets and besides we are more nimble with our hands. We parachuted behind enemy lines, assembled our radios, and called in the artillery shots."

Erwin and Edwin organized the music contingent in the Czech Battalion in the Soviet Army. Edwin composed their anthem, *On To Prague*, and chose to serve and survived service in the front lines as a sanitation worker by day and orchestra musician at night. He knew how to use weapons but preferred the job of bringing food and first aid and carrying the wounded and the dead from between the lines of combat. He returned to Ostrava victorious and only then learned that his parents, sister, aunts, uncles, and cousins had been transported and killed. He found Ruth Erna in the confinement pen into which the local people had forced all of the Sudetan Germans preliminary to transport on foot or cattle car to Germany, where none of them ever lived before and where they were to become pariahs in the German Democratic Republic. Ruth Erna had, when faced with transport to Theriesenstadt, divorced her Jewish husband *in absentia*, resumed her Aryan status and become known as a collaborator with the Nazi regime. Now, six years and a civilization later, Erwin asked her to remarry him. She was reluctant, even though she knew that the alternative was ignominy. But their marriage saved her from transport and they began a life together. His comrades in arms called him crazy. Every place they went to live in Czechoslovakia they were hounded. He was a hero and she a traitor and it seemed no one could get beyond that definition. Erwin had long passed, if ever he had been at, the level of vendetta. Surrounded by death and cruelty, he repeatedly chose life. He changed his surname to Toman to become more readily identified as Czech. Making music was his life and even his religion. By 1956 the anti-Jewish Stalinist purges of Czechs made it impossible for them to remain. Ironically, the Czech Young Pioneers had adopted his anthem, but its composer could not live in such a climate of good death/bad death. They escaped in 1956. Erwin died on a train in the Andes even as he and Ruth Erna were en route to a new life with his relatives in Santiago de Chile.

Erwin's cousin, Ernesto (born Arnst), with his parents, had been among the last of the Czech Jews to escape the Gestapo round-ups in Brno for transports to concentration camps. They found refuge in Chile. Ernesto, then fourteen, lied about his age, volunteered for the Czech Battalion in the RAF, and flew missions over Ostrava and bombed the site of their grandfather's house because it was located near the coal refineries supplying the Nazi war machine. Ernesto survived and returned to Chile where he became a leader in the Chilean Communist Party. He was serving as a deputy Minister for Mines in the Allende government when he was tortured to death by Colonel Roberto Guillard, one of the Chilean Army officers collaborating with Pinochet in the coup.

Individuals have died and been killed, in fact, millions of individuals in the twentieth century died, before their appointed time from war, torture, and genocide. Some deaths are memorialized and some are identified as martyrs. This is a function of attribution that distinguishes certain individuals and ways of dying from others, which have been no less, significant but probably less forged in memory. The human mind struggles to put meaning on six million individuals, but a significant brain icon can form from a symbolic individual. In imagery of the Holocaust, Anne Frank became the one child universally recognized out of millions who perished in the death camps and killing fields of the Nazi genocide. But to be attributed secular martyrdom requires death-for-a-purpose. And hers remains significant because, like millions of others, her life had purpose and her death had none. Sacrifice for martyrdom requires that death occur in the struggle for a higher purpose and in the choice of a behavior or course of action. Anne Frank and the six million Jews killed in the Holocaust had no choice. Only two groups consigned for extermination had a choice. Jehovah's Witnesses could recant their faith and live. Homosexuals were given a pseudo-opportunity to prove that they would be heterosexual and thus save themselves.

The evolution and continuity of civilized humanity is also a product of refugees and exiles who find asylum amongst genetically alien populations and ultimately assimilate and integrate with that population. The second half of the twentieth century was a time of huge waves of people in flight. As identity groups disperse and assimilate or become marginalized in new habitats, their identification with their origins is, in large part, the iconography of their martyrology. A dramatic and relatively recent example of this mass movement is the Vietnamese boat people. They were Christian and Buddhist by religion, but their experience was determined not so much by religious identity as by either Chinese ethnicity or participation in the institutions of the former government, South Vietnam, in collaboration with the United States. Estimates vary, but at least a million people fled in small boats between 1974 and 1992. Their experience of flight united an otherwise diverse population. Every possible calamity beset them: pirates, treacherous seas, and shortages of food supplies. Many landed on inhospitable shores and were raped, beaten, robbed, and killed without a trace. Fortunate survivors were placed in United Nations refugee camps hastily established throughout Southeast Asia. In addition to the administrative records established by the United Nations High Commissioner for Refugees (UNHCR) and co-operating non-governmental agencies (NGOs), the refugees themselves established memorials to boat mates who died en route and besides establishing their own characteristic institutions for living, quickly established cemeteries, both Buddhist and Christian, often across the road from each other and sometimes adjacent to a house of worship. Within their huts many families made ancestor shrines. In some instances, the ashes of a parent accompanied the voyage. Memorialization was a priority much as reproducing their remembered villages was a priority. This was the physical embodiment of spiritual and cultural identity.

Chastity was a high value for Vietnamese women. Many of the refugees had been captive and raped by their captors or by pirates. Many had barely survived multiple rapes and were psychologically so devastated that they retreated into schizoid states of being. Nor was this kind of torment absent from their experience as "protected asylum seekers" in UNHCR camps. Some of the rape victims found themselves pregnant—an even greater dishonor. Self immolation happened more than once and always the place on which it transpired was marked, enshrined, and memorialized. Mothers discovered that children who were orphans had a better chance of re-settlement and so burned themselves to death. (This changed the classification of the children to unaccompanied minors and made their re-settlement in the absence of responsible adults in their homeland a higher priority.) Whether their self-sacrifice constituted martyrdom might be open to debate, but their children were re-settled in third countries and in some instances the family was scheduled for repatriation. These mothers were memorialized as martyrs in the camp and probably addressed as such in the generations of their descendents in the far-off lands and assimilated cultures in which they were finally resettled.

Unlike the Irish hunger strikers, these women did not achieve international recognition and their commitment to faith and life was to their children's future lives or, in the case of the rape victims, to cleansing the dishonor. Whereas the Irish hunger strikers are commemorated by a nation, these refugees, by definition, were neither a nation nor a non-state nation. At most, they were a community of flight. Their actions received little notice outside of the place in which they occurred. In part, this is the politics of memory and also communication to a limited audience. One of the crafts engaged by these boat people as a symbol of memory was to make from the remains of their boat some small piece, often a wooden block but sometimes an elaborate reproduction in miniature. On this piece would be the name and year of the boat and the camp in which they came to rest. The universal human need for transcending time in memory is not always linked to aspirations for wider recognition, even when the act is undertaken as symbolization of political action. As ever, when there is war and flight, parents often consign themselves to death and destruction by using all their resources to get their children out and away. In this act, they attempt to ensure their own immortality through continuity of their progeny.

World War II and the Holocaust were the foundation for the international institutions that became the arbiters of international morality and justice. These became the instruments for memory. But the capacity of the individual for remembering and the gratification it provides are the psychological foundation for community and identity. Remembering martyrs is a shared icon of a common history. Memory and memorializing human beings, as opposed to cathecting god figures and occult immortals, contributes to the social group and gives the individual growing child the possibility for identification with and idealization of values and social norms. Just as the memory of a beloved parent or grandparent can provide an emotionally unifying force for the survivors of an equally divisive implosion if the deceased was the only unifying agent, so the memory of a political martyr serves the polity.

The martyr serves another important function, however. The idea that the sacrifice of this individual for the achievement of the goal of the social or political group becomes personalized into, "He or she died for me." This personalizes responsibility and feelings of guilt, shame, and blame. So we move from the study of the psychology of the martyr to the psychological impact of martyrdom. There is also an implicit test of time in ascription of martyrdom and memorialization.

To be remembered after death is a universal human desire. Death and burial rituals, cemeteries, and memorial shrines are an essential feature of every civilization, historic and contemporary. These provide a location for displacement of grief and alleviate the nagging uncertainty about the fate of the loved one. They also provide a locus for propagation of the name and often some other quality of the deceased. Always in wars there were the unknown soldiers to be accounted and remembered. But every army has had a moral responsibility to account for its dead and retrieve their remains. This repatriation of the honored dead is incorporated into any peace or armistice accord.

The need for the human intelligence to name and identify is incorporated into the idea of memorialization. Not remarkably, there are no nameless great martyrs. There may be abstract sculptures or paintings representing the martyred dead of a time, place, or people, but these are representations. Many western nations have as a national shrine a Tomb of the Unknown Soldier. But this is not an ascription of martyr status for an individual or for a group as such. It is a memorialization of the heroism of unidentified war dead. Recognition as a martyr requires name identity and more.

The most profoundly disturbing irreconcilable injustice is the disappearance of victims with no account and no assignment of responsibility. The rational mind requires an accounting of the past much as it requires connection to the future.

Social and international justice must be systematically formulated if it is to lead to a reintegration of the fractured society. It is through recognition, restitution, and rehabilitation that justice may commence. The injured survivors require more, psychologically, than compensation and therapy. Political victimization imposes feelings of guilt and alienation on the individuals who were its objects. They require recognition as the innocents they were, apologies, and the opportunity to determine the punishment. For survivors of those who disappeared, there is no adequate restitution or acceptable compensation apart from full knowledge of what happened to their missing and locating the remains.

Public recognition and ascription of hero status is accomplished through the means of public communication, now generally referred as media attention. Disappearance, the expunging from existence, is the ultimate denial of any form of immortality and leaves the murderer in the role of divine determiner of who shall live and who shall die. This usurpation of divine right extends beyond the legal fact of homicide—that the torturers and murderers remain inviolate and their crime unacknowledged by assignation of responsibility constitutes impunity.

At this juncture, there is a question of moral judgment from a relativist perspective or the adoption of a universal standard of guilt and morality. It is possible to become mired in rounds of retribution by Justice and perpetrators can become hero/martyr by their loyalties.

The writer Ariel Dorfman (2002) documents the response by his political colleagues to charges brought against General Augusto Pinochet in an international arena through Joan Garces, a Spanish magistrate. The international human rights charges against Pinochet and extradition procedures that followed in British courts raised the prospect that retribution could be delivered through the machinery of international human rights institutions. By that time, 1998, 25 years after Pinochet unleashed terror and torture in Chile, this strong man had become aging, ill, and allegedly demented (suffering senile dementia). The charges, his home detention, and handling by police were protested by a sizeable section of Chileans, mostly the affluent, and were used to portray him in press releases, and in establishing a foundation to celebrate him, as a martyr to the Chilean struggle against the Communist governance by the elected Allende regime. Had Pinochet died during his detention or while on trial in Spain, his adherents might well have established his martyr status in the cause of Chilean democracy. Dorfman writes about his experience as a victim and as a confidante of the multitude of victims of this regime and about the realization that his wish from this turnabout of positions was for redemption rather than revenge. More than anything, he, Dorfman, wanted Pinochet to recognize his responsibility for the years of horror and destruction he had invoked upon the Chilean people. Dorfman wanted Pinochet to recognize the truth of what he had done and seek conciliation with his victims. He writes:

> General Pinochet not only believes in God. He also believes that God believes in him. Saving him over and over again for his divine mission . . . [Pinochet tells a journalist]: "There was no dictatorship in Chile. We are an example for the whole world. The fall of the Berlin Wall was caused by Chile; we were the first to raise our flags against the Berlin Wall. We were the first to defeat communism . . . I wish to be remembered as the best president Chile ever had." (p. 84)

Dorfman recalls how Pinochet viewed himself as the heir of Francisco Franco and that Franco died in old age in his bed and never faced the victims of his terrorism on trial. Dorfman continues to write about the victims but also about the ordinary Chileans who believe either that Pinochet himself neither ordered nor knew about the atrocities and that he had saved their country from governmental impositions on their human rights by the Allende regime which was accused of nationalizing private property—depriving them of their property rights. But what Dorfman recognizes and reports as the great victory for humanity is the recognition by the British Law Lords of the dictator's complicity in torture as extraditable offenses under the international agreement of 1988. To fully appreciate the meaning of the ruling that Pinochet was not immune by reason of his authority from responsibility, regardless of his current status as an honorary Senator for Life. By virtue of the international convention he himself signed, General Augusto Pinochet has been, like Hitler and Mussolini before him, charged before the bar of international justice for crimes against humanity. Unlike them, he is not the leader of a vanquished nation, but was charged instead for his crimes against his own nation. What was probably the signal aspect of the continuing proceedings, then and in the Chilean Supreme Court, is the Disappeared. Disappearances, torture to death, and destruction of the bodies was intended, as mentioned earlier, to insure against political martyrdom. In fact, there is audio taped evidence that Pinochet toyed with the idea of making President Allende the first disappearance by destroying his body.

Although the British court determined that only crimes committed after 1988 could be included in the trial charges, when the international convention outlawing torture was signed by Pinochet and Prime Minister Thatcher, they also deliberated over the Disappeared as an ongoing crime irrelevant to the date of their arrest and disappearance. As noted by Ariel Dorfman:

> The strategy of "disappearing" prisoners, that extreme form of violence that has sullied so many regimes of every ideology all over the world, has proven to be a boomerang that ends up damaging those who use it ... those men and women arrested one night and then never heard of again have refused to accept the destiny of oblivion ... are somehow still alive beyond death. The hidden light of the men and women who gave their lives for what they believed in cannot be totally snuffed out while there is one person somewhere in this world who is willing to remember and resurrect them. (p. 159)

Because the disappearances continued to terrorize and impact the well-being of the survivors, and the date of death and place of interment remained undetermined, all of those who disappeared before 1988 could be counted as continuing crimes against humanity!

Quite recently, on March 7, 2003, a *Washington Post* reporter interviewing personnel in the CIA Center for Counter-terrorism wrote that Attorney General John Ashcroft and CIA Director George Tenet speculated in meetings with their counter-terrorism experts about the outcome for several possible "dispositions of Osama bin Laden":

> "They'd rather have a flash event where he is killed rather than a drawn out event where he is tried," said one person who agrees with the two men and has firsthand knowledge of their views. Two others said the ideal result would be what one of them called a "fade away," a euphemism for killing bin Laden without announcing either his death or those responsible for it. Any disposition of bin Laden risks martyring him in the eyes of supporters, but a second official said that, "for our safety, the best thing overall would be if he disappeared." ("U.S. Steps Up Hunt," 2003)

This indicates that the idea employed by Pinochet and other dictators is not at all foreign to the leaders of the United States who conceive themselves, too, at war against terrorism. The dead body as a prospective icon-rallying image transformed into a blood sacrifice in the minds of followers, has not lost credence even after international justice has condemned these extra-juridical solutions.

These are signal instances of the use of good death/bad death to justify a reign of terror. Several of Pinochet's speeches and conversations are examples of his belief that he is personally saving his country and political system by eradicating the Other. In 1974, the Lutheran and Catholic Bishops met with Pinochet to try to moderate his use of torture. They referred to it as "physical pressure." Pinochet called it "torture," and said:

> Look, you are priests and you work in the Church. You can allow yourselves the luxury of being compassionate and benevolent. I am a soldier and as head of state I have a responsibility towards the entire Chilean people. The plague of communism has invaded the people. I need to exterminate communism. Torture is necessary to exterminate communism. For the good of the fatherland. (Dorfman, 2002, p. 61)

On the second anniversary of his coup, Pinochet spoke on human rights.

Again he told his listeners how he had to choose to whom to grant human rights. As if he were the divine creator who decided that for their transgression in partaking of the fruit of knowledge of good and evil, Adam and Eve would be banished from the Garden of Eden. What hubris!

> Human rights, he says, are universal and inviolable, but not all of them can be exercised unrestrictedly nor are they of the same hierarchy.

When the social body sickens.... It is not possible to enjoy every human right simultaneously. The immense majority of our fellow citizens accept and support.... Because they understand that those restrictions are the price that has to be paid for tranquility, calm and social peace ... when authority is not applied vigorously we fall into depravity ... and into anarchy ... that is why our attitude must remain inflexible for the good of Chile and its children. (Dorfman, 2002, pp. 117–118)

In the same speech he refers to himself as sensitive and grieved by what he must do to preserve a decent life for his countrymen.

After his arrest and extradition trial in London, supporters carried placards reading "Pinochet Our Savior."

The action designed to prevent martyrdom and proof of injustice became at the end of the twentieth century the criminal strategy that would indict the reign of impunity. In all of the wars of the late twentieth century, the Disappeared became the proof of the perpetrators' depravity and violation of international law. The Disappeared of Bosnia, Kosovo, Rwanda, and South Africa, as well as Central and South America were dug up and remains were identified by forensic experts. Even the method of their death and the weapons and their killers are identified and put into the prosecution of the perpetrators.

Pinochet at age 84 was found to be mentally unsound due to brain damage that allegedly destroyed his memory and ability for logical problem solving. He was diagnosed with vascular dementia and the usual prognosis is episodic and unpredictable deterioration of the brain as repeated strokes take their toll. According to the examination report, Pinochet's memory and executive functioning were severely impaired. But the diagnosis remains open to question. The fact is, that neither the British nor Spanish governments wanted to take responsibility for a legal proceeding that might have the effect of Pinochet's death on their soil. Pinochet as a prospective martyr to international justice loomed as a larger threat to international justice than anyone wanted to assume. Nonetheless, in July 2002 the Chilean Supreme Court Justices dismissed the case against Pinochet by reason of his mental deterioration making him unfit to stand trial. Shortly afterwards, Pinochet emerged from his palatial home and publicly resigned from his post of Senator For Life while retaining his impunity as ex-president with a security detail and salary. In a letter he claimed to have personally written he defends his government and historical record. This was accompanied by public pronouncements: "I am not crazy." Coincidentally, that was also the claim of the Unabomber, whose mental status was and remains an issue. In my own experience as a staff psychologist, the majority of patients in a forensic mental hospital who are committed by the court for evaluation or treatment of mental status issues insist that they are not crazy, except if that diagnosis can keep them in the hospital rather than in prison. The question at law then remains competency to stand trial. In most states in the US the criteria for competency are so minimal that the alleged offender is very rarely incompetent to stand trial. At the same time, when individuals are under consideration as to their competency to handle their own affairs, make financial decisions, and care for themselves, the standards for independence are considerably higher.

Thus we return to several of the concepts noted at the beginning of this essay: the capacity for choice, responsibility for that choice, and death inflicted on one who chooses to live his or her beliefs regardless of threat or punishment.

In every generation, in every time and geographic place, the human capacity for conceiving universal justice has been expressed by a few or by many, and civilization itself transcends devastation because that capacity is expressed.

Notes

1. In the sense of promulgation by newspapers, posters, and pamphlets of the time. Media herein refers to any public communication such as leaflets, posters, poems, and ballads, as well as broadcast and journalism.

2. The Thematic Apperception Test is a vehicle for examining and assessing personality dynamics, motivation, relative health, and psychopathology. The TAT is one of the battery of physiological tests used by this author in her studies of children age 6 through 16, members of paramilitary organizations, and torture survivors (Fields 1973a, 1977, 1980).

3. Tapp-Kohlberg Test of Legal Socialization. This is based on the Piaget thesis of levels of moral development equivalent with legal socialization. This test was also given to all of the aforementioned subjects (Tapp & Kohlberg, 1971).

References

Abu-Lughod, I. (1990). Introduction on achieving independence. In J.R. Nassar & R. Heacock (Eds.), *Intifada—Palestine at the crossroads*. New York: Praeger.

Adams, G. (1983). *Falls memories*. Dingle, Ireland: Brandon Book Publishers.

Adams, G. (1990). *Cage eleven*. Dingle, Ireland: Brandon Book Publishers.

Allport, G. (1967). Preface. In R. May (Ed.), *Existential psychology* (pp. xi–xii). New York: Random House.

Ansbacher, H., & Ansbacher, R. R. (Eds.). (1956). *Individual psychology of Alfred Adler: A systematic presentation in selections from his writings.* New York: Basic Books, Inc.

Arnold, M. B. (1960). *Emotion and personality.* New York: Columbia University Press.

Arnold, M. B. (1962). *Story sequence analysis.* New York: Columbia University Press.

Arnold, M. B. (1984). *Memory and the brain.* Hillsdale & London: Lawrence Erlbaum Associates.

Bandura, A. & Walters, R. H. (1959). *Social learning and personality development.* New York: Holt Rinehart & Winston.

Baron, S. & Wise, G. S. (Eds.). (1974). *Violence and defense in the Jewish experience.* Philadelphia: Jewish Publication Society of America.

Beresford, D. (1987). *Ten men dead: The story of the 1981 Irish hunger strike.* Glasgow, Scotland: Collins.

Berne, E. (1972). *What do you say after you say "Hello"?* New York: Grove Press.

Carr, C. (2002). *The lessons of terror.* New York: Random House.

Carson, C. (Ed.). *The autobiography of Martin Luther King, Jr.* New York: Warner Books.

Coogan, T. P. (1980). *On the blanket: The H-block story.* Dublin: Ward River Press.

Dinges, J., & Landau, S. (1980). *Assassination on embassy row.* New York: Pantheon Books, New York.

Dorfman, A. (2002). *Exorcising terror.* New York: Seven Stories Press.

Durant, W. (1950). *The history of civilization: The age of faith* (Vol. IV). New York: Simon and Schuster.

Durkheim, E. (1951). *Suicide.* New York: The Free Press.

Durkheim, E. (1965). *The elementary forms of the religious life.* New York: The Free Press.

Elbedour, S. (1992). *The psychology of children of war.* Unpublished doctoral dissertation, University of Minnesota.

Elbedour, S. (1998). Youth in crisis—The well-being of Middle-Eastern youth and adolescents during war and peace. *Journal of Youth & Adolescence, 45*(4), 57–65.

Elbedour, S., Baker, A., & Charlesworth, W. R. (1997). The impact of political violence on moral reasoning in children. *Child Abuse & Neglect, 21,* 1053–1066.

Erikson, E. H. (1950). *Childhood and society,* New York: W.W. Norton.

Erikson, E. H. (1968). *Identity, youth and crisis.* New York: W.W. Norton.

Erikson, E. H. (1974). On the nature of psychohistorical evidence. In R. & E. Olson (Eds.), *Explorations in Psychohistory: The Wellfleet Papers* (pp. 42–77). New York: Simon and Schuster.

Erikson, E. H. (1975). *Life history and the historical moment.* New York: Norton & Company.

Fanon, F. (1963). *The wretched of the earth.* New York: Grove Press.

Farson, S. K., & Landis, J. M. (1990). The sociology of an uprising. The roots of the Intifada. In J. R. Nassar & R. Heacock (Eds.), *Intifada: Palestine at the crossroads.* New York: Praeger.

Fields, R. M. (1973a). *Society on the run.* Hammondsworth: Penguin Ltd.

Fields, R. M. (1973b, March). Ulster: A psychological experiment? *The New Humanist,* 445–448.

Fields, R. M. (1974). The struggle for a homeland: Striking parallels between Irish Republicanism and Jewish Zionism. *The Holy Cross Quarterly,* 6, 1–4.

Fields, R. M. (1976a). *Society under siege.* Philadelphia: Temple University Press.

Fields, R. M. (1976b). *Torture and institutional coercion.* Paper presented at the American Psychological Association Convention, New York, and American Sociological Association Convention, Washington, D.C.

Fields, R. M. (1977). Psychological genocide. *Repression and Repressive Violence.* Marjo Hofkayels (Ed.). Amsterdam: Swets & Zeitlinger.

Fields, R. M. (1978). Hostages and torture victims: Studies on the effects of trauma induced stress. *Procedings. Second International Conference on Psychological Stress and Adjustment In Time of War and Peace.* Israel: Tel Aviv University.

Fields, R. M. (1979). Children of violence: Violent children. *History of Childhood Quarterly* (fall).

Fields, R. M. (1980a). *Northern Ireland: Society under siege.* New Jersey: Transaction-Society Press, Rutgers University.

Fields, R. M. (1980b). Victims of terrorism: The effects of prolonged stress. In S. Salasin (Ed.), *Evaluation and Change, Special Issue on Survivors* (pp. 78–83). Minneapolis, MN: Minneapolis Medical Research Foundation.

Fields, R. M. (1981). Psychological sequelae of terrorization. In Y. Alexander & J. Gleason (Eds.), *Terrorism: A behavioral perspective.* New York: Praeger.

Fields, R. M. (1982a). Terrorized into terrorist. In F. Ochberg & D. Soskis (Eds.), *Victims of terrorism.* Denver, CO: Westview Press.

Fields, R. M. (1982b). Victims of terror. In D. Rappaport & Y. Alexander (Eds.), *Moral implications of terrorism.* New York: Crane, Russek & Co

Fields, R. M. (1986a). *Children of violence.* Paper presented at Third International Conference on the Psychological Effects of War and Peace, Jerusalem, Israel.

Fields, R. M. (1986b). *Psychological profile of a terrorist.* Paper presented at the American Psychological Association Convention, Washington, D.C..

Fields, R. M. (1987). *Terrorized into terrorist.* Symposium conducted at the Second Annual Conference of Traumatic Stress Studies, New York.

Fields, R. M. (1989). Terrorized into terrorist: Pete the Para strikes again. In A. O'Day & Y. Alexander (Eds.), *Ireland's terrorist trauma: Interdisciplinary perspectives*. London, New York, Toronto: Harvester Wheatsheaf Press

Fields, R. M. (1990a). Children of the intifada. *Migration World, XVII* (1), 13–19.

Fields, R. M. (1990b). Predicted formula for a terror vocation. In J.E. Lundberg, V. Otto, & B. Rybeck (Eds.), *Wartime Medical Services*. Stockholm: FOA.

Fields, R. M., & Elbedour, S. (2002). The Palestinian suicide bomber. In C. Stout (Ed.), *The Psychology of Terrorism*, Vol. 2. Westport: Greenwood/Praeger.

Frankl, V. E. (1962). *Man's search for meaning: An introduction to logotherapy*. Boston: Beacon Press.

Frankl, V. E. (1967). *Psychotherapy and existentialism: Selected papers on logotherapy*. New York: Simon and Schuster.

Freud, S. (1920, 1953). *A general introduction to psychoanalysis*, J. Riviere, (trans.). New York: Doubleday and Company, Inc.

Freud, S. (1925).*Collected Papers* (Vol. IV). London, Hogarth Press.

Freud, S. (1953). The interpretation of dreams. In J. Strachey (Ed. and Trans.), *Collected papers of Sigmund Freud* (Vols. 4 and 5). London and New York: Hogarth Press and Basic Books.

Freud, S. (1961a). *Civilization and its Discontents*, J. Strachey (Ed. and Trans). New York: W.W. Norton & Company.

Freud, S. (1961b). *Totem and Taboo*, J. Strachey (Ed. and Trans.). New York: W.W. Norton & Company.

Freud, S. (1968). *Psychoanalysis and faith*, New York: Basic Books

Fromm, E. (1941). *Escape from freedom*, New York: Holt, Rinehart and Winston, Inc.

Fromm, E. (1955). *The sane society*. New York: Rinehart & Company.

Fromm, E. (1973). *The anatomy of human destructiveness*. New York: Holt, Rinehart and Winston.

Hess, R. D., & Torney, J. W. (1967). *Development of political attitudes in children*. New York: Aldine.

Hoffer, E. (1951). *The True Believer*. New York: Harper and Row.

Huyck, E. E., & Fields, R. M. (1981). Impact of resettlement on refugee children. *International Migration Review*, 246–256.

Jung, C. (1959a). *The Basic Writings of Carl G. Jung*. V Staub De Laszlo (Ed.). New York: Modern Library, Random House.

Jung, C. (1959b). *Four archetypes: Mother/rebirth/spirit/trickster*. Princeton: Bollingen Press, Princeton University Press.

Juergensmeyer, M. (2000). *Terror in the mind of god: The global rise of religious violence*. Berkeley, Los Angeles & London: University of California Press.

Katz, F. E. (1993). *Ordinary people and extraordinary evil: A peport on the beguilings of evil.* Albany: State University of New York Press.

Kordon, D. R., Edelman L. I., Lagos, D. L., Nicoletti, R., & Bozzolo, R. C. (1988). *Psychological effects of political repression.* Buenos Aires: Sudamerica/planeta.

Kritz, N. (Ed.) (1995). *Transitional justice* (Vol. II & III). Washington, D.C.: United States Institute of Peace.

Leach, E. (1969). *Genesis as myth and other essays.* London: Cape.

Lee, A. M. (1983). *Terrorism in Northern Ireland.* Bayside: General Hall, Inc.

Lehman, A. C., & Myers, J. E. (1995). *Magic, witchcraft and religion: An anthropological study of the supernatural.* Mountain View: Mayfield Publishing Company.

Lifton, R. J. (1967). *Death in life—Survivors of Hiroshima.* New York: Random House.

Lifton, R. J. (1968). *Boundaries: Psychological man in revolution.* Clinton: Vintage Books.

Lifton, R. J. (1974). *Explorations in psychohistory: The Wellfleet papers.* New York: Simon and Schuster.

Lifton, R. J., & Olson, E. (1976). The human meaning of total disaster: The Buffalo Creek experience. *Psychiatry, 39,* 1–12.

Lifton, R. J. (1979). *The broken connection: On death and the continuity of life.* New York: Simon and Schuster.

Lustig, A. (1985). *Children of the holocaust.* Evanston: Northwestern University Press.

Maslow, A. H. (1968). *Toward a psychology of being.* New York: Van Nostand Reinhold.

May, R. (Ed.). (1967). *Existential psychology.* New York: Random House.

May, R. (1977). *The meaning of anxiety.* New York: W.W. Norton.

Niebuhr, J. G. (1972). *Black Elk speaks.* New York: Washington Square Press.

Olsson, P. A. (1988). The terrorist and the terrorized: Some psychoanalytic consideration. *Journal of Psychohistory, 16*(1), 47–60.

Piaget, J. (1932). *The moral judgment of the child.* New York: Harcourt, Brace and World.

Piaget, J. (1952). *The origins of intelligence in children.* New York: International Universities Press.

Piaget, J. (1954). *The construction of reality in the child.* New York: Basic Books.

Piaget, J. (1963). *The language and thought of the child.* Cleveland & New York: Meridian Books, The World Publishing Company.

Pincus, J. H., & Tucker, G. J. (1985). *Behavioral neurology.* New York: Oxford University Press.

Pincus, J. H. (2001). *Base instincts: What makes killers kill.* New York: W.W. Norton & Company.

Schneidman, E. S., Farberow, N. L., & Litman, R. R. (1976). *The psychology of suicide.* New York: Jason Aronson.

Seligman, M.E.P. (1975). *Helplessness—On depression, development, and death.* San Francisco, CA: Freeman.

Shansab, N. (1986). *Soviet expansion in the third world: Afghanistan.* Silver Spring: Bartley Press.

Spielberger, C. (1985). *State-Trait personality indices.* Tampa: Psychology Assessment Services & Dr. Charles Spielberger.

Tapp, J. (1971). Socialization, the law and society. *Journal of Social Issues, 27,* 21–33.

Tapp, J., & Kohlberg, L. (1971). Developing senses of law and legal justice. *Journal of Social Issues, 27* (2), 65–92.

Thabat, A. A., & Vostanis, P. R. (1999). Post traumatic stress reactions in children of war. *Child Psychology Psychiatry, 40,* 385–91.

Toch, H. (1965). *The social psychology of social movements.* New York: The Bobbs-Merrill Company, Inc.

Turner, V. W. (1969). *The ritual process.* Chicago: Aldine.

Tylor, E. B. (1893). *Anthropology: An introduction to the study of man and civilization.* New York: D. Appleton & Co.

U.S. steps up hunt. (2003, March 7). *The Washington Post,* p. 26.

Yeats, W. B. (1966). The rose tree. In O. Doubhghail (Comp. and Ed.), *Insurrection fires.* Eastside Mercier Press.

Zamoyski, A. (1999). *Holy madness: Romantics, patriots and revolutionaries 1776–1861.* London: Weidenfield & Nicolson.

CHAPTER 3

THE POLITICS OF MARTYRDOM

Valérie Rosoux

The Politics of Martyrdom

By observing the links between martyrdom and politics, I have sailed into unexpected waters. This subject has not yet been thoroughly covered. However, there is much at stake. Studying the politics of martyrdom brings us closer to some of the most teleological and ambivalent uses of death—teleological as individuals turn into gods, become myths and legitimize whoever may claim them; ambivalent since politically speaking, martyrdom is always open to appropriation, competition, and contestation, even though some political leaders regard martyrs as unambiguous signs of virtue and truth.

The act of martyrdom is basically twofold. On the one hand, it is an individual choice; on the other, it is a social act—that of martyr-making. The psychological approach to the phenomenon tends to analyze the individual *intention* of the martyr. The purpose is to emphasize the motivation explaining the choice to sacrifice oneself. As far as the political approach is concerned, the focus is on the *representation* of those who commemorate martyrdom. As dead martyrs no longer speak, this representation reveals the process of the decision. Indeed "martyrs are made not simply by their beliefs and actions but by those who witnessed them, remembered them and told their story" (Kassimir, 1991, p. 362).

What are the potential representations and political uses of martyrdom? What are the purposes of those who will declare a given demise to be the crowned death of a martyr? The classical definition of martyrdom implies the sacrifice of (his or her) life (for the) in the name of faith. Properly speaking, martyrdom must involve death which can be directly attributed to the faith or the cause which the victim has espoused. On the political stage, the use of the word "martyr" ceases to be literal and becomes metaphorical, the definition of martyrdom depending not upon the manner of death but upon the present context.

This phenomenon is far from new. The ancestral expression "pro patria mori"—to die for one's homeland—goes back to the antiquity. In Athens and in Rome, numerous leaders referred to heroic warriors who were represented as demi-gods. According to Pericles, for instance, the first victims of the Peloponnesian war deserved to be seen as immortal. During the Middle Ages, political leaders went on stressing the religious aspects of self-sacrifice made for the sake of the group. Their argument was that "anyone who was dying for his lord systematically became martyrs of God" (Kantorowicz, 1984, p. 123). For two centuries now, official representatives honor those who died for another sacred cause: the nation. Admittedly, cities, lords, and nations are three contrasting causes to die for. However, in the three instances, the way the political elite commemorate martyrdom is based on the same fundamental mechanisms.

To address these mechanisms, I propose to examine one particular case: the political use of national martyrs in France. The perspective adopted is one based on official statements. Do the French authorities refer to any martyrs? In which circumstances? For what reasons? In doing so, do they have any impact on the population or do they encounter a form of resistance within the civil society? In order to address these questions, I have divided this essay into three main parts. The first one describes the *selective* character of national memory. The second part stresses its *fluctuating* character, whereas the last questions its main *limitations*. Before starting the reflection, I briefly describe the concepts of national identity and official memory.

Introduction

In a speech delivered on September 25, 1999, former French Prime Minister Lionel Jospin asserted that national identities are elaborated on the basis of memory, "Through the ages, an identity is forged with the memories that are adopted, kept alive, lost and sometimes even repressed by people" (Jospin & Schröder, 1999). Ernest Renan, a celebrated French author, referred to the same process in a famous lecture given at the Sorbonne, Paris, in 1882 (Renan, 1997). In this lecture, Renan underlined the "rich legacy of memories" and the "heritage" that constitute the soul and spiritual principle guiding the nation. According to him, "the nation, like the individual, is the culmination of a long past of endeavors, sacrifice and devotion. Of all cults, that of the ancestors is the most legitimate, for the ancestors have made us what we are. A heroic past, great men, glory (by which I understand genuine glory), this is the social capital upon which one bases a national idea. To have common glories in the past and to have a common will in the present; to have performed great deeds together, to wish to perform still more—these are the essential conditions for being a people" (Renan, 1997, p. 31). For Renan, this means that shared suffering is more important than shared joy: "Where national memories are concerned, griefs are of more value than triumphs, for which they impose duties, and require a common effort." This brings Renan to this definition: "A nation is therefore a large-scale solidarity, constituted by the feeling of the sacrifices one has made in the past and of those one is prepared to make in the future." Renan's lecture implicitly indicates the significance of martyrdom regarding the nation. In insisting on notions like "sacrifice," "grief," or "shared suffering," it shows that the liturgy of the fallen has a special urgency in the framework of nation building, for the principle of supreme sacrifice justifies the transcendent character of the nation.

In this conception, the concepts of "memory" and "identity" are mutually dependent and indissolubly linked: "Memory makes us, we make memory" (Tonkin, 1992, p. 97). Memory shapes (us) our minds—we are formed through its action—and we in turn influence its content by our representations. Memory and identity are thus embraced in a dialectic by which they create and reinforce one another.

Identities, whether national or not, can be defined as the social representations adopted by groups. These representations form a basis upon which members perceive some form of group unity and some form of difference, vis-à-vis others. It draws from this definition that identities should not be considered as objective truths. They should instead be understood as the outcome of a process in which social representations are progressively elaborated. There is nothing surprising in these statements. The historical process by which identities are shaped often involves an inventory of those elements belonging to a nation's heritage. Having become popularly accepted within the group, the inventory then becomes an object of "worship" to its members.[1] Several authors qualify this process by describing national identities as "imagined communities" (Anderson, 1991; Hobsbawm & Ranger, 1992). This description does not imply that identities lack solid bases. It rather indicates that identities constitute a reality that is constantly reshaped and updated.

Identities are created in a dual process of convergence and differentiation. They are the result of a process in which members of one group discover what they have in common as well as what differentiates them from other groups. Identities are thus the product of relations within and outside the group. The question does not—or not only—imply, "Who am I?" but also, "What are my characteristics vis-à-vis others?" In this perspective, identities cannot be separated from the concept of Otherness. This emphasizes the significance of the politics of memory by demonstrating that reference to national martyrs is the means whereby political leaders maintain the internal cohesion of the group (a process of convergence) and justify their antagonism vis-à-vis others (a process of differentiation).

What we generally call memory, in the context of human behavior, is the remembrance of lived or transmitted experiences. It also refers to the way in which a society deals with its past through official discussions, commemorations, or monuments. This paper mainly focuses on official, rather than individual, memory—memory that is expressed by official representatives. This distinction is useful but, as we will elaborate further in this essay, the two levels (official and individual) are in dynamic interaction.

Official memory is dependent on the way in which the past is adjusted to present circumstances. The events described in official speeches or texts often occurred long ago. While the aim of these official representations is rarely to inform listeners of past events, they nevertheless contain interesting clues regarding the author's position towards the past.[2] References to the past are rarely made *per se*. Their importance derives from the intentions of the speaker. Events are constantly being reshaped and reconstructed. In this process, nations and individuals select the elements of their memory that will be given greater importance in view of the objectives being pursued.

National Memory as a Selective Process

Memory thus possesses a selective character. This should not, however, be regarded as a negative attribute. It is, on the contrary, inherent to any situation in which a person resorts to memory. It results from a representation of past events. In this thinking memory can be defined, as Saint Augustine defined it, as "the present of the past" (1964). It should not come as a surprise that in the context of official memory, the past is often considered a convenient tool rather than an immutable narrative. Accordingly, the right way to look at the political uses of the past is not to wonder whether historical references are "true" or "false." It is neither to wonder whether they are oriented towards "good" nor "bad" aims. The question is rather: are they *useful* or not? And to whom? The perspective to be adopted here has little to do with the typical concern of historians or with a normative approach. It can rather be seen as a pragmatic approach.

Having said that, one can easily understand why political leaders rarely failed to honor their martyrs. Even if martyrs did not exist, it might be necessary to *invent* them in order to give the nation an intensified sense of identity. The mechanism is similar if not identical with the cult of martyrs within religious communities. The devotion to their heroic memory is a significant means whereby communities—be they political or religious—maintain their internal cohesion and control their social formation (Wood, 1993, pp. 91–92).

Drawing a lesson from the study of the French case, it is apparent that the French representatives employed two main mechanisms in the construction of the official memory aimed at creating and developing national identity. The first mechanism accentuates the heroic and tragic past. Recalling heroic narratives aims to reinforce unity within the national group, whereas emphasizing past persecutions imposes the duty of fidelity on group members. The past was thus valorized in two different fashions, both of which reinforced national cohesion. The second mechanism adopts the opposite approach. Unlike the first, it implies some past events were not overemphasized but concealed. This mechanism was essentially employed when representatives faced embarrassing or shameful past episodes.

In this framework, the figure of martyr is revealed as particularly useful to maintain national identity, especially in a crisis situation. The analysis of attitudes adopted by French authorities towards fallen soldiers and more broadly towards victims of war reveals the selective aspect of official memory. It indicates the importance of two main kinds of national martyrs: the sacrificial figure of the *Poilu* (the ordinary French soldier) in the First World War and the mythical figure of the *Résistant* in the Second World War. By contrast, the reality of the Algerian war explains the quasi-impossibility for French leaders of commemorating any martyrs of the nation in relation with this war.[3]

Remembrance of World War I

By the First World War, the concept of martyrdom had long been secularized, with patriotic and other varieties of martyrdom embodying the values of different political creeds. The martyr status was mainly conferred by reference to the victorious *Poilu*. It was the sacrifice of the soldiers that subsequently determined the political meaning of the war. Accordingly, French leaders made the cult of their national heroes central to each official ceremony. The cult of the fallen was of importance to most of the nation; almost every family had lost one of its members and most of the adult male population had fought in the war and lost a cherished friend. The constant reference to these national heroes not only helped to transcend the horror of war. It also tended to strengthen national identity in post-war France. As has already been suggested, the creation of a strong feeling of belonging to the nation preaches the need for fraternity and solidarity, particularly in suffering. And nowhere are these sentiments and bonds more palpably expressed than in the common grief and collective pity for the sacrifice of war heroes who fell in defence of their homeland. In this respect, the analysis of public commemoration of the First World War confirmed the argument made by Mosse; references to the national martyrs is one aspect of a popular form of civic religion, with a specific liturgy and rites appropriate to a secular and political religion of the masses (Mosse, 1990).

Furthermore, one should stress the fact that the figure of the *Poilu* was not the only one connected with the issue. Three other forms of martyrdom were highlighted during and after the war. Unlike the *Poilus*, these forms concerned civilians and not combatants. Moreover, they did not pretend to symbolize the whole nation. They referred instead to specific groups among the population. The purpose of these local martyrs was not to reinforce national identity as such but to acknowledge particular groups of victims.

The first local group to be recognized as martyr was religious. The killing of French priests by the invading German troops presented a powerful claim of collective martyrdom for the Church. There was much at stake as, in France, official and popular secularism meant that Catholicism had no axiomatic claim to speak for the nation. On the contrary, anticlerical suspicion placed French Catholics on the defensive. As John Horne and Alan Kramer show in their book *German*

Atrocities, 1914. A History of Denial, French priests who had been particularly mistreated by German soldiers served as exemplary martyrs to both faith *and* country (2001, p. 309). Horne and Kramer cite
a number of examples: "The aged priest of Varreddes in the Seine-et-
Marne . . . who had been unjustly accused of signaling to the French
army from his church tower, badly beaten, and killed, soon achieved
martyr status. One publication portrayed him as incarnating the
proud resistance of the 'violated Marne [as] the shield of civilization.'" In similar fashion, the death of a parish priest of Saint-Dié,
Vosges, or the brutal treatment and death of the curé of Sompius, the
Marne, during his deportation provided deaths "which exemplified
Catholic suffering in the hands of the invader."

Second, martyrdom was used as an attribute of the localities that
had suffered from the German atrocities. By late 1914, the term "martyr" was being applied to the worst-affected villages and towns of the
Meurthe-et-Moselle (like No– mény or Gerbéviller, for instance). Some
local authorities even considered preserving the ruins of their town
as a monument attesting of their suffering and the ignominy of their
enemies. This anticipated by 30 years the discussion which was to
occur over Oradour-sur-Glane, the village destroyed with its inhabitants by the SS in 1944, which eventually was commemorated in this
fashion (see below).

In a third step, martyrdom easily encompassed *all civilian victims* of
the invasion. The events of the invasion supplied a number of exemplary cases in which individual martyrdom linked local memory to
national outrage. The German practice of making hostages out of
local dignitaries ensured that there was no shortage of secular martyrs, often suffering their fate with stoic and heroic patriotism. The
executed mayors, for example, were presented as victims likely to
particularize the collective fate of the invaded zone.

Remembrance of World War II

In 1945, the French were still conscious of having fought for their
survival in the First World War, symbolized by their veterans. But
they now had a more recent and complex memory of invasion and
suffering with which to come to terms. It supplied its own imagery of
martyrdom as well as redemption through the mystified history of
the *Resistance*.

In 1945, the main objective of Charles de Gaulle was to restore the
pillars of the Republic, seriously challenged by the defeat of 1940 and
the nature of the Vichy regime. While memories of the Great War

were homogeneous and unanimously heroic, the experience of the Second World War was everything but uniform. There no longer was an obvious distinction between the front line and the home front. Moreover, feelings of defeat and victory were this time paradoxically linked. To focus on the consensual figure of the *Résistant* appeared to be the best way to restore national unity. For decades, French leaders underlined the sacrifice and subsequent martyrdom of numerous *Résistants* and attempted to minimize other aspects of the war. Official representatives could of course not deny the reality of the Vichy regime. From 1944 to 1953, a severe purge—the so-called "épuration" of French collaborators—implied the deaths of about 10,000 people (between 8,000 and 9,000 extra-legal executions and between 1,500 and 1,600 legal executions) and the trial of more than 124,000 individuals (Rousso, 2001, p. 543). However, the importance of the Vichy regime to France has often been de-emphasized in official discourses.

In Charles de Gaulle's speeches, for instance, the accent was put above all on those who resisted the enemy. The only episodes to be solemnly commemorated by the General de Gaulle highlighted the bravery of French *Résistants*. This systematic selection of congruent events inevitably implied the concealment of past events, perceived as "irrelevant," regarding the ancestral notion of the French *grandeur*. As they defend national identity, the formulators and disseminators of official memory were reluctant to admit that violence was committed in the name of the state. Therefore, until recently, they did not readily recognize errors or betrayals attributable to their own citizens during the war.

In the same vein, French textbooks presented Vichy as a phenomenon which remained somehow peripheral. As Suzanne Citron demonstrates, this presentation ignored several aspects of the French experience under occupation and stressed others, particularly the armed resistance against the occupying forces (Citron, 1994). Until the end of the 1960s, textbooks insisted on external reasons (the occupation of France) to explain collaboration. Thus they placed the responsibility for Vichy on the Germans instead of the French. They did not refer to Vichy's share of responsibility for policies pursued during the occupation. Only in 1982 did French textbooks acknowledge Vichy's responsibility for deportations of Jews. Also ignored was the earlier persecution of Jews by the French government and administration. When these events were mentioned, responsibility was attributed to the Germans (Citron, 1994).

Let me take a couple of examples to illustrate this mechanism. In 1946, the President of the National Assembly, Vincent Auriol, called on the nation to forget its disappointments and its disasters and to keep alive "the sublime purity of our Resistance heroes . . . of our martyrs" (Binoche, 1996, p. 231). Charles de Gaulle is rigorously on the same wavelength when he asserted that France "did not need truth, but hope, cohesion and a goal" (Brauman & Sivan, 1999, p. 53). To the General, the only priority of the country was to "fraternally get united in order to heal the wounded France." What he called the "absurd quarrels" of the past absolutely had to be concealed (de Gaulle, 1970, I, p. 298).

It is then not surprising that, in 1945, de Gaulle commemorated November 11, 1918, by paying a common tribute to the "glorious victims" of the two World Wars. He expressively gathered all those who "died for France" in a "triumphant" manner during what he called the "thirty-years war." What is striking here is the connection between a totally glorious period (1914–1918) and a much more ambiguous time (1940–1945). Charles de Gaulle did not hesitate to associate the bravery of the *Poilus* and the courage of the *Résistants*. To de Gaulle, these two martyrdoms were guided by the "same flame"—the flame that "has always inspired the spirit of the eternal France" (de Gaulle, 1970, 4:249–250). Both justified a legitimate feeling of gratitude by the whole country as well as a duty to remain more united than ever. After de Gaulle, the French authorities constantly spotlighted the honor of the Resistance. Each of his successors agreed that reminders of this honor was "to have transformed a prostrated, humiliated and oppressed country"—the situation of France following the capitulation—"into a belligerent, proud and free nation" (de Gaulle, 1970, 4:242–243).

All the *Résistants* who were killed by the enemy had conferred on them the status of national heroes. But among all the "martyrs of the Resistance," Jean Moulin is probably the most emblematic figure. Head of the National Council of the Resistance, Jean Moulin is particularly famous for his actions aiming to unify the Resistance movement in France. Arrested in 1943, he was tortured and then killed. Less than two decades later, his sacrifice became the origin of a profound legend in France. In December 1964, the remains of Jean Moulin were moved into the Pantheon by Charles de Gaulle. Politically speaking, this ceremony was meaningful since the Pantheon is a temple explicitly dedicated to "the great men of France"; among those buried in its necropolis are Voltaire, Rousseau, Mirabeau, Marat, Victor Hugo, and Emile Zola. All the voices and newspapers of Paris—reflecting all political tendencies—unanimously greeted the event. One of the most moving parts of this quasi-religious ceremony was the speech of the French Minister of Culture, André Malraux.

In a few words, André Malraux—who was himself a former *Résistant*—recalled Jean Moulin's attitude when he was facing torture: "As the Gestapo agent gave him a piece of paper [to write the names of other *Résistants*] because he could not talk anymore, Jean Moulin drew the caricature of his torturer. . . . His role was played, and it was the beginning of his calvary. Being scorned, savagely hurt, the head bleeding, the organs burst, he reached the limits of human suffering without betraying one single secret whereas he knew all of them. Let us understand that, during the few days when he could still talk or write, the destiny of France was suspended on the courage of this man" (Malraux, 1973). The emotional impact of this discourse can hardly be denied. The current presentation of Jean Moulin by the Institute Charles de Gaulle in Paris is extremely similar: "Tortured, even though he knew everything about the Resistance, he did not say a word, demonstrating an uncommon courage. Whereas he was asked to write down the names of his companions, he sketched hastily the caricature of his persecutor. . . . Afterwards, he underwent a new *calvary*. His task would have been wrecked by the blows of his torturers. But he resisted. No one was arrested because Jean Moulin won his last battle—to keep silence."[4] This brief biographical presentation ends with one statement by Jean Moulin himself: "There are times when serving one's country whatever the position one assumes is such an imperative obligation that it is naturally and enthusiastically that all honorable men find the necessary power to accomplish their tasks" (May 8, 1939).

This emotional rhetoric and this accentuation of the physical and spiritual suffering of the martyr pursue three main aims.

The first one is *pedagogical*. As Jean Malraux said, "today, youth, think to this man as you would have touched his poor misshapen face of the last day, his lips that did not talk—that day, his face it was the face of France" (Malraux, 1973, pp. 64–67). The message is obvious. The supreme sacrifice of Jean Moulin constitutes an example and a guide for the French population; it implies an imperative to remember him with gratitude. In this respect, it is remarkable that, more than almost 40 years later, Jean Moulin remains one of the key founding references of French national identity (see statistical surveys in Centlivres, 1998, pp. 87–88).

Second, in accentuating the destiny of Jean Moulin, Charles de Gaulle not only sought to edify young generations. The second purpose of this commemoration was directly linked to *political circumstances*. The transfer of Jean Moulin's remains occurred only two days after the vote of a first amnesty law regarding the Algerian war. As we will see, the remembrance of the Algerian war was at that time problematic, to say the least. Only two years after the independence of Algeria, de Gaulle was fully aware of the consequences of the recent past. The experience of the Algerian war and before that, the experience of the Second World War largely traumatized the population.[5] In addition, both events deeply divided the French society.

The Second World War was not limited to opposition between rival nations. It also implied violent hostilities between French collaborators and French *Résistants*. Similarly, the Algerian War cannot be reduced to a war between French and Algerian troops. It was the origin of a situation of quasi civil war too. The bomb attacks by the Secret Army Organization (the OAS was dedicated to keeping Algeria French), the riots on the rue d'Isly in Algiers on March 26, 1962, in which French soldiers opened fire on *Pieds noirs*[6] demonstrating against the French government, and the putsch of French generals against de Gaulle in 1961 are only three examples demonstrating the extent of these divisions. In such context, de Gaulle's primary objective was to restore by all means possible a sense of self-esteem and a form of unity among the population. One of the only ways to do so was to gather all the segments of the French society, from the Gaullist militants to the communists, around one central figure and to focus their attention on an unequivocally heroic fate. From this perspective, the constant representation of Jean Moulin to unify the Resistance, his combat against the enemy, and his tragic martyrdom became *the* unifying narrative par excellence.

Finally, a third purpose can be stressed. The commemoration of the martyr was used to *legitimate de Gaulle* himself. Indeed, in his speech, André Malraux did not hesitate to compare the combat of Jean Moulin and the actions of Charles de Gaulle. He brought forward the direct links between the two men. For example, he recalled that they first met in London in December 1941 and that, two months later, Jean Moulin was sent to France as the main representative of de Gaulle. From that link, André Malraux explicitly emphasized the parallel between the two men: "Considering the unity of the Resistance as the principal means to favor national unity was may be the sign of an attitude that we could qualify today as gaullist. It surely was the way to ensure France's own survival" (Malraux, 1973). Such a direct connection between the two national heroes undoubtedly contributed to the reinforcement of de Gaulle's legitimacy, which was more than appropriate only one year before the presidential election (Rousso, 1990, p. 115).

As in the case of the First World War, the notion of martyrdom also served local interests. The example of the martyred village of Oradour-sur-Glane is telling in this respect. Soon after the war, the term "martyr" was officially recognized by national representatives. However, the choice of this term was originally made by the civil society. A couple of months after the tragedy on June 10, 1944, in which 642 people were killed, among whom there were 247 children, local authorities—both civilian and religious—proposed the creation of the "National Association of Martyrs' Families." The choice of this designation was not neutral. According to the members of the association, the reason was the need to underline the innocent character of the victims. However, one could question such argument. Does it mean that one could set in opposition some innocent victims and some other supposedly guilty victims? The actual reason for insisting on the term "martyr" is somewhat different. After the tragedy, the survivors and the families in mourning wanted to be distinguished and somehow to be recognized as particularly wounded by the war. The status of martyr appeared as one of the means to get such recognition (Fouché, 2002, p. 126). And indeed, this concept appears to be much more dramatic than the usual notion of "victim." Compared to the millions of victims of the Second World War, there were in fact only a few martyrs.

Here again, it is noticeable that the quality of dead as "victim" or as "martyr" is not just a question of vocabulary. The conversion of a victim into a martyr is generally the business of the official representative and its success depends ultimately upon the success of the cause. However, as far as the survivors and their descendants are concerned, it is actually a question of recognition, which appears to be a decisive step to undertake a mourning process. The emphasis put on fighting the Nazis as the basic principle of remembrance implied that only those who had actually fought the Nazis were legitimate victims. By contrast, those who had not fought were not officially commemorated. This was the case of the few Jews (2,500 out of 75,000) coming back from the concentration camps. They were not deported for fighting the Germans, but for being Jews. Things changed with the progressive rising of the Jewish memory in France and subsequent recognition, within the national memory, of genocide. This evolution showed that one of the central issues for the victims and their descendants was to challenge the sort of monopoly that for decades characterized the cult of the martyrs of the Resistance. That move led some sociologists to make a point on the potential competition between groups of victims claiming the status of martyr or, on the contrary, contesting it (Chaumont, 1997). Without going into details at this point, it is worth mentioning that the creation in France of a Jewish Martyr Memorial indicated one of the limitations of national memory as a selective process (see below).

Remembrance of the Algerian War

From November 1954 to March 1962 more than two million French soldiers fought in Algeria in order to keep Algeria a part of France. This was a conflict that, in France, was not officially termed a war at all. The end result was the independence of Algeria under the control of the FLN (National Liberation Front), the departure for France of one million French people, and the deaths of 30,000 French soldiers. However, as it has already been suggested, this un-named war remained an un-remembered war until very recently. For France, the Algerian war presented an unpalatable reflection of past failures and erring ways. The absence of a generally accepted sense of the legitimacy of the war was due to the methods and practices of the French army. French troops committed many crimes, including torture and killings. In addition, the entire war was illegitimate in itself; its goals were not acceptable. Opposing Algerian independence was not legitimate, as the United Nations said openly. The Algerian people had the right to become an independent nation-state. The French government claimed that Algeria was France, and a part of the French population supported that position. They considered that this war was not a war, but an operation to maintain order. However, in their conscience, most French people knew that the domination imposed on the Algerian people had to come to an end.

For decades, French authorities resorted to various schemes to marginalize historical treatment of the conflict. Admittedly, numerous texts and images commemorated this period of French history. But the Algerian war was confined to the register of private memory. The official level was dominated by silence. This "oblivion" was, however, undermined by several signs, among them the evident discomfort of people when referring to the Algerian drama, the censorship of books[7] and films relating to torture that commonly occurred during the war, the struggle to determine who would be allowed to retain control of the archives for the colonial period, the juridical mechanisms (e.g., amnesty and presidential pardon) used to avoid any reactivation of memory, and, above all, the absence—until November 11, 1996—of commemorative tributes to Algerian war veterans.

Completely contrary to the two World Wars, French authorities did not refer to any national heroes or martyrs. This contrast is not surprising since, at the end of the day, French society did not feel that the war in or over Algerian independence was a fully legitimate war. To some specialists, this lack of legitimacy was rooted in the comparison between the Algerian situation and the occupation of French territory by the German troops from 1940 to 1944 (see Winter & Sivan, 1999, pp. 171–172). Even though there is a myriad of differences between those two historical situations, it became almost impossible to avoid the parallels. Were French soldiers fighting the *Fellaghas* entirely different from German soldiers fighting the *Résistants?* Were their methods so different? The point that is made here concerns the link between the non-remembrance of the Algerian war and the remembrance of the Second World War. As Antoine Prost said, "the undeniable legitimacy of the Resistance against the Nazis undermined the legitimacy of the Algerian war."

As a result, victims of the Algerian war were not used by French authorities to establish a tragic narration of the past. Any attempt in this sense would certainly have been counterproductive since these victims appeared to impart a confused feeling of shame among the population. Three different groups were particularly hurt by the Algerian war: the soldiers, the *harkis*, and the *Pieds noirs*. They never formed what one could call positive figures. Soldiers without victory cannot easily become national heroes; victims without good causes cannot become martyrs. It shows—if it was still necessary to do so— that suffering and losses are necessary but not sufficient conditions for martyrdom.

The first group, the ex-soldiers, were so far unable to convert personal memories into a collective memory. Two primary reasons explain this. First, they were deeply divided politically. Their veterans' association (the FNACA, the National Federation of *Anciens Combattants* of Algeria) was controlled by the French Communist Party. This made it impossible for more conservative veterans to enroll in that association. Hence the Rightist association of *anciens combattants* of the First and Second World Wars, the UNC (National Union of Combatants), organized a particular sub-section for Algerians veterans. These two associations opposed each other on every issue, especially on symbolic ones. Therefore, it was impossible, for instance, to find an agreement on the

date on which to commemorate the end of the war. The second reason
is that the Algerian war was meaningless for the majority of soldiers
involved in it. This war was not an opening but a closure, the end of
colonial times. In such circumstances, the death of a companion was
seen as a scandal: "dead for nothing" (Rioux, 1990, p. 84). Unlike the
Poilus and the *Résistants*, they were not heroic combatants, but soldiers
without enthusiasm. Their war was neither glorious, nor victorious—
nothing else than a "dirty war."

The second group of potential victims of the Algerian war were the
Pieds noirs. After independence, most of them had the right to live in
Algeria, with joint Algerian and French nationalities. However, there
was an overwhelming consensus within Algerian public opinion that
their only choice was between leaving and being killed. They chose
to go to France, abandoning in Algeria everything they could not
take with them. After a few months in France, the *Pieds noirs* formed
specific associations of *rapatriés* (people returning to their homeland)
in order to claim reparations from the French state. These associations operated as pressure groups but this action was weakened by
political rivalries and by the willingness to be integrated into French
society. Most of the *Pieds noirs* indeed wanted to be recognized as
Frenchmen like anyone else, to be assimilated, not to distinguish
themselves from the French community. This aim prevented them
from claiming that they were victims of this very community.
Admittedly, the *Pieds noirs* themselves sometimes referred to what
they explicitly called their "martyrs"—describing their "mutilated
children," their "disembowelled wives," their "tortured elderly people" (*Le Monde*, 23 October 1985). However, it was evident that this
category of martyrs could never be underlined as such by official representatives. The issue was far too delicate for that.

The *harkis* were soldiers from the native Muslim community of
Algeria, enrolled as auxiliary forces to supplement the French army.
They did not form regular units enrolled in the French army; they
rather formed a kind of civilian militia with light weapons for night
patrols around the villages. At the end of the conflict, the *harkis* were
in a critical position. They were volunteers, committed to the French
and therefore deemed traitors by the FLN. As some officers thought
it was impossible to abandon them when they left Algeria, approximately 85,000 of them went to France. However, between 55,000 and
75,000 of them—unable to leave their country—were killed after independence. Those who had the chance to go to France were initially
put in camps. They had no family in France, no relations; most of

them were unskilled, and a good proportion of them could not properly express themselves in the French language. Their conditions of living and housing became progressively better. Nevertheless, they were perceived as a burden to the army and to French society as a whole. They actually remained second-class Frenchmen. Then, the second generation of *harkis*, more educated than their parents, suffered at one and the same time for their fathers' commitment to France and their own Algerian origin. Some of them joined in violent demonstrations in several towns of southern France but they were insufficiently numerous to claim any particular status.

These remarks demonstrate the delicate character of any public commemoration regarding the Algerian war. It is striking that in 1968, a French official representative quoted the sixteenth-century Edict of Nantes, at the National Assembly to justify the need to "forget" these tragic events. As King Henri IV said in 1598, "may memory of all the events that occurred since March 1585 as well as memory of the discord that preceded them remain subdued and dulled as a thing that never happened.... We forbid our citizens to remember this period, to attack one another, to insult one another, to provoke one another about what took place for whatever reason ... but we ask them to contain themselves and to live together as brothers, friends and fellow citizens" (Grosser, 1989, pp. 137–138).

This exhortation was expressed on several occasions. In September 1972, French President Georges Pompidou refused to maintain the "eternally bloody" wounds of national discords. According to him, time had come to cast the veil over it and to forget: "Our country, for more than 30 years, went from a national drama to another one. It was the war, the defeat and its humiliations, the Occupation and its horrors, the Liberation and as an indirect consequence the purge and its abuses—we have to admit it; and then the Indo-Chinese war, and then the awful Algerian conflict and its horrors, on both sides ... Is it not the right moment to cast the veil, to forget these times when French did not like one another, tore one another and even killed one another?" (Pompidou, 1972). In the same vein, ten years later, François Mitterrand called on his nation "not to maintain the bones of contention too quick to stir up again." Instead, he said, it was essential to "pacify" the tensions that are tearing the country for a century, these dissensions resulting for example from the Occupation or from the decolonization (Mitterrand & Wiesel, 1995, pp. 109–110).

At that stage of reflection, it is worth underlining that politics of memory are exactly opposite on the other side of the Mediterranean

Sea. Unlike French authorities, Algerian leaders piously maintained a cult of the war memory. The independence war rapidly became a founding myth in Algeria. In particular, the legitimating process that the FLN brought forward was entirely based on the constant reminder of the "glorious martyrs of the nation." As a result, official representatives continuously highlighted the "one and a half million Liberation martyrs." Thus, martyrdom imagery repeatedly appeared in the official speeches and in media. In portraying the sorrow of their martyrs, Algerian representatives tended to epitomize the idea of the nation as a suffering community. This process took root in a religious and cultural heritage. The figure of national martyrs had the advantage of combining Algerian patriotism and the virtues of Muslim faith. The majority of Algerian leaders were not directly motivated by religious grounds, most of them being influenced by a Marxist approach or at least by a secular vision of politics. However, the civic religion of nationalism used religious themes to allow a form of transfer from religious belief to national patriotism. In the same optic, the nation was presented as a transcendent reality that can be compared with the divine law.

The sufferings of the war were regularly reminded to justify political decisions vis-à-vis the former colonizer. French were frequently qualified as "colonialists" or "neocolonialists," whereas Algerians were called to go on the path of independence. The argument was: "Algeria became independent thanks to the sacrifice of its children; it is vital to remember them and to put a definitive end to any "disguised form of colonialism." In this context, references to the martyrs of the nation became a key argument to legitimize their positions. When the Algerian President Houari Boumediene decided to nationalize the oil resources of the country—under the control of French companies up to then—he declared that the Algerian oil was "red from the blood of the martyrs who accepted the supreme sacrifice for their nation" (Boumediene, 1972, p. 232). Similarly, when the Algerian authorities claimed the restitution of the archives relating to Algeria (these archives were repatriated in France, in 1962), one of the arguments was the duty to recuperate the "traces of a history written by the blood of martyrs" (as cited in Stora, 1995, p. 11).

Later, discourses based on the martyrs and the sufferings of the nation were particularly vehement in time of crisis. In 1985, the Algerian Press Agency accused France of having used moudjahidine (independence war veterans[8]) as guinea-pigs for nuclear experiences. A couple of months later, the same agency accused France again of having transformed Algeria into a immense "concentration camp" from 1954 to 1962 and for having committed a "quasi-genocide" ("Paris se refuse à entretenir une polémique" [Paris refuses to enter into an argument], 1985). The same article went into details to describe some of the tortures committed by the French army during the war. It depicted among others the use of a python especially trained to torture, the bites of dogs, the use of electricity and water, and even the rape of a wife or a mother in the presence of a prisoner. The agency added that "the skulls of thousands poor civilians who did not confess what they did not know" had been "broken by blows of sticks." In the same line, the FLN Journal, *Révolution Africaine*, recalled that "they were thousands of Oradour-sur-Glane, Dachau, and Buchenwald in Algeria." The reactions following such accusations in France came essentially from the associations of *Pieds noirs*. The spokesman of one of them explained that it was extremely dangerous to seek to reopen the wounds of the Algerian war. "To this kind of accusations, we could oppose our claims concerning our own martyrs," he said. His point was resumed by the question: what would then be the purpose of a new fight "opposing martyrs from each side?" (Roseau, 1985).

National Memory as a Fluctuating Process

The rhetoric of official memory works by building symbolic bridges between today and yesterday. As it has already been indicated, the primary movement is not from the past to the present but the other way around. On the political stage, references to martyrs, heroes, and victims result above all from fluctuating representations. Admittedly, each of these concepts has a specific definition. According to the dictionary, the word martyr refers to any one who died for having refused to abjure his faith—and by extension to any person who suffers or dies for a cause; the hero designates the person who distinguishes himself by his exploits, a courage extraordinary or a total devotion to a cause; and the victim was originally a living creature being offered in sacrifice to gods—by extension, the word "victim" is applied to any one who suffers and even to any wounded or dead people. The simple enunciation of these definitions indicates that the three notions overlap to a large extent. One of the common elements of these concepts is the idea of *sacrifice*. This common minimal meaning allows numerous shifts from a notion to another. Therefore, although martyrdom is presented as an absolute, it is intrinsically amenable to historical change.

To understand this sort of change in the representation of past events requires us to abandon popular and preconceived notions. It is a widely held belief that the future is open and not yet determined, whereas the past is immutable. In fact, the past is probably never altogether closed. Admittedly, *events* cannot be erased. In principle, one cannot easily undo what has been done, or pretend that what happened never occurred. However, the *meaning* that is attributed to past events is not fixed once and for all (Ricoeur, 2000, p. 496). Accordingly, one can consider that "one never knows what yesterday will consist of" (Brossat, 1991, p. 107).

The analysis of the French case shows that official representations of the past fluctuate according to two main variables. The first one is the context—that is to say the national and international circumstances and the political aims pursued by the leaders. The second variable results from the generation effect. The time factor is indeed often a determining element that explains the conversion of a victim—or even a traitor—into a martyr and vice versa.

The fluctuating character of official memory can be illustrated by Charles de Gaulle's interpretation of past Franco-German conflicts. His interpretation is by no means constant but instead varies from one period to another. De Gaulle often described Franco-German relations before the Second World War as marked by natural hostility, ontological incompatibility, and quasi-visceral mistrust (de Gaulle, 1944). A few years later, however, he underlined the complementary nature of relations between the two nations and the deep affinity that *always* created mutual attraction (de Gaulle, 1967). How can the two statements be reconciled? The explanation lies in a change of circumstances—or context—and a change in de Gaulle's intentions. The first declaration came at a time when de Gaulle saw neighboring Germany building up forces for a possible conflict in the thirties. By contrast, the second took place after the Second World War when de Gaulle was seeking to create a Franco-German rapprochement, since European peace appeared impossible without such a development.

Official representations of the battle of Verdun are also characteristic of that kind of transformation. The number of victims, in addition to the ruthless nature of the fighting, created fearful memories in France and in Germany. As early as 1916, separate patriotic representations of the fighting were being elaborated on both sides of the Rhine. On the French side, Verdun testified to the glory, heroism and victorious spirit of the French combatants. On the other side of the Rhine, Verdun was quickly appropriated by national-socialist ideol-

ogy. After the Second World War, the Franco-German rapprochement and the construction of a united Europe paved the way for a
new interpretation of Verdun. Verdun became a symbol with a similar meaning to all combatants—French *and* Germans. The memories
were no longer presented as national and separate. Instead, they were
unified as a result of the reconciliation that has occurred: the soldiers
who fought in opposite camps were united in a common tribute to the
past. This re-interpretation was given a symbolic expression when
Mitterrand and Kohl stood hand in hand in front of the ossuary of
Douaumont in France in 1984. Past wars fought between France and
Germany were now presented as a common past of collective sufferings. The groups ceased to be described in the official memory as in
opposition. They lost their heterogeneous character of groups living
separately from one another and became brothers who mutually suffered a common tragedy. In June 1962, Charles de Gaulle highlighted
the "the fraternal link" between the two people (Peyrefitte, 1994,
p. 153). A couple of months later, German President Heinrich Luebke
used the same expression and designated France as Germany's
"brother country" (Luebke, 1962). The interpretation was similar
when François Mitterrand depicted the First World War as "fratrici-
dal" (Mitterand, 1994) and when Jacques Chirac celebrated the eight-
ieth anniversary of the battle of Verdun in referring to what he called
a "shared martyr."

These two examples illustrate the fluctuations of official memory
in the context of a *rapprochement* between former belligerents. But it
is also crucial to stress the potential use of the past during the conflict itself. In the context of a war, the accentuation of martyrdom is
a powerful weapon for each party since it can lead to the identification
of the persecutors with the Devil. When tragic events are constantly
recalled during an international or intercommunity conflict, they can
be used as incentives in order to redress past humiliations and suffering. In that case, the purpose is not only to reinforce the national cohesion. It is above all to justify a feeling of hatred vis-à-vis the enemy.

Before the end of the Second World War, the Franco-German relations illustrated very well this mechanism of constant stigmatisation.
In 1870 for instance, just at the starting point of the Franco-Prussian
war, *Paris-Journal,* a French newspaper, encouraged Frenchmen to renewed belligerence: "You will take a revenge on Germany for the evil
they caused in 1814—the elderly people they killed, the wives they
raped, the fathers they shot dead, the children they disembowelled"
(Becker, 1994, p. 257). The war ended in defeat for France. Alsace-

Lorraine, a border region, was annexed by Germany. This loss, as well as other humiliations, was traumatic for the French. This situation conjured up new vehement discourses calling for revenge. Almost forty years later, the fire still burned. When the First World War started, French leaders, authors, and journalists overemphasized the long suffering at the hands of the Germans. They were especially loquacious regarding the martyrdom of children. Numerous caricatures depicted "German atrocities." One of them showed an infant martyr, a little girl with her wrist bandaged, kneeling at the tomb of her own hand. Another one evoked the bad conscience of the German soldier on returning home as he recalled the dismembered infants of the invasion. The French press grounded its perception of "German atrocities" in actual occurrences. Yet the meanings that the press gave events were deeply nationalistic. As Horne and Kramer point out, these representations spoke to real events but they did so "in the language of vilification" (Horne & Kramer, 2001, p. 211). The process was identical in Germany. For more than a century and a half, the incessant reminder of past persecutions contributed to create entrenched positions on each side of the Rhine. These perceptions gave rise to belligerent discourses calling for the crushing of the ancestral enemy. They were based on the same events, but the meaning assigned to these events was in fact totally different. The discourses were thus frequently based on mutually contradictory versions of the past.

This process of stigmatisation is not limited to Franco-German relations. It may also be evident in the conflicts that have consumed the Balkans since the collapse of the communist system. Some Serb leaders have used historical arguments to justify their confrontation with other ethnic groups that made up the ex-Yugoslavia. These leaders view wounds inflicted to the others as revenge for the martyrdom of their ancestors—hence the references to victims of the battle of Kosovo in 1389 and the Second World War. In 1990, while the spectrum of civil war was more and more threatening, the cooperation between the Orthodox Church and the Serb authorities led to a spectacular operation: the Church organized the exhumation of Serbs massacred by pro-Nazi Croats during the Second World War. On several occasions, the Serb television showed nerve-racking images: shattered children's skulls, families in tears in front of the remains of victims killed 50 years ago. The common wish of these families and of the Church—giving a burial place to these forgotten victims—became a major element of the psychological campaign likely to prepare the population to a new confrontation. In 1991, the Church dedicated the whole year to the memory of the historical suffering endured by the Serb people. In his Easter sermon, Patriarch Paul called for forgiveness. However, its message was ambiguous. According to him, if the Serbs wanted to take revenge proportionally to all the crimes inflicted to them during the last century, they would have "to bury living people, to roast living men, to flay them alive, to cut children to pieces in the presence of their parents." He added that it was extremely difficult to smother the voice of human blood regarding martyrdoms of grandparents, parents, and children. Eventually, he asserted that forgetting is a "serious sin" meaning "complicity with the monsters that committed genocide on an innocent people." His argument was that "the events that occur today again, in the same places, by the same actors, prove—that is a fact—that this incomparable crime has not been the object of any remorse and of any expiation so far" (Grmek, Gijdara, & Simac, 1993, pp. 276–278).

The question that is addressed here does not concern the reality of the past to which protagonists refer. No one could deny the bloody feature of the Ante Pavelic's regime, nor the number of crimes committed against Serbs during the Second World War. The point is not the memory itself but the over-accentuation of it. Indeed, to some Serbs, the conclusion of such emphasis was in fact to demand an eye for an eye. To cite an example, a young theologian from Belgrade reminded people in 1991 that "the current war is imposed to us by the greatest criminals ever, the Oustachis, the same people who slaughtered us from 1941 to 1945" (Garde, 1992–1993). The argument was similar regarding the Kosovo battle. As early as 1982, representatives of the Orthodox Church asserted that "the Serb people led their battle of Kosovo since 1389. Kosovo is our memory, our home, the flame of our being" (Miletitch, 1996). More than twenty years later, in an article of the *Orthodox Messenger*, Marko Markovitch explained that "Kosovo was for the Serbs what Jerusalem was for the Jews and Golgotha for the Christians" (Tincq, 1998). Martyrdom thus constitutes a tool that *can* be used in a political process summarized as follows: injuries suffered by ancestors should not be forgotten but should instead be repaid; the best way to do this is to inflict similar injuries on the people who originally did you harm; only in this manner can the memory of martyrs be honored.

How can that situation be assessed? As long as a strong leadership existed in Yugoslavia, mutual hostility was contained. The wounds suffered, including those during the Second World War, were hidden for most of the time. Similarly, the consciousness of belonging to different groups or communities was attenuated. Mixed marriages occurred. The seeds of a common social life were planted. The promise of a joint future, however, disappeared with the end of a united Yugoslavia. Past sufferings and persecutions once again came into the light. Street names, hymns, and flags were changed accordingly. Similar changes took place in textbooks. The past then underwent a process of reconstruction. Underlying this process was the question: why should *we* be administered by *them*? In that framework, *we* and *they* were defined in a Manichean manner and the reciprocal hate, which ex post facto appeared to be eternal, was reactivated.

From this particular moment, identities have been characterized by incompatible beliefs. While the Dayton agreement maintains a united Bosnian state, three separate territorial entities have been allowed to subsist—a Serb, a Croatian, and a Muslim part. In each of these communities, schoolchildren learn that the aggression was perpetrated by *the other*, who remains the enemy. Thus, the author of a textbook in Bosnia-Herzegovina confirms "the genocide of Bosnians by Tchetniks during the Second World War is granted substantial treatment in the new texts" (Uzelac, 1997). A symmetrical scenario takes place in the schools of Sarajevo: young Serbs learn that the "first Yugoslavia" in 1918 created the framework in which Croatians and Slovenes established their domination over Serbs. As for Croatian pupils, they are taught that Yugoslavia was a centralized state "which was founded on Serb domination" (Igric, 1998). In these schools, education confirms the verdict provided by battles. Official memory is not used to promote peace and stability, on the contrary it is used as propaganda to foster conflict. Serbs attempt to forget the events that are recollected by Croats and Muslims of Bosnia—and the reverse is equally true. When the same events are recalled by the different parties, what appears to be a crime for some is interpreted by others as a source of glory. Despite these divergences, one goal seems to be shared by all parties: some willingness to erase any recollection that might encourage reconciliation and peaceful co-existence.

Political circumstances, whether they are dictated by a dynamic of rapprochement or by a confrontational logic, are not the only point that determines the fluctuations of official memory. Time is a second variable to take into account. Time is needed to progressively transform the representations of the past. The renewal of the generations that are in power is a key factor to explain the shifts that characterize the official memory. This phenomenon may once again be illustrated by the Franco-German case. Two main periods can be distinguished regarding the way French presidents and German chancellors describe the relationship between the two nations. The first one is characteristic of the 1960s, while the second starts in the middle of the 1970s.

During the 1960s, the purpose of any discourse about the past was to legitimize the reconciliation. The same argument was made on both sides of the Rhine: "even if cooperation seemed to be a *new* form of relation between the two countries, it was in fact the real *nature* of their link." The accentuation of all the historical signs of a good relationship between French and German citizens aimed at alleviating as much as possible the violent memories lived or transmitted by the population. In the mid 1970s, this perspective was inversed. The memories being gradually alleviated, official representatives reminded their people that the Franco-German friendship was not something to take for granted. Accordingly, they called the new generation to remember that the harmonious relationship between young people from both sides of the Rhine was "historically totally new" (Giscard d'Estaing, 1980). French President François Mitterrand came back to this shift when he explained in one of his last discourses that his own generation had the obligation to "transmit" its memory (Mitterrand, 1995, p. 161).

The generation effect has also an important impact on the official interpretation of the Vichy regime. Neither Georges Pompidou, Valéry Giscard d'Estaing, nor François Mitterrand differentiated themselves from the official history emphasized by de Gaulle. Jacques Chirac was the first one to recognize the responsibility of the French State in the arrest and the deportation of Jews in 1942 on July 16, 1995. Admittedly the social and political context was different. However, the most important point to understand in this change of perspective is undoubtedly the fact that Jacques Chirac was the first President who was only a child during the war. Similarly, the generation effect is determining with regards to the Algerian war. Jacques Chirac expressly mentioned the arrival of a new generation to justify the necessity to look at the Franco-Algerian past on a lucid manner: "Thirty years, forty years, it is a time for a new generation, already mature, the time of the sons and even the grandsons. It is a time when, for those who knew the stupor of the hardship, the efforts to survive and the attempts to forget, even though they are still suffering from too deep wounds, comes the moment of a certain serenity and appeasement" (Chirac, 1996).

Let me cite a last example to show that one cannot neglect the effect of time passing on official memory. This example illustrates the way the French representatives successively considered the French mutineers—the *Mutins*—who were shot during the First World War. Since 1918, the representations of those who were executed "to set an example" were by no means constant, since they appeared as cowards, victims or even martyrs. The identity of the commemorators constitutes the first variable explaining this variation. On the local level, the fate of these soldiers has often been seen as tragic and unjust. According to various local spokesmen, their attitude was perfectly understandable. After undergoing months of cruel and sometimes absurd fighting, after losing their companions, these men were exhausted and desperate. They actually refused to be sacrificed. The argument of local representatives leads to one conclusion: being killed by their own army without any legitimate reason, these soldiers are authentic martyrs—even if they are not recognized as such by the authorities (see Offenstadt, 1999, 194–195). The attitude of official representatives is radically different. For eight decades, the *Mutins* were actually "forgotten soldiers." While the figure of the *Poilu* symbolized the patriotic hero *par excellence*, the memory of these rebellious soldiers was neither consensual nor perceived as edifying. As a result, their memory was put into brackets. Nonetheless, this official version was radically put into question in 1998. At the time, former Prime Minister Lionel Jospin decided to commemorate *all* the French soldiers of the Great War. His words were univocal: the "soldiers who were shot to set an example" in the name of an extremely rigorous discipline "must be fully reintegrated today in our national collective memory" (Jospin, 1998). This sentence implicitly recognizes that the guilty ones may not only be the *Mutins* themselves, but also the Generals and Ministers who were at the origin of offensives that often seemed condemned in advance and therefore useless (Pedroncini, 1996).

This shift in the official strategy is in line with a broader change of perceptions towards the Great War. The French case is indeed not isolated. In England, families of soldiers "shot at dawn" and veterans of the First World War repeatedly called for the rehabilitation of the British soldiers that were executed to set an example. This campaign for the pardon led to an official gesture of repentance. Talking in the name of the British government, the Minister John Reid expressed "a deep sense of regret at the loss of life" (Offenstadt, 1999, p. 172). A similar gesture occurred in Italy when the Minister of Defense, Carlo Scognamiglio, did not hesitate to say that "the poor soldiers shot by our own firing squads were not less heroic than those who died while they were fighting" (p. 198). Admittedly, these three cases are directly linked to a specific national context. However, they did not take place at the same period by coincidence. This general revision of the First World War results to a large extent from a generation effect. After 80 years, all the officers who were responsible for the executions were dead. Accordingly, potential judiciary processes could not lead to condemnations.

This generation factor indicates that the official vs. local character of the commemorator is not the only variable to be taken into consideration in order to understand that the same historical figure passes from the status of traitor and dishonored citizen to the status of victim. The generation effect once again reveals itself to be decisive. Having said that, one must admit that the status of martyr or hero, which was mentioned by some local associations, was absolutely not conceivable in the framework of official memory. The dispute that followed Lionel Jospin's speech is telling in this regard. By calling for their reintegration in the national memory, Lionel Jospin did not really pay tribute to the *Mutins*. He just evoked their memory. However, this symbolic evocation was enough to imply a controversy within the French political elite. The day after the address by the Prime Minister, an official communiqué manifested the intense discontent of the Elysée ("L'Elysée condamne la réhabilitation des mutins de 1917 par Lionel Jospin" [The Elyseum condemns the rehabilitation of the mutineers of 1917 by Lionel Jospin], 1998). Several right-wing voices were raised against the initiative of Lionel Jospin. According to them, his remark could somehow justify "the disobedience of the army" ("Philippe Ségain pursuit la polémique sur la réhabilitation de mutins de 1917" [Philippe Ségain goes on arguing about the rehabilitation of the mutineers of 1917], 1998). Furthermore, they called for the necessary distinction between the *Mutins* and the "good soldiers," reminding the public that the great majority of *Poilus* accomplished their duty until the end, whatever the hardships they suffered. This kind of comment joined the numerous complaints denouncing a climate of "collective expiation" and of "national masochism" in France since official representatives decided to recognize the national past as a whole, with its complexity and its ambiguity, with its heroic pages *and* its "gray zones." Beyond the French case, this polemic reveals that the malleable character of official memory is far from being unlimited.

National Memory as a Limited Process

The political use of martyrdom cannot be reduced to a top-down process. The official emphasis put on the term "martyr" cannot be defined as a pure phenomenon of manipulation or propaganda. The analysis shows that the reference to martyrdom does not always result from an official decision. As it has already been suggested, numerous cases indicate that such emphasis may initially result from a particular initiative within the civil society. On the other hand, when the initiative originally comes from the official level, one question remains essential: what about its impact on individual representations?

Here, we have to come back to the basic distinction between official and individual memory. As it has already been indicated, official representations and individual memories are in constant interaction. Official memory can influence the way people look at the past. For instance, certain symbols emphasized in textbooks or in official commemorations can crystallize elements that are progressively incorporated in the individual memories. In France, specialists argue that the official history taught at school during the third Republic was largely internalized by the French population (Citron, 1987, p. 7). Others confirm that commemorations following the Second World War structured and gave a meaning to the memory transmitted on a private level (Namer, 1983). Official representations of the past have a certain impact on individuals. However, memory cannot be imposed by decree. Indeed, the citizens who are exposed to this official interpretation do not always internalize it.

The potential gap between the official and the individual representations of the same event allow questioning the factors determining the degree of population adherence. Research thus far shows that the impact of official memory on the population depends on three main variables (Rosoux, 2001b, pp. 194–195).

- The first variable concerns the *individual experience*. The room for interpretation towards the past is systematically limited by the impact of events. The interpretation of the past produced by spokespersons cannot normally contradict the experience lived or transmitted by individuals. These people do not always recognize themselves in the official narration concerning the past. Individual resistances were particularly obvious in the framework of totalitarian regimes. For instance, the USSR case shows that the Soviet authorities never succeeded in erasing the memories transmitted by the population.

    One can thus affirm that "the larger the distance between the official interpretation and the individual representations, the weaker its impact."

- *Popular expectations* are the second variable affecting the efficacy of official memory vis-à-vis the population. The degree of accuracy towards the reality of the past is not the only variable to be taken into consideration. Some official representations of the past enjoy popular support even though they do not respect the reality of the past. The "resistantialist myth" elaborated by de Gaulle at the very end of the Second World War is a good example to illustrate this. The official interpretation according to which the whole French population was indeed resisting the Germans during the war achieved a complete success among the population. However, it is obvious that French citizens knew perfectly well that this interpretation did not represent the entire reality of the war. Nonetheless, the great majority of them supported this vision since it corresponded with a collective need of self-esteem. The influence of official memory is then also dependent upon the wishes and/or fears expressed by the population.

  One can thus affirm that "the larger the distance between the official interpretation and the individual expectations, the sharper the resistance within the population."

- Eventually, the *personal variable* turns out to be fundamental. A very important factor of credibility to gain the population's adherence lies in the personal legitimacy of the official representative. For instance, the influence of de Gaulle's interpretation of the national past does not exclusively result from the fact that this interpretation offered a "invented honor" to the French population (Conan and Rousso, 1996, p. 309). It also results from the legitimacy of Charles de Gaulle. Without the credibility of his personal past, de Gaulle would probably never been able to re-write the history of the Second World War in such a way. A similar comment can be made with respect to Nelson Mandela in South Africa.

  One can thus affirm that *"the more legitimate the official representatives in the eyes of the population, the greater the effect produced by their visions of the past on the remembrances shared by individuals."*

At the end of this reflection, the question becomes the following: what is the future of the political use of martyrdom? In countries like France, references to national martyrs seem to be obsolete. Who in France, and more largely in the European Union, would still consent to the sacrifice of his or her children for the sake of the nation? The reasons for this apparent loss of national affection are complex. Among them, it is difficult to deny the progressive removal of the sacred aura surrounding the state. Admittedly, the state is ever-present, but it is neither omnipotent nor transcendent anymore. In civil society, many groups try to work out their own strategies of remembrance alongside the state and sometimes against it. The perspective is therefore much more fragmented than before. The ideal that is internalized by each citizen is not consensual any longer—it is essentially pluralistic. As a result, the idea of self-sacrifice in the name of the state does not make sense anymore.

Another sign of this evolution is the general lack of interest as far as the traditional figure of national hero is concerned. The heroic conceptions that grounded the invention of nationhood during the nineteenth century are more and more replaced by self-critical narratives of the national past. During the last decade, official representatives in several regions of the world admitted responsibility for historical injustices and past discriminatory practices through a critical investigation into their national past. In Europe and in Asia, numerous political leaders acknowledged the historical responsibility of their nations for the sufferings that were inflicted during the Second World War. In South America, several governments launched commissions of truth and reconciliation in an effort to come to terms with the immediate authoritarian past. In Australia, New Zealand, and Canada, official commemorations refer more often to the past and the rights of indigenous nations. Whatever the location, victims of human rights violations and their descendants ask for official recognition. Critical—or post-heroic narratives—emphasize events that do not focus on national heroes but rather on individual victims. From this perspective, the reference becomes less of a state interest and more of a personal suffering matter.

The French case gives a very good illustration of this change. The way the political elite represent the national past can be characterized by three successive stages. As we have seen, they initially focused their attention on two kinds of national heroes (the *Poilus* as far as the World War One was concerned and the *Résistants* in the Second World War). In 1995, they started emphasizing different groups of victims, especially the Jews. Two years later, they stressed the figure of the *Justes*, this concept designating all the people who decided to protect and to save the Jews during the war. This new figure is interesting since it somehow allows reconciling the two faces of the past—the heroic face and the embarrassing face. As President Jacques Chirac said in 1997, "the good and the evil must be equally recognized and assumed. That is the least that one can expect from an elderly people that considers the fight in favor of liberty and human dignity as its highest mission." Thus, after evoking "a combatant and resistant France" and after reminding the hardship of the Jews during the war, Jacques Chirac stressed the "daily and discreet heroism of all the *Justes*" who succeeded to save so many lives (Chirac, 1997). This consensual mention of a "daily and discreet" form of heroism shows that the ultimate reference is more individual than national, more human oriented than state oriented.

Such change seems to confirm the assertion that the notion of national martyr may be no longer needed as a political tool. However, Western European countries constitute one very particular case. If we look at other political contexts, at least two elements tend to deny the political uselessness of martyrdom. Firstly, we have to consider the multiplication of the martyrs in areas of the world devastated by ethnic conflicts. In the aftermath of the cold war we were witnessing the reappropriation of a heroic past and the re-emergence of nationalism. The Balkans remains a tragic illustration of this phenomenon. The second element to be considered is the growing call for self-sacrifice by terrorist leaders. The events of September 11, 2001, and its dramatic consequences tend to indicate that the political use of martyrdom reveals to be more useful than ever.

There is no doubt that the past is still—and will definitely remain—a site of rhetorical struggle over its representation. Controlling discourses about the past may not guarantee political control of the present, but such discourses are nonetheless powerful tools for inspiring mass devotion and self-sacrifice.

Notes

1. The notion of worship is used by Renan himself: "Worshipping ancestors is more than legitimate: they have made us who we are" (Renan, 1997).

2. Memory is thus different from history. History basically attempts to reconstitute events in a manner that depends as little as possible on variable representations. The goal is to attain "historical truth" and to discover events as they happened. By contrast, memory is inherently associated with social representations within a group. It forms a tool and is the result of a process in which identities are construed and/or reinforced (Le Goff, 1988).

3. I decided to take into account the three most traumatic wars of the twentieth century: World War I, World War II, and the Algerian War. The Indo-Chinese (or Vietnamese) War, which ended with the Geneva agreement of 1954, did not have the same impact on French society. Indo-China was quite far from France and French vital interests were not at stake there.

4. http://www.charles-de-gaulle.org/dossier/moulin/biomoul2.htm.

5. A survey published in August 1988 indicates that, according to representatives of the entire French society (whatever the generation and the social and economical status), the Occupation of France (1940–1944) and the Algerian War represent the "two most tragic events of French History" (Rioux, 1990, p. 604).

6. This term designated the French full citizens living in Algeria. They were settlers, workers in the public services, teachers, merchants, and so on. Some of them were wealthy *colons*, but many of them were lower-middle-class, very ordinary people. Their families had migrated to North Africa during the nineteenth century or after.

7. For example, *La Question, La gangrène, Nuremberg pour l'Algérie* or *Les égorgeurs* (see Stora 1998: 28).

8. The concept of "moudjahid" does not literally mean martyr (which corresponds with the Arabic concept of "jahid"). Though, the term "moudjahid" refers to the notion of combatant and to the idea of sacrifice.

References

Anderson, B. (1991). Imagined communities: Reflections on the origin and spread of nationalism. New York: Verso.

Becker, J.-J. (1994). *Guerre et cultures, 1914–1918* [War and cultures, 1914–1918]. Paris: Colin.

Binoche, J. (1996). *Histoire des relations franco-allemandes de 1789 à nos jours* [History of Franco-German relations since 1789]. Paris: Masson— Armand Colin.

Boumediene, H. (1972). *Discours du President Boumediene* [Speeches of President Boumediene], (Vol. 3, 1970–1972). Alger: Ministerí de l'information et de la culture.

Bourdieu, P. (1991). Language and symbolic power. Cambridge: Cambridge University Press.

Brauman, R., & Sivan, E. (1999). *Eloge de la désobéissance. A propos d'"un spécialiste" Adolf Eichmann* [Praise of disobedience about "one specialist" Adolf Eichmann]. Paris: Le Pommier.

Brossat, A. (1991). *Le stalinisme, entre histoire et mémoire* [Stalinism, between history and memory]. Paris: Editions de l'Aube.

Centlivres, P., Fabre, D., & Zonabend, F. (1998). *La fabrique des héros* [The creation of heroes]. Paris: Editions de la Maison des Sciences de l'Homme.

Chaumont, J.-M. (1997). *La concurrence des victimes, Génocide, identité, reconnaissance* [The competition of victims. Genocide, identity, recognition]. Paris: La Découverte.

Chirac, J. (1996). *Allocution du 11 novembre* [Speech of 11 November]. Retrieved from http://www.doc.diplomatie.fr/BASIS/epic/www/doc/SF

Chirac, J. (1997). *Allocution du 5 december 1997* [Speech of 5 December 1997]. Retrieved from http://www.elysee.fr/cgi-bin/auracom/aurweb/search/file?aur_file=discours/1997/DEPOJVIF.html

Citron, S. (1987). *Le mythe national. L'Histoire de France en question* [National myth. The history of France in question]. Paris: Editions ouvrières.

Citron, S. (1994). Au tableau noir de notre histoire [At the blackboard of our history]. *Autrement, 144,* 114–117.

Conan, E., & Rousso, H. (1996). *Vichy, un passé qui ne passe pas* [Vichy: An ever-present past]. Paris: Gallimard.

de Gaulle, C. (1944). *Vers l'armée de métier* [Towards the professional army]. Paris: Berger-Levrault.

de Gaulle, C. (1962). Allocution du 9 septembre à Ludwigsburg [Speech of 9 September in Ludwigsburg]. *Notes et Etudes documentaires, 2947,* 7–8.

de Gaulle, C. (1967). Allocution du 12 juillet 1967 [Speech of 12 July 1967]. *La politique étrangère de la France, 6* (2),40.

de Gaulle, C. (1970). *Discours et messages* [Discourses and messages] vol. I. Paris: Plon.

Farmer, S. (1999). *Martyred village: Commemorationg the 1994 massacre at Oradour-sur-Glane.* Berkeley: University of California Press.

Fouche, J.-J. (2002). Le Centre de la mémoire d'Oradour [The Centre de la Mémoire of Oradour]. *XXᵉ siècle Revue d'histoire, 73* (1–3), 125–137.

Garde, P. (1992–1993). Ex-Yougoslavie: une fausse guerre de religion [Ex-Yugoslavia: A false religious war]. *Politique internationale, 58–59,* 45–63.

Giscard d'Estaing, V. (1980, July–August). Allocution du 10 juillet 1980 [Speech of 10 July 1980]. *La politique étrangère de la France,* 18–19.

Grmek, M., Gijdara, M., & Simac, N. (1993). *Le nettoyage ethnique. Documents historiques sur une idéologie serbe* [The ethnic cleansing. Historical documents on a Serbian ideology]. Paris: Fayard.

Grosser, A. (1989). *Le crime et la mémoire* [Crime and memory]. Paris: Flammarion.

Hobsbawm, E., & Ranger, T. (1992). *The invention of tradition.* Cambridge: Cambridge University Press.

Horne, J., & Kramer, A. (2001). *German atrocities, 1914. A history of denial.* New Haven and London: Yale University Press.

Igric, G. (1998). Relectures de l'histoire yougoslave [Rereadings of the Yugoslavian history]. *Manière de voir, 40* (7–8), 32.

Jospin, L. (1998). *Allocution du 5 novembre 1998* [Speech of 5 November 1998]. Retrieved from http://www.doc.diplomatie. 19 November 1998.

Jospin, L., & Schröder, G. (1999). Memory and identity, *La politique étrangère de la France.* Retrieved September 25, 1999, from http://www.doc.diplomatie.gouv.fr/BASIS/epic/www/doc/SF.

Kantorowicz, E. (1984). *Mourir pour la patrie* [Dying for one's country]. Paris: P.U.F.

Kassimir, R. (1991). Complex martyrs: Symbols and Catholic Church formation and political differentiation in Uganda. *African Affairs*, *90* (360), 357–382.

Le Goff, J. (1988). *Histoire et mémoire* [History and memory]. Paris: Gallimard.

"L' Elysée condamn la réhabilitation des mutins de 1917 par Lionel Jospin," [The Elyseum condemns the rehabilitation of the mutineers of 1917 by Lionel Jospin]. (1998, November 9). *Le Monde*.

Luebke, H. (1962). Discours du 9 September 1962 [Speech of 9 September 1962]. *Notes et études documentaires*, no. 2947, pp. 19–20.

Malraux, A. (1973). Discours du 19 décembre 1964 [Speech of 19 December 1964]. *Espoié*, no. 2, pp. 64–67.

Miletitch, N. (1996). L'Eglise orthodoxe serbe [The Serbian orthodox church]. *Politique étrangère*, *1*, 191–203.

Mitterrand, F. (1994). Allocution du 8 septembre 1994 [Speech of 8 September 1994]. Retrieved from http://www.doc.diplomatie

Mitterrand, F. (1995). *Onze discours sur l'Europe (1982—1995)* [Eleven speeches on Europe (1982–1995)]. Naples: Vivarium.

Mitterrand, F., & Wiesel, E. (1995). *Mémoire à deux voix* [Memory in two voices]. Paris: Odile Jacob.

Mosse, G. (1990). *Fallen soldiers. Reshaping the memory of the world wars*. Oxford: Oxford University Press.

Namer, G. (1983). *Batailles pour la mémoire. Commémorations en France de 1945 à nos jours* [Battles for memory: Commemorations in France from 1945 to the present]. Paris: Papyrus.

Offenstadt, N. (1999). *Les fusillés de la grande guerre et la mémoire collective (1914–1999)* [The shouted soldiers of the great war and the collective memory (1914–1999)]. Paris: Odile Jacob.

"Paris se refuse à entretenir une polémique" [Paris refuses to enter into an argument]. (1985, July 10). *Le Monde*.

Pedroncini, G. (1996). *Les mutineries de 1917* [The mutineers of 1917]. Paris: P.U.F.

Peyrefitte, A. (1994). *C'était de Gaulle* [It was de Gaulle] I. Paris: Fayard.

"Philippe Ségain pursuit la polémique sur la réhabilitation de mutins de 1917" [Philippe Ségain goes on arguing about the rehabilitation of the mutineers of 1917]. (1998, November 11). *Le Monde*.

Pompidou, G. (1972, September 23). Conférence du presse du 21 september 1972 [Press conference of 21 September 1972]. *Le Monde*.

Renan, E. (1997). *Qu'est-ce qu'une nation?* [What is a nation?] Paris: Mille et une nuits.

Ricoeur, P. (2000). *La mémoire, l'histoire, l'oubli* [Memory, history, oblivion]. Paris: Le Seuil.

Rioux, J.-P. (1990). *La guerre d'Algérie et les Français* [The Algerian war and the French]. Paris: Fayard.

Roseau, J. (1985, October 23). Ce qui est passé est mort [What is past is dead]. *Le Monde*.

Rosoux, V. (2001a). *Les usages de la mémoire dans les relations internationales* [The use of memory in international relations]. Brussels: Bruylant.

Rosoux, V. (2001b). National identity in France and Germany: From mutual exclusion to negotiation. *International Negotiation, 6* (2), 175–198

Rousso, H. (1990). *Le syndrome de Vichy de 1944 à nos jours* [The Vichy syndrome from 1944 to the present]. Paris: Le Seuil.

Rousso, H. (2001). *Vichy. L'événement, la mémoire, l'histoire* [Vichy. Event, memory, history]. Paris: Gallimard.

Saint Augustine (1964). *Les confessions* [Confessions]. Paris: Garnier-Flammarion.

Stora, B. (1995). L'Algrie en 1995. La guerre, l'histoire, la politique [Algeria in 1995. War, history, and politics]. Paris: Michalon.

Stora, B. (1998). *La gangrène et l'oubli. La mémoire de la guerre d'Algérie* [Gangrene & oblivion. Memory of the Algerian war]. Paris: La Découverte.

Tincq, H. (1998, March 10). Une terre sainte de l'orthodoxie balkanique [A holy land of the Balkan orthodology]. *Le Monde*.

Uzelac, A. (1997, January 23–29). Apprendre aux petits Bosniaques que leur voisin est un ennemi [Teaching Bosnian pupils that their neighbor is an enemy]. *Gazeta Wyborcza - Courrier International, 325*, 37–38.

Winter, J., & Sivan, E. (1999). *War and remembrance in the twentieth century*. Cambridge: Cambridge University Press.

Wood, D. (1993). *Martyrs and martyrologies*. Oxford: Blackwell Publishers.

CHAPTER 4

The Theology of Martyrdom

Michael Berenbaum and Reuven Firestone

Michael Berenbaum

Martyrdom—The Sanctification of God's Name in Judaism

Thomas Hobbes's classic work, *The Leviathan,* assumes that order is achieved because people prefer stability and security to the state of nature, which he described as the war of all against all, and are willing to sacrifice freedom in order to protect their own lives and to secure the lives of their families. Those in power are willing to risk death a bit longer, to provoke death a bit more, but not to welcome death. What makes martyrdom so perplexing at least to "normal" calculations of power is that the loss of life is not a significant deterrent. Indeed, it is the expected outcome of certain actions and of maintaining certain belief under difficult conditions. That is what is new about the homicide/suicide bombers who cannot be deterred by almost certain death.

Though psychologists will argue otherwise—and properly so—people choose to end their lives for three essential reasons: they do not value life or at least *this* life; they value something more than life or something more than *this* life and they are prepared to offer their life for that which they value more than life; and they despair of this life or of the cost of remaining alive in suffering, indignity, shame, or pain.

Some religious perspectives do not value life; others do not value *this* life, seeing this world as an anteroom to the next. Viewing death without much sadness and without regret, they insulate the believer from the highs and lows of life by achieving a spiritual equilibrium that provides stability in the face of death. Others negate this life as one of sin and iniquity, unworthy and therefore something that can be given up for a better life that awaits. Still other faiths do not take death as final. They see it as a passageway. There are echoes of this in the Roman Catholic Mass of the Resurrection and also in the commonly used phrase at funerals and at moments of intense grief that seemingly offers consolation: "He is in a better place now."

Some despair of this life.

A patient suffering with a terminal illness, seeing each tomorrow as less than yesterday, experiencing pain and only expecting more, may wish to die. Recently, I personally confronted this very situation. Early this winter my mother, who was suffering from terminal lung cancer, asked a profound question masked with her typical humor: "Where is Kevorkian when I need him?" Her own anguish mirrored the experience of so many others and has led to a reevaluation in some states of the practice of assisted suicide. In the next breath she said: "My husband was too religious and my son is too religious to permit that." She understood full well that Judaism frowns upon suicide because it does not regard life as an individual choice but as the gift of God who alone can decide who shall live and who shall die and thus life is sacred and not within the prerogative of human beings to end. Rabbinic sages and their successors onto our very days have written tomes regarding the practice of such values under the conditions of modern medicine where even for most devout, the physician and the medical system play an active role in decisions of life and death.

It is noticeable that a significant number of Holocaust survivors who as young men and women faced death and provoked death and survived, now in their later years when diagnosed with a fatal illness choose suicide rather than endless suffering. John Roth and I edited a book titled *The Holocaust: Religious and Philosophical Implications* that brought together more than 18 classical essays on the Holocaust. Almost half of the authors and more than half of the survivor accounts that we had collected had committed suicide by then or when faced with a terminal illness shortly thereafter. Despite the teachings of Judaism, it makes psychological sense. Once they prolonged life no matter what, but then they were young and could hope to outlast the enemy and outlive the enemy—*iberlausen* is the word they used, to outlive, but that was then and now is now. Then they were young and now they are old. Then they could hope to outlive the enemy by endurance and now they know they will not outlive. Death awaits them; their battle will be lost. Once they lost control and could come back. Now when they lose control, there will be no return. The loss is final and irrecoverable. So they preserve choice and control and choose to die rather than cede that last bit of control.

Given the depth of the Rabbinic opposition to suicide, one is surprised to see that the Hebrew Bible treats self-chosen death in a rather matter of fact manner. The fear of shame, not pain, is the reason that the Bible gives for the self-chosen death of Abimelech and Saul in the Bible, voluntary deaths that pass surprisingly without even a pejorative comment.

The account of Abimelech's death from *Judges:*

> Abimelech proceeded to Thebez; he encamped at Thebez and occupied it. Within the town was a fortified tower; and all the citizens of the town, men and women took refuge there. Abimelech pressed forward to set it on fire. But a woman dropped an upper millstone on Abimelech's head and cracked his skull. He immediately cried out to his attendant, his arms bearer, "Draw your dagger and finish me off, that they may not say of me, 'A woman killed him!'" So his attendant stabbed him, and he died.[1]

Though the Bible has no problem with the manner of Abimelech's death, the same cannot be said for the way in which he lived.

The story of Saul as narrated in *Samuel I:*

> The battle [with the Philistines at Mount Gilboa] raged around Saul and some of the archers hit him and he was severely wounded by the archers. Saul said to his arms bearer, "Draw our sword and run me through so that the uncircumcised may not run through me and make sport of me." But his arms-bearer in great awe refused: whereupon Saul grasped the sword and fell upon it.[2]

Saul's arms bearer also chooses to end his own life either in an act of solidarity or to avoid witnessing the shame of his King.

Two other instances of self-chosen or voluntary death in the Hebrew Bible, Ahitophel and Zimri, pass without comment on the manner of death though not on the manner of the life led by the deceased. Ahitophel was an advisor to David and his son Abshalom but he sided with Abshalom in his battle for succession with David. In essence, he backed the wrong candidate and lost out in the battle for succession. The Bible recounts Ahitophel's death *en passant:*

When Ahitophel saw that his advice had not been followed, he saddled his ass and went home to his native town. He set his affairs in order and then he hanged himself. He was buried in his ancestral tomb.[3]

Zimri, who served for a brief and bloody time as King of Israel, began his seven-day rule by slaughtering all the male kinsmen of his predecessor. He fought in opposition to the army commander Omri who prevailed:

When Zimri saw that the town was taken, he went into the citadel of the royal place and burned down the palace over himself. And so he died—because of the sins he had committed and caused Israel to commit, doing what was displeasing to the Lord and following the ways of Jeroboam.[4]

The Bible's judgment is harsh. Zimri is a traitor, but he is condemned not for the way in which he died, but for the manner in which he lived and ruled.

The case of Samson is rather different and more akin to the contemporary homicide/suicide bombers. He took his own life and took others' lives with him. Samson was experiencing humiliation rather than anticipating it. His motive was vengeance not honor, and God was portrayed the enabler, at least according to the Biblical narrative. But rather than offer no comment on the manner of death, the Bible is rather laudatory of Samson's death and recounts that he is given an honorable burial by his family.

Then Samson called onto the Lord: "O Lord God! Please remember me and give me the strength just this once, O God to take revenge on the Philistines if only for one of my two eyes." He embraced the two middle pillars that the temple rested upon, one with his right arm and one with his left, and he leaned against them. Samson cried, "Let me die with the Philistines!" and he pulled with all his might. The Temple came crashing down on the lords and on all the people in it. Those who were slain by him as he died outnumbered those who had been slain by him when lived.[5]

Rabbinic Judaism did not sanction voluntary death nor would it withhold its judgment and let such deaths pass without comment. Its opposition was vehement. Life was a gift from God and God alone was to decide who is to live and who is to die. The human being has no right to usurp the divine prerogative.

The first major story of sacrificial death—at least in potential—is the test of Abraham, which later became known as the *Akedah*, the binding of Isaac. Genesis 22, the story of the command to Abraham to offer Isaac as a sacrifice, has intrigued generations. The Torah frames the narrative as the test of Abraham, "After these things, the Lord tested Abraham."[6] The drama of the Patriarch who waited so long—until he was 100 years old—for a son from Sarah, toward the end of his life received a command from God to offer his son, his only son [from Sarah] whom he loves, Isaac, and to offer him as an *olah*, sacrificed whole on one of the mountains that will be shown him. This Scriptural reading has an honored place in Jewish tradition. It is read on the second day of *Rosh Hashanah*, the Jewish New Year, and is one of the themes associated with God's mercy, demanding symbolic not actual sacrifice. It is part of the daily morning prayers.

The story is classical. Each generation reads their struggles through the narrative. Each generation wrestles with the sacred text, viewing themselves as Abraham, perceiving themselves as Isaac or Sarah, who waited at home unknowing of the drama, or as one of the lads, left behind before father and son set out together. During the Crusades when fathers offered their sons rather than permit even the possibility of conversion, they saw themselves as more severely tested than Abraham. We shall return to this theme.

The story has continued to fascinate Jews even today—especially today—when Isaac is depicted in Modern Jewish commentary and even in secular Israeli poetry as the first survivor, the first to see death face-to-face and return. Genesis 22 reads *"And* Abraham returned to the young men."[7] No mention is made of Isaac, nor does the Torah describe his presence at Sarah's funeral. Isaac is next mentioned when he meets his bride Rebecca.

In post-Holocaust literature the question is often raised: where was Isaac? What happened in the period of time when he witnessed his own impending death and when he was prepared to marry and to bring children into the world? There is a debate in Rabbinic tradition as to the age of Isaac at the *Akedah*. Was he three, a mere child too young to understand but not too young to remember? The evidence: Isaac says so little; his questions are so basic. Was he thirteen and the *Akedah* his rite of passage to adulthood, his Bar-Mitzvah, so to say? The father-son drama seems quite adolescent. Or was he 37, a grown man. The argument for the later age is that his mother was 90 when he was born and died at 127, and since her death immediately follows Genesis 22, then Isaac may well have been 37 and of the age where he could have easily resisted. Hence the Torah tells of his binding, which according to some sages implied his consent.

The three years from 37 to 40—if indeed they were three years—are all the more symbolic since only three years separate the liberation of the camps from the establishment of the Jewish state. How does one see death face-to-face and return to life, marry and bring children into the world?

In the Christian narrative Jesus is the consummated Isaac, the atoning sacrifice, and in medieval Jewish literature, the fathers offered their sons. There was not one father and one son, but thousands upon thousands. They felt superior to Abraham: "Yours was a trial, mine was an accomplished fact. Yours was a trial, mine were the performances."

In a slim, but wondrously powerful volume written more than a half century ago in honor of Mordecai Kaplan's seventieth birthday, Shalom Spiegel reviewed the legends of the *Akedah* as an introduction to a poem that is so startling; for it contradicts the Torah even as it argues that it is the normative meaning. Ably translated by Judah Goldin and titled *The Last Trial: On the Legends and Lore of the Command to Abraham to Offer Isaac As a Sacrifice,* in the poem by Rabbi Efraim ben Jacob of Bonn wrote:

Then did the father and the son embrace,
    Mercy and Truth met and kissed each other.
Oh, my father, fill your mouth with praise,
    For He doth bless the sacrifice.

I long to open my mouth to recite the Grace:
    Forever blessed be the Lord. Amen
Gather my ashes, bring them to the city,
    Unto the tent, to Sarah.

He made haste, he pinned him down with his knees,
    He made his two arms strong.
With steady hands he slaughtered him according to the rite,
    Full right was the slaughter.

Down upon him fell the resurrecting dew, and he revived.
    (The father) seized him (then) to slaughter him once more.
Scripture, bear witness! Well-grounded is the fact:
    And the Lord called Abraham, even a second time from heaven.

The ministering angels cried out, terrified:
    Even animal victims, were they ever slaughtered twice?
Instantly they made their outcry heard on high,
    Lo, Angels cried out above the earth.

We beg of Thee, have pity upon him!
    In his father's house, we were given hospitality.

He was swept by the flood of celestial tears
  Into Eden, the garden of God.

The pure one thought: The child is free of guilt,
  Now I, whither shall I go?
Then he heard: Your son was found an acceptable sacrifice,
  By myself I have sworn it, saith the Lord.

In a nearby thicket did the Lord prepare
  A ram, meant for this mitsvah even from Creation.
The proxy, caught its leg in the skirts of his coat,
  And behold, he stood by his burnt offering.

So he offered the ram, as he desired to do,
  Rather than his son, as a burnt offering.
Rejoicing, he beheld the ransom of his only one
  Which God delivered into his hand.

This place he called Adonai-Yireh,
  The place where light and the law are manifest.
He swore to bless it as the Temple site,
  For there the Lord commanded the blessing.

Thus prayed the binder and the bound.
  That when their descendants commit a wrong
This act be recalled to save them from disaster,
  From all their transgressions and sins.

O Righteous One, do us this grace!
  You promised our fathers mercy to Abraham.
Let then their merit stand as our witness,
  And pardon our iniquity and our sin, and take us for Thine
  inheritance.

Recall to our credit the many Akedahs,
  The saints, men and women, slain for thy sake.
Remember the righteous martyrs of Judah,
  Those that were bound of Jacob.

Be Thou the shepherd of the surviving flock
  Scattered and dispersed among the nations.
Break the yoke and snap the bands
  Of the flock that yearns toward Thee
  O GOD! O KING . . . [8]

"Scripture, bear witness! Well-grounded is the fact"; the words are
most startling for plainly they contradict the ordinary readings of
Scripture. Death and resurrection rather than near death was the re-

quired interpretation, psychologically necessary to those who had slaughtered their children rather than permit apostasy.

Two non-canonical sources deepen and complicate our understanding of the attitude of early Jews toward martyrdom. The story in the Book of Maccabees II is haunting. In the presence of their mother, seven sons are brought before King Antiochus and offered their life in exchange for a transgression by eating swine's meat. The first son refused and was burned alive.

The second son also refused. In his final words, death is regarded as a release, the temporality of this world, an anteroom to everlasting life and dying for the sanctification of the divine name seemingly an assurance of his fate in the world to come:

> You wretch you release us from this present life, but the king of the world will raise us up, because we have died for his laws, to an everlasting renewal of life.[9]

The third son, stretching forth his hands to King Antiochus, is confident of what he must do, but a bit less confident in its reward. His deed is absolute, his assurance tentative:

> I got these from heaven for the sake of its laws: I disregard them and from it I hope to receive them back again.[10]

The fourth son shares the conviction of the third, but understands that while his reward may be uncertain, the punishment of the evil king is quite certain:

> It is better to die by men's hand and look for the hopes God gives of being raised again by him; for you will have no resurrection to life.[11]

The fifth son refuses to see his fate as a sign that God has abandoned the righteous. The true manifestation of God is postponed.

> Since you have authority among men, though you are mortal, you do as you please; but do not suppose that our people have been abandoned by God. But follow your course and see how his mighty power will torment you and your posterity.[12]

The sixth son sees his fate as linked to his sins and fully expects the same fate to be meted out against the King:

> Do not be falsely deceived; for we suffer these things because of ourselves, for we have sinned against our own God, so these amazing things happened. But you must not suppose that you will go unpunished for having attempted to fight against God.[13]

The mother beseeched her final son to share the fate of his brothers and also their faith:

> My son have pity upon me, who carried you nine months in the womb and nursed you for three years and brought you to your present age . . . Do not be afraid of this butcher and show yourself worthy of your brothers so that by God's mercy I may get you back again with your brothers.[14]

God's anger, the seventh son believed, was only temporary, His compassion enduring. Before his mother could finish, the young man said to the king.

> What are you waiting for? I will not obey the command of the king but I obey the command of the law that was given to our forefathers through Moses . . . for we are suffering because of our own sins. And though the Lord is angry for a little while, to rebuke and discipline us, he will be reconciled with his own slaves again . . . I like my brother give up body and soul for the laws of my forefathers calling upon God speedily to show mercy to our nation.[15]

Notions common to Jewish theology of their time fortified the seven sons. Death was but temporary. It would be followed by resurrection and eternal life. The authority of the king is temporal; divine authority is eternal and everlasting. The punishment of death is immediate and undoubtedly painful, but the king is mortal and he, too, will meet his own form of justice. As to punishment of the seemingly innocent: God's anger is but temporary, the wrath against the oppressor shall surely come. These views were consoling. They offered each of the brothers the strength to maintain their own religious integrity and to refuse to capitulate.

Perhaps the most influential depiction of voluntary death for contemporary Jews—though not for classical Judaism—comes from the speeches that Jewish historian Flavius Josephus placed in the mouth of Eleazar Ben Yair, the leader of a group of Jews encamped on a fortress atop Masada who refused to surrender to Rome after the defeat of the Jews and the destruction of Jerusalem in the year 70 C.E. Roman encampments had surrounded all sides of the mountaintop fortress; those camped out at Masada had adequate food and water to hold out against Rome and the strategic advantage of their location. They could not contemplate victory, merely surrender or another alternative.

The speech is a creation of Josephus, seemingly based on the testimony of a woman and five children who survived but widely and correctly regarded as a projection of his own views onto Eleazar, a projection of views and values that he may have held but did not practice when faced with somewhat similar choices. As a Jewish commander, Josephus surrendered rather than risk his own death and the death of his soldiers, a course that Eleazar, as depicted by Josephus, vehemently rejected. Josephus wrote:

> My loyal followers, long ago we resolved to serve neither the Romans nor anyone else but only God, who alone is the true and righteous Lord of men: now the time has come that bids us prove our determination by our deeds. At such a time we must not disgrace ourselves: hitherto we have never submitted to slavery, even when it brought no danger with it: we must not choose slavery now, and with it penalties that will mean the end of everything if we fall alive into the hands of the Romans. For we were the first of all to revolt, and shall be the last to break off the struggle. And I think it is God who has given us this privilege that we can die nobly and as free men, unlike others who were unexpectedly defeated. In our case it is evident that daybreak will end our resistance, but we are free to choose an honorable death with our loved ones. This our enemies cannot prevent, however earnestly they may pray to take us alive; nor can we defeat them in battle.
>
> From the very first, when we were bent on claiming our freedom but suffered such constant misery at each other's hands and worse at the enemy's, we ought perhaps to have read the mind of God and realized that His once beloved Jewish race had been sentenced to extinction. For if he had remained gracious or only slightly indignant with us, He would not have shut his eyes to the destruction of so many thousands or allowed His most holy City to be burnt to the ground by our enemies. We hoped, or so it would seem, that of all the Jewish race we alone would come through safe, still in possession of our freedom, as if we had committed no sin against God and taken part in no crime—we who had taught the others—Now see how He shows the folly of our hopes, plunging us into miseries more terrible than any we had dreamt of. Not even the impregnability of our fortress has sufficed to save us, but though we have food in abundance, ample supplies of arms, and more than enough of every other requisite, God Himself without a doubt has taken away all hope of survival. The fire that was being carried into the enemy lines did not turn back of its own accord towards the wall we had built: these things are God's vengeance for the many wrongs that in our madness we dared to do to our own countrymen.
>
> For those wrongs let us pay the penalty not to our bitterest enemies, the Romans, but to God—by our own hands. It will be easier to bear. Let our wives die unabused, our children without knowledge of slavery: after that, let us do to each other an ungrudging kindness, preserving

our freedom as a glorious winding-sheet. But first let our blow to the Romans that I know, to find our persons beyond their reach and nothing left for them to loot. One thing only let us spare—our store of food: it will bear witness when we are dead to the fact that we perished, not through want but because, as we resolved at the beginning, we chose death rather than slavery.[16]

In contemporary Israel, the myth of Masada has been created, or as some would say rediscovered, and the tradition of Masada fortifies contemporary Zionist emphases on political freedom and independence, the refusal to surrender and the notion—so very contrary to Rabbinic tradition—that political freedom merits the sacrifice of one's life.

In the early 1960s Masada was a site of massive government-sponsored excavations by Israel's most prestigious archeologist and War of Independence hero Yigal Yadin. It is a site of pilgrimage for youth groups. It is climbed by Israel Defense Forces recruits who vow that "Masada will not fall again," and thus reaffirm their own commitment to the defense of their homeland. So it is an understatement to say that the first century collective suicide/martyrdom, which passed virtually unmentioned through nineteen hundred years of exile, plays a significant symbolic role in the psychology of contemporary Israelis and impacts directly on the psychology of its youth and even in the values of its military.[17]

Rabbinic Judaism did not speak of martyrdom but of *Kiddush Hashem* and *Chilul Hashem*, the sanctification or defamation of the Name of God. The classical reference point is Biblical from the book of Leviticus, "You shall not profane my holy name that I may be sanctified in the midst of the people Israel—I am the Lord who sanctify you."[18]

There is a tension within Biblical and Rabbinic tradition as to whether Sanctification of God's name is the act of the Lord—God acting in a redemptive manner—or at human initiative. Ezekiel would seem to maintain the former with but one notable exception, while the admonitions of Amos, "You who trample the poor into the dust of the ground and make the humble walk in a twisted course Father and son go to the same girl and thereby profane my holy name,"[19] and Jeremiah, who regards slavery as a similar profanation of God's name, point to the human initiative in the sanctification and profanation of God's name. As with most things Biblical, the initiative is often God's prerogative, but by the time of Rabbinic tradition the sanctification of the name of God is more of a partnership between the divine and the human.

The daily prayer book underscores this partnership while highlighting the divine initiative for the sanctification of God's name. By redemptive acts of God, God's name is sanctified. It underscores the partnership and prays for the response. The first part of the service has an early declaration of Sh'ma Yisrael, "Hear oh Israel, the Lord is Our God, the Lord is One," followed by this blessing:

> Sanctify Thy Name among those that sanctify it, yes sanctify Thy Name throughout thy world and through Thy salvation let the horn be exalted and raised on high. Blessed art Thou Oh Lord, who publicly sanctifies Thy Name.[20]

Pious Jews from a young age were raised on stories of *Kiddush Hashem*. They were repeated in the schoolrooms and in liturgy. Schoolboys could recite the stories of Hannah and her seven sons. The death of the greatest of the rabbinic authorities, Rabbi Akivah, is recounted in a powerful non-historical poem recited on the Day of Atonement as a centerpiece of the Additional Service (Mussaf) that speaks of the murder of ten rabbis during Hadrianic persecution. Rabbi Akivah is smiling at his death and his students audaciously interrupt his dying, a practice explicitly forbidden by Rabbinic tradition, to demand an explanation for his joyous faith.

Akviah's answer is moving and bold: "All my life I have recited the verse 'You shall love the Lord with all your heart, with all your soul and with all your might' and now even as God takes my soul, I can love the Lord with all my might."[21] With that explanation, his soul departs the world.

The behavior of the students is disturbing. Why interrupt, why interfere in this most personal, most intimate of moments. The response: they have accorded their master the highest honor, seeing him to the very end as their teacher and not as a victim, permitting him to instruct them even with his death. It is a majestic moment in the student/teacher encounter. And the young rabbinic student wonders were circumstances to impose such a fate would he (now she) be equal to that faith?

Because Rabbinic Judaism valued something more than life, it imposed three conditions under which a Jew—it is unclear whether such a requirement falls on non-Jews—must willingly sacrifice his life. One must die rather than commit idolatry, incest, and murder.

> Rabbi Johanan said in the name of R. Simeon b. Jehozadak: By a majority vote it was resolved in the upper chambers of the house of Nithza in Lydda that in every other law of the Torah if a man is commanded:

"Transgress and suffer not death, excepting idolatry, incest (including adultery) and murder . . ."

Whence do we know that if a man was bidden "Engage in idolatry and save your life," that he should do so and not be slain? From the verse [You shall therefore keep my statutes and my judgments, which if a man do,] he shall live in them but not die in them. I might think that it may even be openly practiced, but Scripture teaches, "Neither shall ye profane My holy name, but I will be hallowed . . ."

When R. Dimi came he said: This was taught only if there is no royal decree, but if there is a royal decree one must incur martyrdom rather than transgress even a minor precept. Rabin came, he said in R. Johanan's name: "Even without a royal decree it was only permitted in private, but in public one must be martyred even for a minor precept rather than violate it."

In Rabbinic Judaism one must be prepared to die rather than violate three essential commandments; death was seen as more honorable than compromising the essential of one's faith or the essence of the other. In the Christian narrative, the stakes are much larger. The willing death of Jesus as the Christ, the Crucifixion is a redemptive act. The death of the purely innocent was a choice essential to the atonement for sin, for salvation and for redemption. Imitation of Christ was an invitation for self-sacrificial death.

It bears reiteration that Rabbinic Judaism was established in the aftermath of the defeat of the year 70 C.E. by Rabban Yochanan ben Zakkai, who compromised with Rome and sacrificed political independence to maintain the physical survival and spiritual independence of the Jews. It was he who transformed Judaism from a land-centered, Jerusalem Temple–centered religion to a portable religion that could be reconstituted in exile wherever a quorum of Jews existed with a synagogue consisting of a Torah and a community and a house of study where God's word could be studied.[22] Rabbinic Judaism, those who came after Rabban Yochanan, clearly did not sanction the behavior at Masada.

The test of rabbinic theology came in the lives of the Jewish people as they experienced a history that certainly brought with it many instances of persecution and too many opportunities to pay the ultimate price for the sanctification of the Divine Name.

During the Crusades, community after community faced the acid test. Would Jews submit and convert to Christianity or would they offer their lives—and the lives of their children—rather than violate the teachings of their faith. Clearly, having lived in a Christian ambiance and, whether directly or indirectly, absorbed some Christian teachings, they were clearly more willing to consider the redemptive character of the sacrificial offering. Let us pay attention to an unknown author writing of Mainz on the third of Sivan in the year 1096. According to Robert Chazan, the protection of the local authorities was no longer viable. Self-defense had failed. Yes, Jews had resorted to self-defense, they had fortified themselves and prepared arms, but their fortifications were overcome and their arms insufficient. The options were stark.

> The enemy immediately upon entering the courtyard, found there some of the perfectly pious with Rabbi Isaac ben R. Moses the subtle thinker. He stretched out his neck and they cut off his head immediately. They [Rabbi Isaac and his followers] had clothed themselves in their fringed garments and had seated themselves in the midst of the courtyard in order to do speedily the will of their Creator. They did not wish to flee to the chambers in order to go on living briefly. Rather, with love they accepted upon themselves the judgment of heaven. The enemy rained stones and arrows upon them, but they did not deign to flee. They [the Christian attackers] struck down all those whom they found there, with blows of sword, death and destruction.

Some did not wait. They chose self-sacrifice rather than death after surrender. The Chronicle continues:

> Ultimately we must not tarry, for the enemy has come upon us suddenly. Let us offer ourselves up before our Father in heaven. Anyone who has a knife should come and slaughter us for the sanctification of the unique Name [of God] who lives forever. Subsequently, let him pierce himself with his sword either in his throat or in his belly or let him slaughter himself.—They all stood—men and women—and slaughtered one another. . . . They were all slaughtered. The blood of the slaughter flowed through the chambers in which the children of the sacred covenant were. They lay in slaughtered rows—the infant with the elderly— . . . [making sounds] like slaughtered sheep.

Not all had the courage to match their conviction. Not all children agreed to be bound as Isaac had been bound.

> There was a notable lady, Rachel the daughter of the R. Isaac ben R. Asher. She said to her companions: "I have four children. On them as well have no mercy, lest these uncircumcised come and seize them and they remain in their pseudo-faith. With them as well you must sanctify the Holy Name."—One of her companions came and took the knife. When she [Rachel] saw the knife, she cried loudly and bitterly. She

beat her face, crying and saying: "Where is your steadfast love, O Lord?"—She took Isaac, her small son—indeed he was very lovely—and slaughtered him. She had said to her companions—"Wait—Do not slaughter Isaac before Aaron."—But the lad, Aaron, when he saw that his brother had been slaughtered cried out—"Mother, Mother, do not slaughter me!"—He then went and hid himself under a bureau. She took her two daughters, Bella and Matrona, and sacrificed them to the Lord God of Hosts, who commanded us not to abandon pure awe of him and to remain loyal to him. When the saintly one finished sacrificing her three children before our Creator, she then lifted up her voice and called out to her son—"Aaron, Aaron, where are you—I shall not have pity on you either."—She pulled him by the leg from under the bureau, where he had hidden, and sacrificed him before the sublime and exalted God. She then put them under her two sleeves, two on one side and two on the other, near her heart. They convulsed near her, until the crusaders seized the chamber. They found her sitting and mourning them. They said to her—"Show us the money which you have under your sleeves."—When they saw the slaughtered children, they smote her and killed her. With regard to them and to her it is said—"Mother and babes were dashed to death together."—She died with them, as did the [earlier] saintly one with her seven sons [a reference to the Jewish mother-martyr of the Antiochene persecution]. With regard to them it is said: "The mother of the child is happy."

The Jews who chose death in the Crusades were honored in the Sabbath Prayer Book. The anger of the author is apparent, so too is the plea for God to be manifest swiftly and the hope for retribution. The sentiments are not exactly modern and thus the Reform movement omits the prayer altogether and the Conservative movement omits the final line and limits its recitation to special Sabbaths that mark the Hadrianic persecution, the Holocaust, and the destruction of Jerusalem. Yet no one who reads this prayer can deny the reality of the sentiments and the intensity of the fury. Written in the aftermath of persecution by an author who had internalized its pain, the prayer reads:

May the compassionate Father, enthroned in high, remember with sublime compassion the pious, the good and the innocent, the holy communities who laid down they lives in the sanctification of his name. Beloved and beautiful in their lives, in their death they were not parted. They were swifter than eagles, stronger than lions in doing the will of their Creator. May our God remember them for good together with the other righteous of the world and render retribution for His servants' blood which has been shed, as it is written in the Torah of Moses, man of God: "Acclaim His people, O nations, for He will avenge the blood of His servants, render retribution to His foes and cleanse His people's land." And by your servants the Prophets it is written, "Though I cleanse them, I shall not cleanse them in regard to their bloodshed; and the Lord dwells in Zion." And in the Psalms it is said: "Why should the nations ask, 'Where is their God?' Let your retribution for the blood of Your servants be know made known among the nations in our sight." And the Psalmist declares, "He who renders retribution for bloodshed remembers them; He has not forgotten the cry of the humble." And it says: "He judges among the nations: the land is full of corpses: he smites the head over a wide land. He drinks of the brook in the way: therefore shall he lift up the head."[23]

Clearly the behavior of many Jews during later persecution was different. The deaths during some later Crusades were less though still significant. The Marrano phenomena associated with the Spanish Inquisition could only exist because Jews were willing to convert rather than lose their lives, convert rather than submit to expulsion. They converted in name alone and continued to live an underground life as Jews, at least for a time until they could return to Judaism or until assimilation took its toll.

In the popular imagination and liturgical formulations, and most especially among survivors, the Jews who were murdered during the Holocaust are referred to as martyrs. The publication of one prominent survivor group is called *Martyrdom and Resistance,* as if the two were equal in weight as a description of the Holocaust and also as if martyrdom is an appropriate description of the dead. In Hebrew liturgical formulation for memorial prayers the words *kedoshim utehorim,* holy and pure, are used to describe the dead, traditional words employed to mark the martyrs of earlier generations; the largest commemoration in New York City that annually draws thousands to fill the massive sanctuary of Temple Emanuel also refers to the *kedoshim and martyrs.* Though commonly called martyrs, most of the Jews who were murdered in the Holocaust were more properly victims. They faced what literary scholar Lawrence Langer called "choiceless choices.—Critical decisions did not reflect the options between life and death, "but between one form of abnormal response and another, both imposed by a situation that in no way was of the victim's own choosing."[24]

The Nuremberg law of 1935 defined Jewish based on the religion of one's grandparents and thus persecuted as Jews even those who had previously converted to Christianity or whose parents had con-

verted. With rare, notable, and important exceptions, Jews did not die
for the values they affirmed or for the religion they practiced but for
the sheer accident of the religious affiliation of their grandparents. It
was sufficient to be victimized as a Jew if two or more grandparents
were of Jewish origin.

In actuality one group of Nazi victims were truly martyrs in the
classical sense of the term, namely they had a choice of victimization
or freedom. Unfortunately, Jews faced no such choice nor did many of
the Nazis' other victims.

Throughout Nazi rule, Jews were the major Nazi targets of animus,
yet they were not the only ones. Political dissidents—communists,
socialists, and liberals alike—and trade unionists were persecuted because of their politics. Dissenting clergy were arrested when they
spoke out against the regime. Mentally retarded, physically handi-
capped, or emotionally disturbed Germans were not suitable raw material for breeding the "master race." They too suffered at the hands
of the Nazis. By September 1939, a state-sponsored murder program
was in place. Henry Friedlaner has argued that the roots of genocide
must be seen in this so-called "euthanasia" program. Gypsies, traditional outsiders, were distrusted and despised. Regarded as a menace,
they were deported and incarcerated. Still later, many were killed.
Male homosexuals were arrested and their institutions destroyed because of their sexual practices. Lesbians were exempt. There is no
credible evidence of the systematic persecution of lesbians as lesbians.
In the Nazi mind-set, the world was divided into a series of lesser
races by color, ethnicity, culture, or national identity. Blacks and Slavs
were a special target of Nazi animosity.

Jehovah's Witnesses were persecuted for their faith; Jews for the
accident of their being of Jewish ancestry.

Witnesses, who would not swear allegiance to the state nor serve
in the army of the Third Reich, were targeted as pacifists. They were
isolated and harangued from 1933 onward. Suspicion and harassment
turned into bitter persecution as the Witnesses refused to surrender.
They refused to enlist in the army, undertake air raids drills, stop
meeting or proselytizing. "Heil Hitler" never passed their lips.

Twenty thousand among 65 million Germans, the Witnesses entered the spiritual battle against the Nazis as soldiers of Jehovah in
the war between good and evil. They taught that Jehovah's forces
would defeat Satan. The Nazis could not tolerate such "false gods."
Persecution began immediately in 1933, and continued until 1945.
After 1937, Witnesses were sent to concentration camps. Outside the

camps, Witnesses lost children, jobs, pensions, and all civil rights. Throughout their struggle Witnesses continued to meet, to preach, to distribute literature. Five thousand Jehovah's Witnesses were sent to concentration camps, where they alone were "voluntary prisoners." The moment they recanted their views, they could be freed.

No Jew could renounce their Judaism or could consider conversion. It simply would not help. Some Witnesses lost their lives in the camps, but none renounced their faith. Because they understood why they were suffering, they maintained themselves spiritually to a degree unusual among prisoners. The document that would have freed them is remarkable.[25] It demonstrates that the Witnesses had a choice, freedom or incarceration. Clearly, Jews had no similar choice. Even the choices made a generation or two before to escape Jewish fate by conversion did not protect their descendants.

Why then the persistent use of the term martyrdom among the Jews and most especially among the survivors?

Primo Levi wrote that had the camps lasted a little longer, they would have had to invent a new language. We are drawn back to familiar language because we lack the vocabulary and perhaps the imagination to give voice to a new experience that shatters the previous categories of understanding. The best of the writers invent a new vocabulary; create a distinct language to speak of the Shoah. One such leader, Rabbi Yitzhak Nissenbaum, invented a new category to speak of the experience of the Jews within the Warsaw Ghetto. He deliberately would not use the term *Kiddush Hashem;* instead he spoke of *Kiddush Hahaim.*

> This is the time for *kiddush hahaim*, the sanctification of life, and not for *kiddush ha-Shem*, the holiness of martyrdom. Previously, the Jew's enemy sought his soul and the Jew sacrificed his body in martyrdom [i.e., he made a point of preserving what the enemy wishes to take from him]; now the oppressor demands the Jew's body and the Jew is obliged to defend it, to preserve his life.[26]

And indeed if anything characterizes the dignity of the destroyed, to use the term that the late Saul Esh argued, it is the notion of the sanctification of life, the mighty will to live as defiance of the enemy's desire to kill the Jews.

All this is not to argue that there were not instances of the deliberate choice of martyrdom during the Holocaust. Rabbi Shimon Hubberband argued that there were two forms of *Kiddush Hashem* during the Holocaust possible in the ghettos of Poland: A Jew risking his life to save another Jew or many Jews and a Jew killed while fighting in the defense of Jews.[27] There is also a third, exemplified by the behavior of the Jewish Councils, whose leaders were given a black eye by Hannah Arendt and others for submission and compliance. But those who paint the Jewish leaders with one brush as inadvertent collaborators do not consider the several instances of true martyrdom. Members of the Jewish Council of Bolgoraj, in the Lublin District of Poland, were shot when they refused to surrender their people. Dr. Joseph Parnas, the first Jewish Council president in Lvov, then in German-occupied Poland, was shot when he refused to deliver several thousand Jews for deportation. On October 14, 1942, the entire Judenrat of Bereza Kartuska committed suicide rather than participate in the deportation. The leader of the Jewish Council at Nieswiez Magalif marched to his death rather than turn Jews over to the Germans, saying:

> Brothers, I know that you had no trust in me. You thought I was going to betray you. In this my last minute I am with you—I and my family. We are the first ones to go to our death.

Although there are many other examples, most especially in halachic literature when religious Jews asked guidance of their rabbis and then willingly accepted their judgment and often the divine decree it represented, these cannot obscure or overwhelm the far larger and more prevalent experience of victimization.[28]

Why then do survivors resort to the language of martyrdom? Perhaps because it is comfortable to use such language. Martyrdom has an honorable place in the literature. In part, because the new language seems to offer meaning to the reality of a meaningless death. As Langer wrote:

> Those who died for nothing during the Holocaust left the living with the paralyzing dilemma of facing a perpetually present grief. To the puzzled inquiry why interest in the Holocaust seems to grow as the event recedes into the past, one answer may be that there is no inner place or time to bury it in.
>
>   The fault lies not in our own deficient vision, but in the nature of the experience, which challenges our imagination with a near impossible task. Confrontation with conduct in the death camps represents less a recollection of time past . . . than a collection of past moments whose intrinsic chaos urges us to invent a new moral and temporal dimension for its victims to inhabit.[29]

Those who do not invent such a language resort to the old, familiar language, which both comforts and misleads.

Reuven Firestone

Martyrdom in Islam

The English word, martyr, derives from the Greek word for witness, *martys*. This finds a semantic parallel in the Arabic term for
martyr, *shahid*.[30] While *shahid* is a common qur'anic term, in the
Qur'an it almost always means witness in the sense of one who observes or who attests and can furnish proof. In post qur'anic religious
literature the term is quite common as a designation for martyr, but
it rarely corresponds to that specific meaning in the Qur'an itself[31]
and is not attested as such in pre-Islamic literature.

The Arabian Context

Like any religion, Islam emerged out of a cultural and historical context that exerted a powerful influence on its worldview. Just as Biblical
religion emerged out of an ancient Near Eastern context and Christianity and Rabbinic Judaism emerged out of a context that might be described as combined Greco-Roman and Biblical, the context of Islamic
emergence is seventh-century Arabia. Islamic sources always refer to
the pre-Islamic period of Arabia as the *jahiliyya*, a time of darkness and
ignorance prior to the enlightenment of Islam. According to Islamic references, pre-Islamic Arabia was the last remaining stronghold of per-
vasive idolatry and its permanent correlate, immorality. It was home to
a level of barbarity and cruelty in such dire need of fixing that God sent
his final revelation through the last Prophet Muhammad.

And indeed, Islam radically reformed the cultural and ethical and
well as theological landscape of the pre-Islamic Arabian world.
Nevertheless, Islam emerged out of Arabia as an *Arabian* religion. As
such, its very discourse as well as worldview naturally reflects many
shades and nuances of pre-Islamic Arabian cosmology.

Arabia, then as now, was a harsh physical environment: arid, hot,
or extremely hot for most of the year, and unable to sustain more
than a small population anywhere outside of a few oasis communities.
There was never an overarching political organization, no great
kingdoms or empires that could organize and protect large populations. Because of the lack of any overarching system, kinship remained both the organizing principle for human relations and its
institution. It offered economic sustenance and physical protection
against harsh elements and human threat. One was usually safe
within the kinship group. One was never safe outside of it.

The harshness of the environment and limited space in oases resulted in a large but diffuse population of Arabian nomads and semi-nomads: herders of sheep, goats, and camels that wandered the arid steppe. Even with high mortality rates, natural population growth encouraged customs that would ensure a manageable population size in order to secure survival of the collective, if not always of the individual. These included infanticide at a still undetermined level, and the ubiquitous raiding between kinship groups.

Raiding not only helped keep the population at a tolerable level, it also redistributed resources, mostly in the form of flocks, to the strongest and most able kinship groups. According to the pre-Islamic social system, there was nothing inherently wrong with raiding a different kinship group, though raiding from one's own tribe was absolutely forbidden. Raiding also allowed young men to prove their bravery and skill, thereby moving up the social ladder within the clan or tribe. Pre-Islamic poetry is the only literary source from this period, and it repeatedly records and extols the bravery of young men in the martial world of inter-tribal warring.

Religious martyrdom was not known in pre-Islamic Arabia, but killing and dying through tribal competition over scarce resources was. One killed as a tribal member and one was killed in the same way. If a member of one's tribe was slain, the equation could not be settled until the perpetrator or another member of the perpetrator's closest kinship group was killed in an act of vengeance. Death was death as a member of the tribe. It was built into the cosmological system. There was, therefore, a sense of belongingness in death at the hands of the other. This was not martyrdom, but it was death with a meaning that transcended that of simply ending an individual life.

It is impossible to determine the actual rate of killing in the pre-Islamic period, and it is possible that it was not as common as the poetry would lead one to expect. Pre-Islamic poetry makes the point, however, that death prior to old age was such a part of life that it was considered one's likely fate or destiny. Pre-Islamic Arabian poetry contains a great amount of material on the vicissitudes of fate; *hummat maniya*[32] in this literature refers to the fated determination of one's death, and the old Arabic words for fated decree, *qadar* and *qada'* later became the primary terms in Islam for the divine decree.[33]

Pre-Islamic poetry repeatedly expresses the view that death is preordained. Time (*dahr* and *zaman*) is personified and carries a sense of destiny as it brings on the death of the victim. "Time overcame Ad by

force, and Himyar, troups after troups."[34] "Time has killed him. . . . "
"Time is a thief who snatches away friends and relatives. . . . "[35]

Because one will meet one's demise at a particular time and in a
particular way, it is no use trying to avoid it. *Sabr*, or patient endurance, is the best approach to a life that has, built into it, one's own
destined demise.

> O my friends, a respected death
> Is better than an illusory refuge;
> Anxiety does not ward off the decree (*qadar*)
> But endurance is a cause of victory.
> Death (*maniya*) is better than vileness,
> And having death before oneself is better than having it behind.
> Thus, courage! There is no escape from death.[36]

This, clearly, is not martyrdom. One of the most important elements lacking in these descriptions, for example, is the promise of an
afterlife. There is virtually no evidence that indigenous Arabian religious ideas included such a notion, though formulations of Judaism
and Christianity with afterlife concepts existed around and within
Arabian communities prior to the emergence of Islam. Nevertheless,
one can see elements in this general pre-Islamic world view that
might contribute to the development of martyrdom ideologies in
later, emerging Islam.

Martyrdom in Early Islam

Precisely as in the case of emerging Biblical religion and Christianity, the most contemporary sources we have for the emergence of
Islam are the classic sources of the emerging religion itself: Scripture
(the Qur'an) and Tradition (the Hadith).[37] Although less obvious
from a critical reading of the Qur'an, the Hadith certainly considers
Islam coeval with the last of God's great prophets, Muhammad.
According to the sources, Muhammad was born and raised in Mecca,
a town populated by a single tribe, the Quraysh, and the home of an
idolatrous cult center for a large part of west-central Arabia. The
economy of the city depended on the religious pilgrimage of thousands of people to its cultic places, and the pilgrims required the services of religious guides and institutions of hospitality.

In about 610 c.e., when Muhammad began preaching the divine rev-
elations that would later be collected into the Qur'an, he was largely
ignored by his tribe. But as his denunciation of idolatry attracted a fol-

lowing and people began to question the assumptions of polytheism—including the need to worship and make pilgrimage to the gods of Mecca—he and his mission began to raise eyebrows. As might be imagined, opposition began verbally, but when vocal opposition did not end Muhammad's mission, it became increasingly physical.

Some of Muhammad's early followers, such as Sa'd b. Abi Waqqas, Hamza b. 'Abd al-Muttalib, and 'Umar b. al-Khattab were warriors who could protect themselves and intimidate their opponents, but the status of his community of believers became increasingly precarious. According to Muhammad Ibn Ishaq (died 767), the earliest authority on the life of Muhammad who constructed his authoritative biography from the Tradition literature, the early followers of Muhammad were subjected to the kinds of treatment that one encounters in Christian and Jewish martyrologies: "Every clan which contained Muslims attacked them, imprisoning them, and beating them, allowing them no food or drink, and exposing them to the burning heat of Mecca, so as to seduce them from their religion. Some gave way under pressure of persecution, and others resisted them, being protected by God . . . " One famous early Muslim, the black slave, Bilal, used to be brought out "at the hottest part of the day and throw[n] on his back in the open valley and have a great rock put on his chest; then [his tormentor] would say to him: "You will stay here until you die or deny Muhammad and worship al-Lat and al-'Uzza."[38] Ibn Ishaq cites Hakim b. Jubayr:

> I said to 'Abdullah b. 'Abbas, "Were the polytheists treating them so badly that apostasy was excusable?" "Yes, by God, they were," he said, "they used to beat one of them, depriving him of food and drink so that he could hardly sit upright because of the violence they had used on him, so that in the end he would do whatever they said." If they said to him, "Are al-Lat and al-'Uzza your gods and not Allah?" he would say, "Yes" to the point that if a beetle passed by them they would say to him, "Is this beetle your God and not Allah?" he would say yes, in order to escape from the suffering he was enduring.[39]

In the end, one woman was killed when she refused to abandon Islam, though she is not extolled in this text as being a martyr, and perhaps the first in the history of Islam.[40] According to Ibn Ishaq, Muhammad then sent a group of his suffering followers to Abyssinia to escape the violence and persecution. However, his problems only increased. The next year his entire clan was subjected to a boycott by the Meccans, and then his most powerful protector, Abu Talib, died.

This led, eventually, to Muhammad's own tribe of Quraysh expelling him from Mecca. He and his followers found shelter in the oasis settlement of Medina.

It was in Medina where the believers made the transition from a small and persecuted community to one that was increasingly bold and self-confident. More Muslims died for their convictions during this Medinan period (circa. 622–632 C.E.) than during the previous Meccan period (circa 610–622), but their deaths occurred on the giving rather than receiving end of the stick.

Martyrdom in the Transition from Vulnerability to Power

Mecca was a trading depot, while Medina was an agricultural community. Muhammad and the early believers were offered shelter in Medina, but all the productive land had long since been claimed by the local inhabitants. After almost two years living at least partially on the public dole, Muhammad began sending some of his followers to engage in raids to gain needed resources. Muhammad had attracted followers from a number of different tribal groups, but his multi-tribal following, as might be expected, behaved according to the traditional tribal customs with which they were familiar. The natural "other tribe" for them—the target for their raids—was not unexpectedly the tribe that had banished Muhammad and his earliest and most loyal followers from their home in Mecca. But this tribe was the Quraysh, the very tribe to which Muhammad and his earliest followers belonged. Muhammad's daring raids stirred up the entire region because it broke from the old tribal taboo forbidding raids against one's own kinship group.[41]

Muhammad's community of believers rapidly began to view themselves as a kind of "super-tribe" (in Arabic, *umma*) that functioned in many respects like the tribes of the traditional pre-Islamic system. There were important differences as well, of course, as certain aspects of a general Islamic worldview began to emerge. One extremely significant difference was what would become the deep and abiding belief in an afterlife.

The afterlife is one of the most ubiquitous themes in the Qur'an. There is the Garden (*al-janna*),[42] and there is Gehenna (*jahannam*) or the Fire (*al-nar*).[43] The sheer number of references suggests the need to implant the concept of heaven and hell in the minds and hearts of a people that were initially uncomfortable with it. One of many contexts for the repetition of this theme is that of raiding or fighting the opponents of the early Muslims. The Qur'an repeatedly calls on the community to engage in raids as members of the new super-tribe of Islam, and the idiom for describing activity on behalf of the community is *fi sabil Allah*—in the path of God.

In a context in which God condemns those early Muslims who complained about the many casualties in the fighting, we find: "And what if you be killed or die in the path of God? Forgiveness and mercy from God are better than all that they amass. What if you die or are killed when you are gathered unto God?" (3:157–8). "Do not consider those killed in the path of God as dead. On the contrary, they are living with their Lord, who gives them sustenance" (3:169). Other verses explicitly mention a reward for dying while fighting in the path of God: "Let those fight in the path of God who sell the life of this world for the other. Whoever fights in the path of God, whether he be slain or victorious, We shall give him a vast reward" (4:74). "God has purchased of the believers their lives and their possessions in that they have the Garden, they fight in the path of God and kill or be killed. . . . So rejoice in the bargain that you have made with Him, for that is the mighty bliss (*al-fawz al-'azim*—or, supreme triumph)" (9:111). Some verses, such as 47:6, explicitly promise the victim entry into the Garden for dying while fighting in the path of God.

In the later Tradition literature, these who fight on behalf of God's religion are called *shuhada' al-ma'raka*, "battlefield martyrs," and they have the distinction of being referred to as martyrs both in this world and the next (*shuhada' al-dunya wal-akhira*). Other martyrs, such as those who are killed for their beliefs or while defending their families against brigands, are martyrs in the next world only (*shuhada' al-akhira*). According to Kohlberg, the category of martyrs was extended greatly after the decrease in the number of battlefield martyrs following the early conquests.[44] The extension moved in two directions. On the one hand, martyrdom became a means of extolling certain behaviors, such as performing one's religious duties as a Muslim.[45] On the other hand, those killed innocently by disease, fire or accident, in childbirth, or defending their homes were considered martyrs as a way of ensuring their entry into the Garden.[46]

Death in combat thus became established as "the noblest way to depart this life."[47] One finds in the Tradition literature the motif of the old man who rushes forth to die in battle, and some medieval Sunni sources depict mothers expressing gratitude at the news of their sons' death through battlefield martyrdom and forbidding mourning over them. At the same time, martyrdom became reduced to such a mundane level that some considered virtually any kind of painful death and suffering a form of martyrdom. Among Sufis, adepts could be living martyrs who are engaged in the "greater *jihad*" of fighting their own evil inclinations. According to this view, the battlefield martyr is only a martyr externally (*fil-zahir*) while the true martyr is one who has successfully slain his own person (*nafs*) while continuing to live according to the Sufi way of life.[48]

Martyrdom in Shi'ite Tradition

The idea of martyrdom and the redemptive nature of suffering reaches its apogee in Shi'ite Islam. Annually during the first ten days of the month of *Muharram*, devotees gather in Karbala, the place where Husayn, the grandson of the Prophet, was martyred by the forces of the Sunni religious establishment. There they lament and mourn his death with ritual self-flagellation and real physical distress in a kind of passion play of suffering and commemoration.

The death of Imam Husayn became a paradigm of selfless sacrifice and a source of salvation for Shi'ites through the intercession of the imams, as well as the interiorization and emulation of his suffering by the community.[49] This concept of redemptive suffering finds a parallel with the Jewish concept of "merit of the ancestors" (*zekhut avot*) and the Christian concept behind the act of granting indulgences. Although the martyrdom of Husayn is of greatest importance in Shi'ite martyrologies, among the Imami Shi'ites the martyr list is long and therefore, so is the list of those who may intercede on behalf of the believer.

As a result, various Shi'ite communities visit the graves and commemorate the martyrdoms of the martyrs through *ziyara*s (visitations at a level below the official hajj pilgrimage), the recitation of elegies (*marathi*), and the *taziya* or passion play, especially in relation to the shrine of Husayn. This particularly Shi'ite form of devotion tends to be condemned as a kind of idolatry by mainstream Sunnis and establishment figures.

While the power of martyrdom in Shi'ite ritual and consciousness has tended to encourage the emulation of martyrdom more among Shi'ites than among Sunnis, this trend seems to have shifted by the beginning of the twenty-first century. Modern Shi'ite "battlefield martyrdom" has become deeply acculturated by radicalized Sunni Muslim militants among Arab groups such as *al-Qa'ida* and its offshoots, and among Palestinian militants such as *Hamas*, *al-Jihad al-Islami* (Islamic Jihad), and the *Tanzim* of *al-Fatah*.

Notes

1. Judges 9:50.
2. I Samuel 31:4.
3. II Samuel 17:23.
4. I Kings 16:18–19.
5. Judges 16:30.
6. Genesis 22:1.
7. Genesis 22:19.
8. Shalom Spiegel, *The Last Trial: On the Legends and Lore of the Command to Abraham to Offer Isaac as a Sacrifice: The Akedah*, trans. Judah Goldin (New York: Schocken Books, 1969), 148–52.
9. II Maccabees 7:9; Edgar J. Goodspeed, trans., *The Apocrypha: An American Translation* (New York: Vintage Books, 1959).
10. II Maccabees 7:11.
11. II Maccabees 7:14.
12. II Maccabees 7:16.
13. II Maccabees 7:18.
14. II Maccabees 7:27.
15. II Maccabees 7:38.
16. Josephus, *The Jewish War*, trans. G.A. Williamson (Middlesex and Baltimore: Penguin Books, 1959), 360–61.
17. See Nachman Ben-Yehuda, *The Masada Myth: Collective Memory and Mythmaking in Israel* (Madison and London: The University of Wisconsin Press, 1995).
18. *Leviticus* 22:31.
19. *Amos* 2:7.
20. *Daily Prayerbook*.
21. *Sanhedrin*, 74a.
22. Jacob Neusner, *From Politics to Piety* (Englewood Cliffs: Prentice Hall, Inc., 1973).
23. Siddur, *Sim Shalom*, trans. Julius Harlow (New York: The Rabbinical Assembly and the United Synagogue of America, 1985).
24. Lawrence Langer, "The Dilemma of Choice in the Deathcamps," in *The Holocaust: Religious and Philosophical Implications*, ed. John K. Roth and Michael Berenbaum (New York: Paragon Books, 1989), 224.
25.　　Concentration Camp _____
　　　　Department II

I, (Mr./Mrs./Miss _____
born on _____
in_____
Herewith make the following declaration:

1.　　I acknowledge that the International Jehovah's Witness Association is disseminating erroneous teachings and using religion as a disguise merely to pursue subversive goals against the interests of the State.

2.   I have therefore completely left that organization and have also spiritually freed myself from the teachings of that sect.

3.   I herewith pledge that I will never again participate in the International Jehovah's Witness Association. I will immediately denounce any individual who solicits me with the heresy of the Witnesses or who in any manner reveals his affiliation with the Witnesses. Should Jehovah's Witnesses publications be sent to me, I will immediately deliver them to the nearest police department.

4.   In the future, I will obey the laws of the State, and particularly in the event of war, I will defend the Fatherland with weapon in hand and totally become part of the national community.

5.   I have been informed that should I violate today's declaration, I will again be arrested.

_____(place)_____(date)

_____
(Signature)

26. Saul Esh, "The Dignity of the Destroyed," *Judaism* 15, no. 1 (Winter 1966).

27. Yosef Gottfarstein, "Kiddush Hashem Over the Ages and its Uniqueness During the Holocaust Period," in *Jewish Resistance During the Holocaust: Proceedings of the Conference on Manifestations of Resistance*, ed. Meir Grubsztein (Jerusalem: Yad Vashem, 1972), 453–483.

28. See Irving Rosenbaum, *The Holocaust and Halachan* (New York: Kt'av Books, 1976) among other works for a description of religious Jewish and religious law's response to the Holocaust.

29. Lawrence Langer, *Versions of Survival* (Albany: State University of New York, 1982), 79–80.

30. The accent is on the second syllable. Arabic terms are here rendered in Latin characters and without diacritical marks.

31. Of 56 verses in which are found the term, *shahid*, only three refer to martyrs, and all appear in the context of martyr prophets rather than martyr warriors.

32. Helmer Ringgren, *Studies in Arabian Fatalism* (Upsala, 1955), 6–9.

33. Helmer Ringgren, 9–14; L. Gardet, "Al-qada' wa'l-qadar," in *The Encyclopaedia of Islam*, New ed. (henceforth, *EI²*) , 4: 365–67.

34. Both Ad and Himyar are tribal names.

35. Reuven Firestone, *Jihad: The Origin of Holy War in Islam* (New York: Oxford University Press, 1999), 28–29.

36. Ringgren, 57.

37. On the vast compendium of literatures that is called the Hadith, see J. Robson, "Hadith," EI², 3: 23–28.

38. Alfred Gulliaume, *The Life of Muhammad, A Translation of Ibn Ishaq's Sirat Rasul Allah* (Oxford: Oxford University Press), 143–144; Arabic, *Al-Sira al-Nabawiyya* (Beirut: Al-Dar al-Thiqafa al-Arabiyya, n.d.), 1: 317–19. Al-Lat and al-'Uzza were gods among the Meccan pantheon.

39. Guillaume, 145; Arabic, 1:320.

40. Some later texts, however, do consider her the first Muslim martyr. She is identified by Ibn Ishaq only as the mother of 'Ammar b. Yasir, but later tradition (and the editors of the Arabic edition) identifies her as Sumayya bt. Khayaat (Arabic, 1: 320, n.1).

41. It is interesting to note how the sources insist that Muhammad sent only members of his own tribe of Quraysh to engage in the first raids against the Quraysh tribe. This might have protected other tribes from retribution from the Quraysh, but it most certainly turned the old pre-Islamic tribal system upside down.

42. *Janna*, related to the Hebrew word *gan* (and Aramaic *ginna*), represents the Garden of Eden of Paradise. I count 148 references.

43. *Jahannam* is clearly related to the Hebrew *gey hinnom* (Gehenna), with 78 references. Another roughly 100 verses in the Qur'an refer to Hell as "the Fire" (*al-nar*).

44. Eitan Kohlberg, "Shahid," *EI²*, 9:205.

45. Ahmad b. Hanbal, *Musnad*, 6 vols. (Beirut: Dar al-Sadr, n.d.) 1:63, 237; 4:200.

46. "The man or woman who dies of plague is a martyr (*shahid*)" (Bukhari, *Sahih* [Lahore: Kazi, 1983] 7:422); "one who drowns is a martyr" (Abu Daud, *Sunan*, 4 vols. [Cairo: Dar al-Misriyya wal-Lubnaniyya, 1988] 3:7; "One who goes forth in the path of God and dies or is killed is a martyr . . . or [suffers] any kind of death is a martyr and has [a future life of] the Garden" (Abu Daud, 3:8–9); even, "The dead away from one's native country are martyrs (*mawt ghurbat^{in} shuhada'*)" (Ibn Maja, *Sunan*, 2 vols. [Beirut: al-Maktaba al-'ilmiyya, n.d.] 1:515).

47. Kohlberg, *EI²*, 9:205.

48. Kohlberg, *EI²*, 9:206.

49. Mahmoud Ayoub, *Redemptive Suffering in Islam* (The Hague: Mouton, 1978).

PART II

CHAPTER 5

A Conversation among the Collaborators

R. Fields: Let's start with a conversation about some of the connections between religion and politics. There are also several other issues about how martyrs are identified in literature and what is the role, as you see it, of literature in ascribing martyrdom? And what is the connection between suicide and martyrdom? This comes up because Valérie believes that in Islam the suicide bombers are recognized as martyrs. And there is evidence in the writings of Islamic theologians on both sides of that issue. Also, I have another perhaps side issue to consider; individuals immolate themselves in protest. I mentioned the Vietnamese mothers as an example and the Czech student, but returning to the definition of the term, they would not be so identified, right? I'm concerned that in attempting to be "Politically correct," the meaning of the idea becomes so diluted that there is nothing and everything.

C. Owens: OK. To begin with, in common usage (as indicated by the *American Heritage Dictionary*), the word "martyr" has four usages: one who chooses death rather than renounce religious principle; one who sacrifices something very important to further a belief or principle; one who endures great suffering; and one who makes a great show of suffering in order to arouse sympathy. Thus, this range of common usage raises a couple of the basic questions here: the choice of death (originating in the will of the martyr), the "witness" to a religious or other principle (larger than a material or self-interest); the price paid (one's life or something similarly valuable); and the way this is viewed by the outside world.

V. Rosoux: The phenomenon of suicide martyrdom is not specific to Islamic societies. From a historical perspective, we know that the phenomenon is also connected with other religions, for instance the Christian faith. Thus, even if numerous suicide attacks are nowadays linked with Islam (especially in the Middle East), it is by no means specific to that religion. The suicide attacks committed by Tamil Tigers in Sri Lanka provide a good example. Their cause is a national one, which means that religion is not a necessary condition to become a martyr. What is needed is the sacralisation of a cause presented and perceived as more important than individual life. Most of the time, this cause is national (that is the case in Kashmir, in Sri Lanka, in Palestine, or even in the war between Iran and Iraq from 1980 to 1988).

R. Fields: So if the winners, which I believe is correct at least in the short run, write history, their heroism would not be recognized immediately, of course.

M. Berenbaum: Actually, I have never accepted the idea that history was written by winners because my people seldom won and yet they continued to write. I think the "losers" authored some of the most powerful work ever written.

R. Fields: In the cases I described in my essay, those who were ascribed martyrdom met criteria numbers 2 and 3 on the definitions Cóilín provided. But what you are saying is that the protests and suicide bombing might meet the criteria in definition 4? In the cases I described, about the psychology of the martyr, these are individuals who meet criteria 2 and 3 and have chosen to live their beliefs, regardless of the hazards, rather than murder themselves or murder others in the course of murdering themselves. But you are suggesting that perhaps the age of martyrdom is not in the past, but for some individuals and groups in some parts of the world, is very much in the present?

V. Rosoux: Farhad Khosrokhavar also stresses a profound change in the number of martyrs. He explains that, in the history of Islam, the phenomenon of martyrdom traditionally had an exceptional character. Before the fourteenth century, cases of martyrdom were extremely rare. That aspect is in sharp contrast with the current proliferation of the term and the phenomenon.

C. Owens: In the strictest sense—validated by the great religious traditions (represented in my perspective by Christianity)—the term is reserved solely for those who willingly suffer violent death at the hands of others, for the sake of the Kingdom of God: that life has a transcendental meaning. This narrowest definition thus excludes those who did not die violently (who died natural deaths), who died by accident, or simply as victims of some outrage from which they could not have escaped even if they had the opportunity to do so, and those who are not recognized by any third party.

M. Berenbaum: There is no virtue in suffering according to Judaism though one may do much that is virtuous in response to suffering. At the core of Christianity is the image of Christ on the Cross, the suffering of the innocent, which redeems a sinful humanity. No such powerful image is found at the core of Judaism. In fact, the argument can be made that the core experience that shapes Judaism is the exodus from Egypt, the end of suffering. Now if there is no virtue in suffering, much virtue can be found in how we respond to suffering, which is prevalent in traditional literature and featured most prominently in post-Holocaust literature. Suffering confers no virtue. In fact, if we believe Holocaust survivors' testimonies, it destroys virtue. Wiesel writes, "Saints are those who died before the end of the story." Primo Levi writes, "Survival without the renunciation of any part of one's own moral world, apart from the powerful and direct interventions by fortune, was conceded only to very few superior individuals made of the stuff of martyrs or saints."

C. Owens: The cult of the martyrs in Christian tradition, while essentially rooted in the suffering and death of Christ, does not figure largely in the official liturgy except in cultures where the Church is under threat. So, while all Christians are required to bear witness to their faith in Christ Jesus, only the few are called to do so even unto death. Their witness bears witness to Christ who died and rose, to whom he is united in charity. The Church calendar commemorates the lives of the saints and the deaths of the martyrs as models for Christian emulation. The commemoration of the saints proffers examples of the virtuous quotidian—of lives of patient waiting of which little notice is taken by the world at large. Such lives require discipline, steadfastness, and to reach the goal, the cardinal virtue of hope. Of course, it is (happily) more relevant to most of us to learn to live well than to die heroically, knowing that one will enjoy a posthumous glory. The cult of the martyrs serves as an instruction on the virtue of fortitude in dealing nobly with extreme circumstances—where the delivery is swift and dramatic. So, in sum, whereas the saint faces the perils of despair, the martyr risks the adulteration of motive.

V. Rosoux: I would like to make another point: the necessity of avoiding a stereotyped view of Islamic societies. It is important not to deny the diversity and plurality that characterize these societies. In this respect, it might be useful to clarify the distinction between the dynamics of suicide attacks in Palestine, for instance, and suicide attacks by al Qaeda members in New York and Washington on September 11, 2001. In my view, the objectives and the profile of actors involved in these two cases are completely different. In his book called *Les Nouveaux Martyrs d'Allah* [The New Martyrs of Allah] (Paris: Flammarion, 2002), Farhad Khosrokhavar shows that there is no unique model of martyrdom. He stresses the distinction between martyrs of a "national cause" (in the Lebanese or Palestinian context) and martyrs of a "transnational cause" (for example, al Qaeda). According to him, the first ones are characterized by a deep feeling of humiliation—this humiliation resulting from a direct and daily experience of pain and suffering in the region where they live. By contrast, the humiliation of al Qaeda members who committed the suicide attacks of September 11 is of a more indirect nature. There is a second main difference between the two phenomena: Palestinian or Tamil martyrs identify themselves with a nation, while members of al Qaeda are culturally heterogeneous. They often speak various languages (some of them being fluent in three to six languages); some traveled all over the world and most of them have lived in the Western world (Paris, London, New York, Hamburg, and so on).

M. Berenbaum: We are also talking about innocent life, making no distinctions between combatants—actual or potential—women and children, the elderly, even Arabs and foreigners who have no relationship to the political situation.

R. Fields: In Islam, there is the *Shaheed* idea. That is, the person-soldier or civilian who dies as a consequence of the invasion of their country by an infidel is immediately martyred and goes to paradise. The concept of paradise in Islam is somewhat different from Judaism and Christianity, isn't it? I think that in all three monotheisms, there is no glorification of deliberately inviting death, or is there?

M. Berenbaum: The concept of paradise is present in all three faiths. It however is not present in the same form and not given the same credence in all three faiths at this moment in time. Martyrdom requires either a renunciation of this life as unimportant or unworthy or the sense that something is much more important than this life and that sense must be credible to the individual and perhaps the community.

C. Owens: Modern usage—journalistic, political, and even religious—embraces many actions that do not meet this definition. Early Church arguments went over these same grounds, and arrived at the strict definition I cite. Among the considerations that clearly exclude one from the claim of martyrdom is death by accident, suicide, or even drawing the fate upon oneself (deliberately taunting the would-be executioner), and committing heinous crimes in the process (such as the suicide bomber does). The suicide bomber thus meets only some of the criteria—enduring death for a disinterested cause, and gaining recognition (entering the tribal memory) for that action. The suicide bomber fails to meet the criteria that forbid suicide (the death must be primarily caused by another) and the taking of the lives of others who do not pose an immediate threat to oneself.

R. Fields: I am thinking that by the use of these definitions, we have a category under which to consider political ascription of martyrdom, but also to recognize the juncture between political and religious as suggested in my essay and in Michael's comments in our earlier discussion.

V. Rosoux: I would like to add something on the hypothesis of a pretended martyr's profile. In an article devoted to young Palestinians' martyrdom (*Politique étrangère*, October–December 2001), Pénélope Larzillière explains that it would be naive to think that the phenomenon can be reduced to a specific social category that would be particularly underprivileged. Politically speaking, suicide attacks are generally presented as the "power of the weak." In 2001, one of the leaders of Islamic Djihad in the Gaza Strip asserted: "We only have that option. We do not have bombs, tanks, missiles, planes, helicopters" (*ABC*, August 21, 2001). Accordingly, it is often argued that a disastrous political and economical context leads the population to a form of despair (to the feeling that "there is nothing to lose"). However, as Larzillière shows, suicide bombers are not always those who can be seen as having no future, some of them having a job and a family.

R. Fields: In my chapter on Palestinian suicide bombers, in Volume 2 of the *Psychology of Terrorism*, I reported on my clinical and social psychological study of the personality dynamics, demographics, and social histories/behaviors of the seven Gazan suicide bombers who acted in the early nineties after the Oslo accords had been generally accepted. These aspects were noted and compared with later suicide bombers and with members of terrorist groups from many other parts of the world. In conclusion, I had to recognize that whatever their chronological age, they were attracted to this course of action because they were truncated at the level of moral development/political socialization of Vendetta and had been persuaded that the act provided immediate transformation to a perfect way of being.

C. Owens: By the same criteria, then, neither the victims of the Holocaust nor of 9/11 are martyrs. Whether willing or not, they do not bear witness to a transcendent set of values. Both suffer death because of their ethnic or political identity. The hijackers are not martyrs because they took their own lives immediately and willingly. Claims to the title of "martyr" are political propaganda. This is evident in the quick denial of the status by mainstream Muslim clerics. In this condemnation, they are both correct and politically correct, in that seeming approval would have given Islam the disrepute of leading the naive to think that they would enjoy a Garden of Carnal Delights for their suicides.

M. Berenbaum: They actually were killed by accident. They were in the wrong place at the wrong time. They may have happened on the scene and the individuals were killed as a collateral damage of the desired carnage. So it is not correct to speak of suffering death—or being murdered to be more precise—for ethnic or political identity. The dead of 9/11 were from diverse nations and many different religions, rich and poor, American and non-American; that is what made reading the *New York Times*'s portraits so fascinating.

R. Fields: It seems to me that many violent acts that have resulted in martyrdom have been committed in the name of one or another "true religion" or "true God."

V. Rosoux: Khosrokhavar underlines two main arguments that are often presented to justify the death of innocent people. First, it is argued that the importance of the cause (national or religious) is such that it allows the sacrifice of innocents. The second argument is that the Western world behaves in a similar way (the classical example being the deaths of Iraqi children). The reasoning is then based on *reciprocity*: if they can do it, why would we not have the right to do it as well?

R. Fields: That is precisely the kind of moral reasoning that is Vendetta! Although King in his sermon after the bombing of the church in Birmingham and the death of the little girls does refer to them as martyrs or as a blood sacrifice, but not as martyrs because of willing their own destruction. They are martyrs because they were innocents who were murdered because they were, in King's words, "Negroes." I think that, sociologically and psychologically, this marks the distinction between heroes, martyrs, and victims. Thus, those who died as a consequence of the 9/11 attacks on the World Trade Center and the Pentagon were victims. Those responsible for their deaths are murderers except to their sympathizers, who have ascribed them martyr status and this also goes to the reason, Michael said, Holocaust victims were deaths without choice except for the Jehovah's Witnesses who had a chance to recant, or in the case of homosexuals (who were not Jewish), prove themselves otherwise.

M. Berenbaum: Certainly that is the case. There is a basic argument to be made that the Holocaust was committed in the name of God. At least, many perpetrators felt that they were acting in the name of the Lord for the sake of the Lord . . .

R. Fields: Of course we know that religion is as often hijacked, as are airplanes, to provide an excuse for violence or self-righteous indignation.

M. Berenbaum: . . . fulfilling the mandate of the Churches. Islam also has a violent side—most especially with the concept of *Dar al Islam,* Islamic lands and Judaism—at least in its Biblical and also in its current manifestation.

R. Fields: I wonder if there is a psychological archetype that legitimates violence justifying it on the grounds of divinity. Please elaborate on that.

M. Berenbaum: Judaism has the capacity for violence. Look at the commandment regarding the eradication of Amalek where the commandment is to eradicate even its remembrance, and some—few but a significant enough number to be worrisome—invoke Amalek to justify actions even today. Invoking God allows one to move beyond conventional morality and to accept the responsibility for acting like God, choosing who shall live and who shall die.

R. Fields: That is often cited as the basis for ethnic cleansing or genocide and the blame is placed on Jews, as if the God of the Jews invented it!

M. Berenbaum: Again, just because anti-Semites invoke certain teachings to cast aspersions on the Jews does not mean that these teachings cannot be problematic, though I hesitate to add fuel to the flames of anti-Semitism. I think we have to grapple with Amalek, but Amalek was no innocent; they refused an overture of peace and attacked from the rear, slaying women and children—the innocent.

R. Fields: As frequently cited are the instructions to Joshua to destroy the Canaanites.

M. Berenbaum: Again here, the reality is that the conquest of the land took time and evolved over centuries including the absorption of native populations into the children of the Israel. The Joshua story gives a harsh impression of conquest and is certainly vaulted in the Bible. That is why Biblical Judaism is more militant than its Rabbinic successor and some contemporary Israelis have returned to Biblical roots bypassing the cautions of Rabbinic Judaism.

R. Fields: In Biblical Judaism there are no martyrs, are there? There are prophets and heroes, but no martyrs.

M. Berenbaum: There are actually figures who chose to die. Saul chose to die rather than be shamed and be humiliated in defeat. Samson chose death as revenge. The concept of *Kiddush Hashem,* the Rabbinic term for martyrdom, clearly was later than the Bible, but it was present in contemporaneous literature to the Bible that did not quite make it into the canon, such as the book of Maccabees.

V. Rosoux: Among the various elements that can be at the origin of such actions (as suicide bombing) are: the attractive effect of a longer temporal perspective (the concept of *djihad* allows one to frame the fight in the very long run and therefore allows the individual to pass from the status of victim to the status of millenarian hero; the will to compete on the spiritual level with the Western world seen in the daily life as dominating at the economic, technical, and political level. In this line, the extreme aspect of self-sacrifice is perceived as the guarantee of one's absolute superiority vis-à-vis a Western world in distress. (Larzillière depicts this idea as a mixture of reject and fascination towards the Western world). We get back here to the humiliation aspect that has already been highlighted.

C. Owens: It is in the historical interest of any public religion or political entity to recognize martyrs—they advertise the values that justify the cause and encourage the members to remain faithful to their inheritance. Since religions deal with matters of conscience—the individual's relationship with the divine—they must take into primary consideration matters of intentionality. Political or ethnic identities are less intrusive and scrupulous in this regard, and thus can afford a broader or external definition, concerned with objective action and the perception of that action by the world at large. As you observe, in the secular world, modern psychology makes distinctions that parallel and refine those that we find in the religious culture of previous ages. Would you agree?

R. Fields: We generally recognize people like Gandhi and Martin Luther King, Jr., as martyrs, but, and this is the question I tried to raise in my essay, what about those who are tortured to death and made to disappear? Or, when a dictator ascribes to himself martyr-dom, as did Pinochet, most people laugh or scoff or become infuri-ated. But his followers equate his "sacrifice" with the crucifixion!

M. Berenbaum: In my essay I argue that there is a distinction be-tween the formal teachings of Judaism regarding martyrdom and its actual practice, most especially in the middle ages, when Jews lived in close proximity to Christians and absorbed willingly or unwillingly some of their teaching. The formal teaching of Judaism is that mar-tyrdom is required and indeed permitted only under the most rare of conditions and to avoid the most unacceptable of behavior: murder, impermissible sexual violation, and idolatry. Certainly in the Israeli emphasis on the Masada story where death was chosen over surren-der, and political freedom was placed above the value of life, you have a clash between the normative teachings of the tradition as they de-veloped in the Rabbinic period and the actual behavior of Jews in an earlier era and the reverence for such behavior in contemporary Israel where the Israeli Defense Forces would visit Masada and pledge Masada will not fall again, invoking the image of a battle unto death for freedom.

R. Fields: How does Judaism deal with the homicide/suicide of Masada?

M. Berenbaum: Josephus created the Masada myth as his way of grappling with the death of a community that refused to surrender. In the early Zionist period, preceding and just following the estab-lishment of the state of Israel, the Masada myth was important to in-culcate the value of freedom and the determination to fight unto death for that freedom. It is still a national shrine in Israel but, given the empowerment of Israel, there is less likelihood of a fight unto death and hence Masada plays a less prominent role than it once did. Rabbinic Judaism, which sought to restrict martyrdom only to those times when one would have to violate the life of another or the essence of life, regarded Masada as non-normative, indeed as anti-normative. It would not have been condoned by the rabbis who preached a path of compromise and who, indeed, trace their roots to Yavneh where Yochanan Ben Zakkai sacrificed political independence for religious continuity.

R. Fields: How does time and distance influence the ascription of martyrdom? For instance, I think according to Jewish folk religious tradition there was a time during the Crusades when all who died for the sanctification of the Name were ascribed martyrdom. That is, they refused to convert. There were also those who killed their children to prevent their being converted. In response to your last comments, however, I think that's the most universal description. Intentionality, or commitment with knowledge of the possible deadly consequences but determined to live the belief and to live to profess and act on the belief would express the psychology of the martyr. I think the capacity to make these choices, an indication of brain development, and the emotional and moral maturity that characterized the individuals I studied. The contrast is, of course, those motivated by vendetta, morally truncated at the second level of moral development, who, when inspired to act, commit carnage.

C. Owens: As Michael Berenbaum rightly observes, Christianity is founded on the martyrdom of Jesus Christ. The first Christian literature, the New Testament, is an account of that martyrdom (the Synoptic Gospels), an account of the beginnings of the historical reflection on that martyrdom (the Acts of the Apostles), the first theological reflections on it (John's Gospel, the Epistles), and its completion in history (Apocalypse/Revelation). Outside of this canonical body of texts, Christian literature about the martyrs begins with the Martyrology—a staple of early and medieval Christian pious reflection. Besides these and other official texts in Christian culture, there is the whole tradition from the mystery plays to treatments of the deaths of martyrs in the genres of secular literature. Broadly speaking, these texts celebrate the links between national cultures and Christian belief.

R. Fields: So the basis in some national cultures for ascription of martyrdom would be the similitude with the martyrdom of Christ? But of course, the question remains, if a tree falls in the forest and no one is aware of it, did the tree fall? And so also with martyrs. If an individual is tortured for their beliefs and their identity and dies of the torture but "disappears" they cannot be ascribed martyrdom, or, only after their fate is ascertained? I question the role played by the media response to the death. I think that the quality of communication in the last century and how it is possible now for general recognition to occur simultaneously whereas in the past it was a convergence of the historical and political moments that ascribed the status.

M. Berenbaum: It adds many voices to the conversation, but history is not merely the amassing of facts but their interpretation and I am not sure that we could see the story amidst the many sources of information.

R. Fields: At the beginning of my essay, or early in it, I suggested that in the blood sacrifice of the principals to the Easter Rising (in

Ireland), the media of the time contributed to the popularization and recruitment to the struggle for Irish nationhood. I was challenged about the use of the word "media" so I explained that the pamphlets, posters, and broadsides were the media of the day and place. Later, plays, poems, and other literature took over and mythologized or reported on these individuals and events. If history is written by the winners, then it takes a very long time for the proponent of an unpopular cause to reach the moment of recognition. Today, with instant international communications, we are still subject to the balance of power in determining whose bravery we recognize and who becomes dust. And now, to the question of literature: I mentioned at the beginning of my essay, "the media," in reference to the deaths of Pearse et al, in the Easter Rising. I meant of course, that the literature that evolved from their blood sacrifice identified them as martyrs to Irish nationalism. The media of the time was poetry and prose in broadsides and pamphlets. How does this fit with the literary determination of ascription of martyrdom and can it only be post hoc? Does the contemporary literary or media make a definition?

C. Owens: Secular literature about martyrs acknowledges the links between a national culture and religious belief: Chaucer's pilgrims—whatever their differences in temperament and storytelling capacities—share a double allegiance to Christianity and Englishness. We get a whole variety of treatments of Joan of Arc from Voltaire, Mark Twain, G.B. Shaw, Verdi, Tchaikovsky, and Shakespeare: where she is celebrated and derided as visionary, naif, slut, saint, deluded, goddess, hero. The weight of memorialization finally brought the Church around, so that her Christian martyrdom was not acknowledged until 1920, over 400 years after her fiery exit.

R. Fields: I think we want to consider Jeanne D'Arc in much the same way. She became a religious/political martyr and her Sainthood was attributed 400 years after the fact. I think that psychologically we need "martyrs" and we need heroes. Some people need to view themselves as victims whether or not it can be objectively ascribed. And in some instances, in order to conceive a hero there must be a vulnerable population of victims or prospective victims for the hero to save and then, if the hero meets an untimely death while advocating for these people or cause he or she may be martyred. But the definitions Cóilín puts forth also require suffering, and accepting suffering might be an important criterion. Another question I have is about whether a particular action, like protest actions, have resonance as martyrdom. I mentioned the Vietnamese mothers in the refugee camp and also Jan Palach, who immolated himself in Prague to protest the Russian occupation, and now five more young people have immolated themselves in Prague to protest the war in Iraq. Then there are people protesting who got their beliefs, like the anti-war protesters at Kent State University did many years ago. They were protesting the extension of the war to Cambodia and were shot and killed by National Guardsmen. Are they martyrs? For a while they were icons for the anti-war movement. Now they are generally considered victims of the ill-considered violence of a group of soldiers, many of whom were no older than the students they killed.

V. Rosoux: Since 1431, Jeanne d'Arc is a very important symbol in France. In 1997, a survey indicated that she was considered as the fifth most important figure in French history—after de Gaulle, Napoléon, Charlemagne, and Louis XIV, but before Robespierre, Henri IV, or Clémenceau (*L'Histoire*, May 1997). The most interesting point about the political uses of Jeanne d'Arc during the twentieth century is that they pursued contrasting and sometimes contradictory finalities. At the end of the nineteenth century, Jeanne d'Arc was simultaneously evoked by French political leaders from the Left and the Right of the political spectrum: Socialists depicted her as defending the poor and destitute people, while the Catholic French bourgeoisie described her as the messenger of God. During the First World War, the function of Jeanne d'Arc was not any longer to defend one particular component of the French society but to foster national unity. In that light, official representatives highlighted her unceasing resistance against the external enemy. The purpose of national unity remained decisive after the war. The number of statues and monuments representing the young Jeanne is telling in that regard. During the Second World War, Jeanne d'Arc was compared with Philippe Pétain *and* Charles de Gaulle, according to the speaker. For some, Jeanne d'Arc was the symbol of the resistance against the British, depicted as the ancestral enemy (*La Gerbe*, May 15, 1941). For others, Jeanne d'Arc was associated with the action of Charles de Gaulle. In this case, the enemy was not Britain but Germany. This ambivalent and teleological character of Jeanne d'Arc's memory did not only appear in connection with the two World Wars. During the Algerian War, people from both camps (in favor of or against the independence of Algeria) underlined their fidelity towards Jeanne d'Arc. Those who were against independence considered that, as Jeanne d'Arc, they were saving the "Patrie" in great danger, whereas some others stressed that she was a symbol of the liberation of oppressed people. More recently, political leaders like Jean-Marie Le Pen (on the far right) and Jacques Chirac have also referred to her memory. In a very nationalistic speech, Jean-Marie Le Pen called on her to save France from the "new invaders"—referring to the immigrants (May 1, 1996). In reaction, President Jacques Chirac emphasized that the attitude of Jeanne d'Arc has nothing to do with the ideas of hatred and contempt: "Her words are at the opposite of any discourse of intolerance, reject, violence that some people did not hesitate to express in her name" (May 8, 1996).

These examples show that the symbol of Jeanne d'Arc has been used by almost all political tendencies. In 1884, Joseph Favre, a French deputy, explained that "Jeanne does not belong to any specific party because she belongs to France." Ten years later, Monsignor Gonthe-Soulard claimed that in fact "Jeanne belongs to the Church." Like him, almost each representative seemed to consider that "Johanna nostra est." There is not *one* memory of Jeanne d'Arc but *various* memories of her, according to the context and the political objectives pursued by the actors. This should not come as a surprise since political uses of the past are always dictated by present realities.

R. Fields: But her martyrdom, as celebrated in literature, defined her with so much certainty that many statues were erected before 1920, and what would make the difference amongst the literary treatments on how her martyrdom or not was perceived by the public? And of course, her ascension to sainthood would mean that miracles were ascribed to her. Was that all pre-1920? I guess what I'm trying to examine is the way ascription of martyrdom is at least in part the function of literature (or the media in the broadest sense). But literature plays a second part in martyrdom, besides the ascription, it establishes icons for the imagination or memory/emotion of the larger public.

C. Owens: I chose the Eliot play because it scrutinizes the levels of motivation most scrupulously. In writing the play, Eliot had plenty of circumstantial documents concerning the conflicts between Henry and Thomas, Rome and the English monarchy. But he developed the dramatic argument from the distinctions made by the theological tradition, and not from any spiritual diary or posthumous autobiography. In the cases of other martyrs—the Irish ecclesiastic Oliver Plunkett who was executed in Tyburn in 1681, for example—we have a similar set of externals: a conflict which is overdetermined by political and religious and, indeed, personal considerations. Oliver Plunkett (belatedly, Saint) was executed on the official justification of treason against the English state, although he was not a political agitator. His offense was his station as archbishop in a proscribed church. And doubly ironically, some minor ecclesiastics whom he had censured for simony betrayed him.

R. Fields: Plunkett, Becket, and Jeanne D'Arc all held to their beliefs, recognizing their endangerment therefrom and choosing to live practicing these, but were betrayed and killed. Their beliefs were at the time of their martyrdom, unpopular beliefs and politically adverse.

C. Owens: I wonder whether you would agree that the roles of literature, religion, and psychology are similar in the respect that each seeks to distinguish, for the purpose of proper memorialization, the true from the opportunistic claim?

R. Fields: Certainly in clinical practice, it is essential to determine whether a patient is presenting a predicament of bona fide persecution or is paranoid as diagnosed. In that sense, of course, the idea of commitment regardless of consequences may be a symptom of grandiosity typical of mental illness, or a genuine, sincerely held belief and value system. I suppose that the way a clinician would make this determination is through knowledge of the patient's objective circumstances, and lengthy interview/psychological testing. It is quite common for hospitalized patients to present their confinement as proof of their martyrdom and persecution. It's quite another matter, for an individual who is a political exile and has a declared price on his head or public threat against his or her life to remain steadfast and determined to profess his or her beliefs. In some instances, among those I examined and referenced in my essay, they have clear indices of traumatic stress syndrome, but that has not contradicted the reality of their vulnerability. And of course, it's legion that every convicted offender, almost, proclaims that he was "framed."

C. Owens: Plunkett, Becket, and Jeanne D'Arc are parallel cases in that they are Christians martyred by other Christians. The complications arise from the cross-purposes of sectarian, political, and ecclesiastical interests. Nothing as clear as in the cases of the Maccabees or Saint Catherine, where pagan monarchs do the damage. Hitler's no-god is Nietzsche. In an effort to vindicate his predecessor (by six) Henry VIII had Thomas's bones dug up and destroyed. Eliot's play is an attempt to reverse this reversal. The belated canonization of Jeanne was, no doubt, in large part due to the fact that the Church allowed itself to be the tool of the English in trying and condemning her in the first place. The Church is not given to the *volte-face*! Plunkett's case was not pursued until the twentieth century. No doubt, the Irish Church in the nineteenth century did not wish to play into Fenian hands and embarrass the British.

R. Fields: It is political in ascription, but psychological insofar as the individuals who become these icons. Literature provides a "mass memory," a nearly indestructible and accessible record that is, albeit susceptible to politics, less limited than the historian in recounting winners and losers as politically driven distinctions.

M. Berenbaum: Actually, in Judaism, martyrdom does not require a witness who will tell the story, merely the oppressor and the killer. There are many martyrs whose stories were never told and whose names were never known. Nevertheless, they were martyrs.

C. Owens: The issue of the mental state of any claimant to martyrdom must naturally arise. What they all have in common is an indomitable antipathy to the prevailing culture. And in the short term at least, that culture gets to write the diagnosis. It is only when the sharers of the martyr's values get to write their account that the subnormal become reevaluated as supernormal.

R. Fields: And because the human brain and the capacities of the human being have remained constant over time, the expression of ideas more than the mortal flesh provides the evidence for judgment in the larger arena. But also for this reason, there are constants and consistencies among the individuals and acts accepted as heroic even if there are religious differences in attribution of martyrdom. Shakespeare's statement, that "evil men do live on after them while the good is oft interred with their bones," is contradicted when the literature renews their existence. I suppose that the elevation of a dissident into a deity or the depiction of the Deity as dissident is the totem (in Freud's terminology) that guides the psyche of the "martyr elect." On the other hand, in Biblical terms, women who suffered were answered when they prayed for relief; for example, Hannah, who was childless, and Sarah, who was answered with pregnancy.

M. Berenbaum: Yes, but that is not martyrdom; that is the fate of the barren women at a time when having children was both an important confirmation of status and significant to one's own self worth.

R. Fields: Perhaps Samson's choices reflect the human condition as regards the choice of martyrdom, but also tinged with his own sense of guilt, which is what many of the psychoanalytic theorists would define as the nexus of violence.

M. Berenbaum: There is a basic difference between suffering and martyrdom. Suffering can be for the sake of God or not. Please explain Samson in psychoanalytic terms. I do not understand it.

R. Fields: That psychoanalytic interpretations of violence, as in martyrdom, engage the apocalyptic idea of death and rebirth, but are fueled by feelings of shame and guilt: sexual fantasies of the forbidden.

M. Berenbaum: I still don't understand it in Samson's case. He was duped by his sexual companion and humiliated by the Philistines and thus took them out with him. He did not initiate the violence but was responsive to it—answered it with violence.

R. Fields: But the psychoanalytic interpretation would be that he wanted Delilah and the sexual fantasies that her being promote, and that fueled his guilt and erupted into violence. But you see, that could also be argued to explain the 9/11 suicide bombers! The explanation would be that these surging and complex feelings generated by self denial, guilt, and displaced anger were mobilized through the Jihad directive to kill and thus achieve redemption (rebirth) in Islam.

M. Berenbaum: I'm not sure what we do with the interpretation except to recognize the ingredients that go into such violence.

R. Fields: But as we know, Freud, in *Totem and Taboo*, utilized Biblical metaphors to explain the Oedipal drives. I think it is important to distinguish between theology and religion as such. Is there a theological basis for ascribing martyrdom and criteria, or not, and in which theological framework?

M. Berenbaum: Theology is the legitimation by doctrine and elite formulation of what may have an entirely different origin and takes religious forms. Certainly on a manifest level religion is an important motivation and theology is offered as an explanation and justification, offering a plausibility to an act that seems implausible.

R. Fields: Let's go back to your comments, Valérie, on the definitions. I like what you said about the place of political memory in the establishment of martyrdom. I think that cuts across all theological perspectives. So I think we are on pretty good ground when we consider the definitions as presented by Cóilín Owens.

V. Rosoux: Politically speaking the qualification of an act as martyrdom does not really depend on the act itself or on an abstract definition but rather on the political interests and circumstances. It was obvious in the French case and I have the feeling that the process is the same as far as suicide bombers are concerned. One element in support of that view is that some extremist leaders call for actions leading to martyrdom whereas other spiritual leaders explicitly reject the religious character of these acts. It is striking that those condemnations of suicide attacks are made on behalf of Islam, arguing that such actions result from a wrong interpretation of the faith (see,

for example, the reactions of the Saudi Mufti Cheikh Abdel Aziz al-
Cheick). These two contradictory reactions (active encouragement
on the one hand and clear condemnation on the other) indicate that
the claim to the title of martyr does not exclusively depend on the act
itself. I fully agree with the comments of Cóilín here.

R. Fields: I recall the very chaotic days of 1982–84 in Beirut when I
was with reporters and discussing crimes in the street against foreigners and the danger threatening all of us. (This was prior to the kid-
nappings of reporters and professors.) None of them wanted to report
these instances and indicators because of constraints by the Lebanese
government and the governments of the media they represented. In
fact, on another level, as an academic, I brought my students with me
to meet with and study the survivors of the Sabra/Shatila massacre. At
the time, the Lebanese secret police were taking men and boys away
and they were never heard from again. We saw that. And because I was
documenting this with students, the CIA gave the message to the administration of the university, that I was a hazard to security. In fact, it
was a hazard to the secrecy and political will of all of these "powers."
They felt such knowledge was dangerous and I was ordered to leave
the university. That was the beginning of their strategy to turn,
through terrorism, the losers into the political powers of Lebanon. The
effort by the government to squash communication eventuated in their
own demise. I think that the current war in Iraq provides excellent opportunities to realize the varieties of media presentations and the many
directions that "facts" can be taken. At the end of the day, instant or de-
layed, the means of communication are themselves political. I am reminded of the quote, "Freedom of the Press belongs to those who own
it." If we accept the idea that martyrdom is designated by the community, then haven't we lost a sense of universality? Is martyrdom an in-
strumental idea, or a purposeful act?

M. Berenbaum: No act, so deeply personal, can be undertaken in the
abstract. It is concrete—undertaken by a person either for the most
personal of reasons or because he or she values something communal
above their own personal life. But these suicide/homicides are thinking of the group or are so immersed in the group or the spirit that
they are willing to pay with their life.

R. Fields: The sense of one's own mortality, or mortality itself,
comes even later than 16—possibly at 18 or 20 years old or older, depending on the individual's experiences and education. There is little
recognition at 13 or 16 of mortality. The value of a human life as
irretrievable and irreplaceable is incomprehensible in adolescence.

That's why adolescent drivers take risks, and that's also why people under the influence of alcohol whose frontal lobes are dulled do not recognize hazards and consequences.

M. Berenbaum: So is it the youth of these suicide/homicide that leads them to action? The reality is that the perpetrators of 9/11 were older. Some were married so something else was operating there.

R. Fields: But there are individual exceptions and I mentioned one, the young Cambodian boy, and another, of course, was Gandhi. I think that perhaps if one were to take Biblical texts as descriptive formulations of valued traits and behaviors we might look at the young Samuel, or as Christians do, the young Jesus. Suicide/homicide/martyr seekers who are chronologically older are not necessarily emotionally mature. Some, many in fact, become truncated at a level of moral development Piaget that described as Level 2-Vendetta. This has more to do with motivation and emotion than with cognitive processes. They view their suicide/homicide as a "good for action" because they do not value the lives of their victims and believe that their own lives are immortally enhanced by this action—the ultimate vengeance. Members of terror organizations identify only with their own group. They live in a we versus they cosmos and if they are dictators or leaders of insurgent groups, declare that a good death is the death perceived for and a bad death is when one of their own is killed. Can we relate this phenomenon to the Biblical interpretations on the choice of life or death? For instance, the sacrifice of Isaac and other interpretations that deal with this choice of life or choice for death.

M. Berenbaum: Martyrdom involves choice. The decision to undertake an act with the full knowledge that one will die and perhaps that one may die. Victims can be heroes, but not martyrs. Heroes can be victors and not martyrs. Victims can be heroes in the way they bear their suffering, in their dignity and self sacrifice, decency and compassion for others. The image of Christ on the cross, the suffering of the innocent, which by its "chosenness" redeems a sinful humanity, represents the centrality of Martyrdom in Christianity. No such powerful image is found at the core of Judaism. In fact, the argument can be made that the core experience that shapes Judaism is the exodus from Egypt, the end of suffering. Now if there is no virtue in suffering, much virtue can be found in how we respond to suffering, which is prevalent in traditional literature and featured most prominently in post-Holocaust literature. In fact, if we believe Holocaust survivors' testimonies, suffering destroys virtue. Wiesel writes, "Saints are those who died before the end of the story." Primo Levi writes "Survival without the renunciation of any part of one's own moral world—apart from the powerful and direct interventions by fortune—was conceded only to very few superior individuals made of the stuff of martyrs or saints."

R. Fields: If we take the core experience of Judaism as the exodus which symbolized freedom from suffering, might we also take the forty years in the wilderness as a kind of self-sacrifice for purification? From the mentality of slavery, to the dignity of freedom? Is that self-sacrifice the expurgation or the exhilaration? What does the promise of a hereafter in Judaism contribute to making the self-sacrifices for purification through the mitzvot?

M. Berenbaum: This speaks to the valuing of something communal over the individual's own personal life, but it is not martyrdom.

R. Fields: Some have described the use of martyrdom as the designation and the practice of homicide/suicide as the hijacking of religion. How do you, as a theologian, view it?

M. Berenbaum: By its very definition, homicide/suicide violates everything I regard as religious.

R. Fields: Choice itself is predicated on maturity. It requires alternatives and recognition of alternatives. When I score the motivation of a subject, I attribute varying values to the recognition of alternatives. The young people who immolate themselves in protest are killing themselves but not others. The suicide bomber may be the same age but they are motivated differently. Choice, or motivation, to achieve an objective is the psychological definition of commitment. But how might we account for the choice of death to communicate a protest or to prove a commitment?

M. Berenbaum: There is no achievement without risk, most especially dangerous achievement or provocative ones. Martyrdom is another matter. Do they hate themselves or are they in love with the world so much that they seek to transform it and improve it, make it more wonderful, just, beautiful. Certainly in my essay I am exploring the question of this world and the next, the values that are essential in this world and what is forbidden to transgress even at the cost of death.

R. Fields: But if they love life, they do not love enough to live in it and seek and take actions that would make life more wonderful, just and beautiful.

M. Berenbaum: On that we are agreed.

R. Fields: . . . make choices on a mature level. Yet, children or adolescents age 13 are confirmed and have bar and bat mitvahs in Christianity and Judaism, respectively. How does that commitment comport with adult choice?

M. Berenbaum: Wars are also fought by the young. I wonder if the sense of vulnerability increases with age and relates to maturation.

R. Fields: Choice, psychologically, requires alternatives and recognition of alternatives. When I score the motivation of a subject, I attribute varying values to the recognition of alternatives and realistic means for achievement. That's why youngsters and adults who have been politically and economically suppressed have less realization of the choice possibilities. But equally significant is the development of the brain that permits mature judgment and initiative because the capacity to imagine alternatives is inherent in that brain development.

M. Berenbaum: Perhaps in our age such adult-like maturity comes at 16, not 13, comes at the age of the driver's license and not at puberty.

R. Fields: An individual at the second stage of moral development determines their response to a perceived injustice on the basis of who is the "hurter" and how he (the chooser) is related to the victim.

M. Berenbaum: But when one lived to only 40 or 45, by 15 one had lived one-third of one's life.

R. Fields: And at that level, the choice of behavior, as well as the judgment of the behavior at issue, is based on identification with the recipient/victim and vendetta. At that level of development or age it is a rare child who can think abstractly in universals. And that is probably why tribal warfare and intergenerational vendetta were so commonplace in the historical periods when the majority of people died earlier and probably developed or truncated in a different manner. That was one of the descriptions of Gandhi's early life that struck me as remarkable—the report that he engaged in games of moral judgment and choice at an early age.

M. Berenbaum: An opposition to the culture that persecutes and kills them or demands their sacrifice, but they may well be deeply rooted in another culture.

R. Fields: You had suggested in our live talk something about different interpretations of the sacrifice of Isaac and I would like to know more about that and other interpretations that deal with this choice of life or choice for life.

M. Berenbaum: The sacrifice of Isaac is a problematic story on so many levels. The Bible actually records it as the test of Isaac. See the introductory lines of the story. The binding of Isaac is but a subtheme and certainly not the overriding one until much later when commentaries understood that continuing faith entailed a price and a risk not only for oneself but for one's children. Later in the middle ages there were even those who claimed Isaac was slaughtered and resurrected, believing against belief and against the plain meaning of the text that their own children—their Isaacs—might be resurrected.

R. Fields: What does the belief and promise of a hereafter contribute to realizing the commandments, the *mitzvot?*

M. Berenbaum: The simplest answer is that since reward is not apparent in this world, it is deferred into the next. And in the next the accounting for deed and fate will be balanced. The result is justice.

R. Fields: According to Lifton's arguments in *Death After Life* and *The Broken Connection,* every person has a desire for immortality and there are several different ways to achieve it. Perhaps for them martyr ascendance to the next world is that achievement. But one cannot seek immortality that way if the individual doesn't believe in a "hereafter" either for justice or paradise.

M. Berenbaum: As to Lifton, surely we each have a desire for immortality either through our descendants or our reputation or through prolonging our own life to the immortal. One can achieve immortality through accomplishments in this world without belief in the next.

R. Fields: This is an important issue—the timing of recognition. I think Gandhi and King were recognized as such at the time of their death. So also with the Irish hunger strikers. But many of the others are belatedly recognized. So what is the role of literature in ascribing and memorializing the lives of martyrs? There are some examples you mentioned in earlier conversation, for instance Oliver Plunkett and Thomas Moore and Jeanne D'Arc and of course, the significance of T.S. Eliot in memorializing Thomas à Becket through *Murder in the Cathedral.* It seems to me that Eliot managed in that play to define Martyrdom. I think also that Shakespeare significantly did not define as martyrs most of his heroes in tragedies, and there must be a reason for that.

C. Owens: The movement in modern Christian studies to ascertain who precisely is "the historical Christ" produces the pattern that whereas he thought that he was giving people a reasonable advice with respect to the imminent end of the world, the second generation of followers (not having seen that occur), turned him into a martyr for a transcendent set of values, presaged by his resurrection. Official memorialization takes on an ecclesiastical cast, and produces the tradition of self-deluded imitators. Nevertheless, even in this reading, Jesus is still a martyr in behalf of a purified Judaism or in resistance to an imperial Rome. The notion of literature as transcending history by a process of elevation into "classic" and "inferior" has been much argued about in recent literary theory. The argument that all literary values are fundamentally political—and thus, in our context here merely a form of memorialization for the more socially ascendant classes—is the exaggeration of a position that is quite reasonable: that we are all—writers and readers—historically contingent, but some of us, to paraphrase Orwell, are less contingent than others. That is why I think that Eliot's play is a superior memorialization of a martyr than, say, Greene's *The Power and the Glory*. It is superior in its uses of the resources of the English language, the literary tradition, and its investigation of the essential issues attendant upon martyrdom, whether viewed politically, theologically, or psychologically.

R. Fields: And that is precisely the reason I wanted you and your interpretation of this work to be the literary preamble that sets the parameters of discourse on the idea of martyrdom. Can you bring your earlier definitions into summarizing our conversation?

C. Owens: Defined in my perspective and contemporized, I would add that martyrdom is a radical protest on behalf of transcendent values against social conventions that always threaten those values. Sacrifices like that of Masada serve as a notice to Rabbinic Jewry that being faithful to God requires vigilance against comfortable compromises that slowly erode the transcendent values without which a religious worldview has no meaning. Similarly, the peace and justice witness of the Berrigan brothers, costing them years of imprisonment, requires us to examine our own assumptions about the justice of the development of a nuclear force capable of total mutual destruction.

R. Fields: I believe this conversation is endless and absorbing. We find ourselves stimulated to new ideas through each other's reflections. Hopefully, our ideas about martyrdom and our conversation about each other's ideas and our own will be elaborated through each reader's contribution to a public and international conversation. We have reached the end of our allotted space long before exhausting the subject.

INDEX

About the Series Editor and Advisory Board

CHRIS E. STOUT, Psy.D., MBA, holds a joint governmental and academic appointment in Northwestern University Medical School, and serves as Illinois's first Chief of Psychological Services. He served as an NGO Special Representative to the United Nations, was appointed by the U.S. Department of Commerce as a Baldridge Examiner, and served as an advisor to the White House for both political parties. He was appointed to the World Economic Forum's Global Leaders of Tomorrow. He has published and presented more than 300 papers and 29 books. His works have been translated into six languages.

BRUCE E. BONECUTTER, Ph.D., is Director of Behavioral Services at the Elgin Community Mental Health Center, the Illinois Department of Human Services state hospital serving adults in greater Chicago. He is also a Clinical Assistant Professor of Psychology at the University of Illinois at Chicago. A clinical psychologist specializing in health, consulting, and forensic psychology, Bonecutter is also a longtime member of the American Psychological Association Taskforce on Children & the Family.

JOSEPH FLAHERTY, M.D., is Chief of Psychiatry at the University of Illinois Hospital, a Professor of Psychiatry at the University of Illinois College of Medicine, and a Professor of Community Health Science at the UIC College of Public Health. He is a Founding Member of the Society for the Study of Culture and Psychiatry. Dr. Flaherty has been a consultant to the World Health Organization, to the National Institutes of Mental Health, and also the Falk Institute in Jerusalem.

MICHAEL HOROWITZ, Ph.D., is President and Professor of Clinical Psychology at the Chicago School of Professional Psychology, one of the nation's leading not-for-profit graduate schools of psychology. Earlier, he served as Dean and Professor of the Arizona School of Professional Psychology. A clinical psychologist practicing independently since 1987, his work has focused on psychoanalysis, intensive individual therapy, and couples therapy. He has provided Disaster Mental Health Services to the American Red Cross. Dr. Horowitz's special interests include the study of fatherhood.

SHELDON I. MILLER, M.D., is a Professor of Psychiatry at Northwestern University and Director of the Stone Institute of Psychiatry at Northwestern Memorial Hospital. He is also Director of the American Board of Psychiatry and Neurology, Director of the American Board of Emergency Medicine, and Director of the Accreditation Council for Graduate Medical Education. Dr. Miller is also an Examiner for the American Board of Psychiatry and Neurology. He is Founding Editor of the American Journal of Addictions and Founding Chairman of the American Psychiatric Association's Committee on Alcoholism.

DENNIS P. MORRISON, Ph.D., is Chief Executive Officer at the Center for Behavioral Health in Indiana, the first behavioral health company ever to win the JCAHO Codman Award for excellence in the use of outcomes management to achieve health care quality improvement. He is President of the Board of Directors for the Community Healthcare Foundation in Bloomington, and has been a member of the Board of Directors for the American College of Sports Psychology. He has served as a consultant to agencies including the Ohio Department of Mental Health, Tennessee Association of Mental Health Organizations, Oklahoma Psychological Association, the North Carolina Council of Community Mental Health Centers, and the National Center for Health Promotion in Michigan.

WILLIAM H. REID, M.D., MPH, is a clinical and forensic psychiatrist and consultant to attorneys and courts throughout the United States. He is Clinical Professor of Psychiatry at the University of Texas Health Science Center. Dr. Miller is also an Adjunct Professor of Psychiatry at Texas A&M College of Medicine and Texas Tech University School of Medicine, as well as a Clinical Faculty member at the Austin Psychiatry Residency Program. He is Chairman of the Scientific Advisory Board and Medical Advisor to the Texas Depressive & Manic-Depressive Association, as well as an Examiner for the American Board of Psychiatry & Neurology. He has served as President of the American Academy of Psychiatry and the Law, as Chairman of the Research Section for an International Conference on the Psychiatric Aspects of Terrorism, and as Medical Director for the Texas Department of Mental Health and Mental Retardation.

About the Author and Contributors

RONA M. FIELDS, Ph.D., is a psychologist and sociologist whose research and publications have centered on violence and social change. Her work on terrorism and the psychological profile of the prospective terrorist has been widely published. Her work on the psychological effects of terrorization has been internationally recognized and is seminal to programs dealing with the psychological consequences of the current state of terrorism alert in the United States. Beginning in 1962 as one of the first Community Psychologists in the country for the Board of Health, City of Chicago, she worked with impoverished young adolescents in a black ghetto, to southern California where she became involved with the then nascent Chicano movement. Her work has wedded clinical psychological assessment with sociological research on social and political issues such as racism, gender discrimination, human rights, and intercommunal violence. She taught at California State University–Northridge, California State University–Los Angeles, and California State University–Long Beach, as well as Pacific Oaks College and Pasadena City College. She founded, in east Los Angeles, with the Brown Berets, the first Chicano Free Clinic. She was awarded, in 1969, the Gamma Phi Delta Award for Distinguished Community Service. In 1970 she was granted her doctorate by the University of Southern California. She received the Sterling Price Williams Award for the Outstanding Graduate in Psychology from Lake Forest

College and her M.A. in Psychology from Loyola University of Chicago. She is Senior Research Consultant and Fellow at The Center for Advanced Defense Studies (CADS) in the School of Engineering at George Washington University in Washington, D.C.

Her research and work in Northern Ireland, Israel, Lebanon, South Africa, southeast Asia, Chile, Portugal, and the former Portuguese African colonies has been reported in her books *Society on the Run*, *Society Under Siege, Northern Ireland*, and *The Portuguese Revolution and the Armed Forces Movement*. She was Associate Professor of Sociology and Women's Studies at Clark University. Her book, *The Future of Women*, is a compilation of her data-based research and wide-ranging studies of the social psychology and politics of gender. She has authored American Psychological Association Monographs, book chapters including "The Science of Forensic Opinions" in Schiffman et al., *Ethics in Forensic Science and Medicine* and "Palestinian Suicide Bombers" in the four-volume set, *The Psychology of Terrorism*, edited by Chris Stout. She is a frequent media commentator. Her research on the cognitive and affective development of children growing up in violence was featured in the CNN series, *Waging Peace*, 1989.

She is a Fellow in the American Psychological Association and has been recognized by her peers with many citations. Dr. Fields lives in Washington, D.C., where she is the founder and Director of Associates in Community Psychology, a clinical and consulting organization.

Her children, now grown and themselves professional writers, educators, and entrepreneurs, accompanied her on many of her research studies, ranging from the Los Angeles Zoo to Northern Ireland and the European continent.

CÓILÍN OWENS is Associate Professor of English at George Mason University in Fairfax, Virginia. He has published widely on the Literature of Ireland, including Irish drama, Maria Edgeworth, the Irish language, and James Joyce. His education in Scholastic Philosophy and Theology has enabled him to develop his interest in Christian Literature. He has taught courses in Bible as Literature, Christian classics, and the Catholic tradition in twentieth-century literature. In addition to his university teaching, he has conducted many popular courses in Irish culture and literature and on Joyce's *Ulysses* for the Smithsonian Institution in Washington, D.C., and for the Learning in Retirement Institute at George Mason. He is currently completing a study of the relationship between the Christian idea of grace and Celtic myth in Joyce's early works. His contribution to this volume is focused on the idea of martyrdom developed in T.S. Eliot's *Murder in the Cathedral.*

VALÉRIE ROSOUX has a Ph.D. from the Université Catholique de Louvain (UCL), Belgium, in International Relations. She graduated in Political Science and Philosophy. She is a research fellow at the Belgian National Fund for Scientific Research (FNRS). She is a member of the Center of International Conflicts and Crises Studies (CECRI) and teaches International Negotiation at the University of Louvain.

MICHAEL BERENBAUM is a writer, lecturer, and teacher consulting in the conceptual development of museums and the historical development of films. He has just been named Director of the newly established Sigi Ziering Institute: Exploring the Ethical and Religious Implications of the Holocaust at the University of Judaism where he is also an Adjunct Professor of Theology. In the past he has served as the Ida E. King Distinguished Professor of Holocaust Studies at Richard Stockton College for 1999–2000 and the Strassler Family Distinguished Visiting Professor of Holocaust Studies at Clark University in 2000. For the prior three years, he was President and Chief Executive Officer of the Survivors of the Shoah Visual History Foundation. He was the Director of the United States Holocaust Research Institute at the U.S. Holocaust Memorial Museum and the Hymen Goldman Adjunct Professor of Theology at Georgetown University in Washington, D.C. From 1988 to 1993 he served as Project Director of the United States Holocaust Memorial Museum, overseeing its creation.

Berenbaum is the author and editor of thirteen books, scores of scholarly articles, and hundreds of journalistic pieces. Berenbaum is a graduate of Queens College (BA, 1967) and Florida State University (Ph.D., 1975), and also attended the Hebrew University, the Jewish Theological Seminary, and Boston University. He has won numerous fellowships including the Danforth Fellowship, the George Wise Fellowship at Tel Aviv University, and the Charles E. Merrill Fellowship at FSU. Berenbaum was an elected fellow of the *Society for Values in Higher Education.* He was given a Doctor of Divinity (*honoris causa*) from Nazareth College in 1995 and a Doctor of Humane Letters (*honoris causa*) from Denison University.

REUVEN FIRESTONE was born in Santa Rosa, California, in 1952 and educated at Antioch College; the Hebrew University in Jerusalem; Hebrew Union College, where he received his M.A. in Hebrew literature in 1980 and Rabbinic Ordination in 1982; and New York University, where he received his Ph.D. in Arabic and Islamic studies in 1988. From 1987 to 1992, he taught Hebrew literature and directed the Hebrew and Arabic language programs at Boston University. In 1992 he was awarded the Yad Hanadiv Research Fellowship at the Hebrew University, where he spent the year conducting research on holy war in Islamic tradition. In 2000, Professor Firestone was awarded a fellowship for independent research from the National Endowment for the Humanities for his research on holy war in Judaism, and was chosen to be a fellow of the Institute for Advanced Jewish Studies at the University of Pennsylvania in 2002. Since 1993 he has served as associate and then full professor of Medieval Judaism and Islam at Hebrew Union College in Los Angeles, where he directs the Edgar F. Magnin School for Graduate Studies.

Professor Firestone authored the books *Journeys in Holy Lands: The Evolution of the Abraham-Ishmael Legends in Islamic Exegesis, Jihad: The Origin of Holy War in Islam, Children of Abraham: An Introduction to Judaism for Muslims* (Ktav), and dozens of articles on Judaism, Islam, and comparative studies between Judaism, Christianity, and Islam. His articles appear in *The Journal of Semitic Studies, The Journal of Near Eastern Studies, The Journal of Religious Ethics, The Journal of the American Academy of Religion, The Journal of Jewish Studies, Jewish Quarterly Review, Judaism, Studia Islamica, The Muslim World, The Encyclopaedia of Islam,* and *The Encyclopaedia of the Qur'an.*